...urn to ....

CT/UB/£10.00

TRANSPORT
AND
DISTRIBUTION

Second Edition

TRANSPORT AND DISTRIBUTION

G. J. MURPHY

Senior Lecturer in Economics of Transport
Lanchester Polytechnic

BUSINESS BOOKS
COMMUNICA - EUROPA

First published 1972
Second edition 1978

© GEORGE JOHN MURPHY, 1972, 1978

ISBN 0 220 66321 1

*This book has been set 10 on 11 point IBM Press Roman by
Ebony Typesetting, Liskeard, Cornwall, and printed
in England by The Anchor Press Ltd, Tiptree, Essex
for the publishers, Business Books Limited,
24 Highbury Crescent, London N5*

Contents

Part 4   ORGANISATION AND CONTROL

Preface

The aim of this book is to try to strike a balance between too academic an approach to the problems of physical distribution and too much simplification of the situation. On too many occasions an attempt is made to introduce methods of control which, because of their content, are too complex to be operable in the real work context. At the same time, because of experiences like this, operating management become suspicious of any means of improvement that differs from their past practices.

* * *

Thanks and appreciation are tendered to Temple Press Limited's staff and management who first introduced me to the methodological approach to the total costs of distribution through *Freight Management* and who also kindly allowed the use of material already published in that magazine.

Part 1

TRANSPORT — THE BASIC FACTOR

1 Total distribution costs

The role of transport and distribution is so basic to the modern industrial economy that its efficiency is often taken for granted. The economic function has been carried out by firms since they first came into being.

The industrial society rests on trade, i.e. the movement of materials from where they are found to a processing point and then the finished product to the market. It is only in very exceptional circumstances that the source of the raw materials, the manufacturing point and the market place are all in the same location. The usual situation is that they are geographically separated, and even where they are not, it can often happen that other areas may be able either to produce the same materials or finished products more cheaply than the one under consideration, or the market may be larger or more wealthy.

In all of these cases the most important act that must take place if the 'economy' is to develop is that of transportation and distribution. Without these the regions would have to rely solely on their local resources and markets. The proposition can be made that transport and distribution are the bridging costs between the cost of material and manufacture, and the prices charged to the ultimate consumer (after profit, of course).

The universality of the transport and distribution function would at first glance seem to ensure that it received the greatest of attention from management, but this is not always the case. Indeed, very often this very universality has resulted in the function being fragmented and passed under the control of so many different departments that no single person within the organisation really knows the full extent of the firm's commitment in this area.

The purpose of this chapter is to examine the basic characteristics of transport and what methods can be put into use to try and increase the effectiveness of its contribution to the firm's overall performance. First, however, we will look at the influence that transport can have on other functions within the organisation.

One of the major burdens that the transport and distribution function has had to labour under has been that of attitude. Until very recently the two areas were treated and thought of as separate entities. The usual reaction was that transport was a minor function, responsibility for which could be pushed well down the management scale. Worse, it was thought that the transport services of the firm could make little contribution to profit. It is a fair generalisation that the transport department was often looked upon as some sort of parasite by the other areas of activity within the firm.

Distribution was in a similar position, for it was often the case that the normal industrial firm did not see itself as engaged in distribution at all. Distribution was something to do with the retail trade, not with manufacturing industry. The combination of these two operations into a single department was very seldom considered, never mind evaluated. There were exceptions to this frame of mind. These were, however, usually in those industries where they had little choice, such as brewing and the food industry. With such a large part of these firm's activities being concentrated in the transport and distribution function they ignored it at their peril — the successful ones did not.

Even as short a time ago as the late fifties and early sixties transport and distribution was being called 'the last cost-saving frontier' and 'the dark continent of economics'. Surveys carried out in the UK over the last five years have supported American experience and tend to show that as many as 60 to 70 per cent of the firms approached had no immediate knowledge available on the total cost of distribution within their organisation.

It is this total cost of distribution that has caused the two areas we have mentioned to draw together once more, i.e. transport and distribution are progressively regarded now as one management function.

TOTAL DISTRIBUTION COSTS

In simple terms transport involves the physical movement of goods. In the same way distribution, while it may also include transport, has as its major components the holding of goods in stock-holding points, the deciding of what amounts to hold and the administration of the system. All of these activities affect each other and benefit from coordination; the total distribution cost approach is the name given to the method of dealing not with transport as a function and distribution as another area, but combining the two.

Transport, warehousing, distribution inventory, protective packaging and the administrative procedures involved all fall within a single umbrella. Whenever possible the treatment of them as such can result in very substantial benefits to the firm. All of these factors make up the total distribution cost triangle (see Exhibit 1.1). If the market is dispersed and demand fluctuates, then certain functions are brought into existence. Inventory must be held to act as a buffer between fluctuations in demand and production so that the predetermined service level can be met. The market is dispersed, therefore service stock will be held in warehouses to facilitate distribution to the individual markets. Both the location of the warehouses and the level of inventory will be affected by the time factor which in its turn depends on the efficiency of the transport operation. Packaging and administration will be affected by all of the above. Therefore we cannot regard any of these functions as separate compartments to be operated individually. There must be overall coordination if they are to make their maximum contribution to the firm.

In the particular arrangement shown in Exhibit 1.1, transport has been taken as the base of the triangle. This is not the only way to look at the situation as any number of variations can be used. The real importance of the triangle does not lie in the pattern of its contents but the fact that it exists. The total distribution cost triangle illustrates the point made, namely that all the factors mentioned are important to the overall performance of the organisation and that they influence one another. To see how this operates we must again look at the role played by transport and distribution within the firm.

For the individual organisation, as opposed to the economy in general, the real contribution that these areas make is simply to provide service. By the term customer service we mean, at this stage, giving the customer the type of product that he wants at the time he wants it. Later in this volume greater time is spent on this question of customer service levels and their costs, but for the moment assume that the management of the firm is aware of the decisions involved and has taken the best ones for the firm. We can then say that the function of transport and distribution is to maintain this customer service level at the minimum possible cost consistent with the level of reliability decided upon. The transport and distribution function will normally have this level of customer service before them. There will also be one other factor over which they will have little control — the location and distribution of the markets to be serviced.

Return now to the total distribution cost triangle and examine it under the above conditions. Taking market location and dispersion together with the service level that has been decided upon, we have immediately created an inventory holding function. This requires both inventory and points to hold it in, i.e. warehouses.

Exhibit 1.1   The TDC triangle

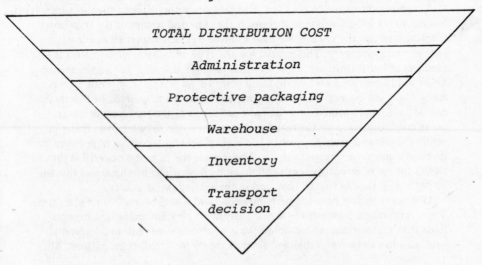

The role of inventory is to act as a buffer between variations of demand and production. If we are faced with a demand pattern such that we are in a position to know exactly what tomorrow's demand will be, and if this rate of demand corresponds exactly with the most profitable rate of production, we would have no inventory problem. The normal situation is not like this. Usually demand fluctuates and these variations are difficult to forecast. We must therefore have a reservoir between the uncertain patterns of demand and the best rate of production. This is inventory. When we decide on a service policy we have said that a certain number of customers coming to us for our product will always be satisfied. To do this we must hold inventory.

But the patterns of demand are not the only influence that will affect the amount of stock we shall hold for a given service level. The location of our markets *vis-à-vis* the location of production points will also have a direct influence.

Suppose that our plant is located in the midst of our market, then we might possibly be able to maintain our service levels by holding inventory at the factory, and since the market and the stock-holding point are in such proximity there will be short lines of communication between them. Thus any change in the expected pattern of demand within this market can be easily detected and extra inventory obtained with the minimum of delay.

The delay point is important. Reduced to its most basic conditions let us suppose that it takes three days for the inventory controller to spot a change in demand, make the order and receive the merchandise. If these times are always possible (we are also assuming that plant can produce to order), then it is obvious that there will always have to be three days' consumption on hand. If the market were not next door to the plant, and if because of this the interval between ordering goods and receiving them was six days, then there would have to be greater levels of inventory held in the system.

We can say this: that as the number of warehouses included in a distribution network increases then the amount of inventory in the 'pipeline' will also increase, and as inventory costs money the costs also go up. Therefore if we have dispersed markets, then the higher the service levels we desire then the higher the costs of providing them.

This brings us to the base of our triangle — transport. One of the most important influences on what we have said above is the type and nature of the transport employed within the system. We have pointed out that higher service levels require more inventory. This is true, but the type and character of the transport used can affect the proportion of this increase. We also said that higher service levels would require more warehousing points if we were dealing with a geographically dispersed market. This is also true, but again the magnitude of this increase can be profoundly affected by the basic influence of the transport decision. As far as inventory levels go the real decision is often one between low, cheap inventory levels and more expensive, fast and reliable transport, or high expensive inventory and slow, cheap transport. The shorter the time the material is in transit the more inventory levels should come down. The mechanics of this will be dealt with later in this section, and in the section on inventory.

One point should be made here, however, and it will be·made time after time. There is no magic ingredient in any management area, including distribution. Each firm's circumstances are unique to a greater or lesser extent. No general formulation can be made that will solve all problems for all organisations. All that can be done is to give broad recommendations that will bear some elements in common with most situations. These must be adapted to solve the problem at hand. Moreover what works in one situation may not do so in another.

This being said, we will return to the distribution triangle. From what has gone before it can be seen that far from these functions of service inventory, warehousing and transport being separate and distinct, they belong under the same overall control, each bearing a very important relationship to the other.

It will be noticed that the administrative block has been left from this discussion, which does not imply that it is considered unimportant. This is an extremely important area indeed. Simple changes in administration can have a great influence on distribution. The reason for not discussing it here is simply that it is universal to all management, and as such is often subject to central control, at least as far as investigation goes. For this reason it is felt that the ordinary appraisal of procedures that will take place for overall administrative efficiency will be best left to the already existing departments. The point about the other functions is that it is only in a small number of cases are they subject to central control, hence they will receive the most attention here. Where special cases for attention arise, administration will be dealt with throughout the text.

The important question that must be examined now is, of course, cost. There is little virtue in directing greater attention to an area if the total commitment of the firm in that function is too low to warrant expenditure. Exhibit 1.2 shows the results of a survey carried out for the Department of Employment.

There are two important facts that must be remembered when looking at Exhibit 1.2. The first is that the details refer to manufacturing industry, and do not include retail trade. This is important because figures in the retail industry would naturally be very much higher, and had these been included then this would have drawn the data upwards reflecting higher figures for manufacturing industry than are given here. Even so, 16 per cent of sales figures is a high average for a function that very often does not exist in the thoughts of the management of the firms in question. This 16 per cent is, of course, an average. The data range from a low of about 2 to 4 per cent up to a highest value of around 43 per cent and even this is misleading for in some industries, exceptional statistics of upwards of 55 per cent were encountered.

The next important factor concerns the state of knowledge in the firms approached. About 70 per cent of firms surveyed had no detailed breakdown of their distribution costs similar to the one given. In other words they were just simply not aware of the fact that on average 16 per cent of their sales revenue

Exhibit 1.2 Total distribution cost as a percentage of sales

Administration	2.0
Transport	5.5
Inventory	3.0
Warehousing	2.5
Packaging (including display)	2.0
Order processing	1.0
TOTAL TDC	16.0

was going on the costs of physical distribution. This can almost certainly be attributed to the fact that very few firms have any form of account which would show the total costs of distribution in a consolidated form. The figures exist within the firm but they are compartmentalised (like the function) to the extent that the overall picture has been lost.

Therefore the data given will be from firms that have realised the importance of this area and are paying it more attention. These should of course be more effective and we can reasonably expect the figures given to be on the optimistic side.

This survey was carried out some years ago, but smaller surveys by myself and others have tended to support the situation as being very similar at the present time and investigation has tended to support the assumption that for a large section of industry in the United Kingdom the average figure going on total distribution costs is higher than 16 per cent, perhaps as high as 20 per cent. The difference can in most cases be traced to inventory and warehousing costs, especially to confusions concerning the real costs of inventory.

Here we have the situation, then, of a considerable amount of costs in the firm being traced to an area that has suffered grievously from a lack of attention in the past and whose real importance is very often not known to the firm concerned.

REASONS FOR LACK OF ATTENTION

It was mentioned above that one of the most important reasons for the lack of attention to the total cost of distribution has been attitude and its very universality. This is true, but there were other considerations as well. These are important because one of the greatest tasks faced by the modern distribution man is to change these attitudes and one of the best aids is to understand how they arose in the first place.

After the Second World War the greatest accent was on production, and rightly so. During the war years a great deal of consumption desire had been pent up. After the war the greatest desire was to satisfy the delayed consumption of the 'lean times'. There was, of course, the usual short-lived postwar boom, and this also lent itself to the push for more effective production methods.

The economic history of the UK after the Second World War shows that there was something missing. Since 1945 we have gone through some dozen major economic crises and one of the most common underlying influences in these crises has been the low productivity of the home economy. This continuous succession of problems has tended to make the UK very production-orientated. There is absolutely nothing wrong with this, but like any other movement you can go too far in one direction; for the best results advance should take place on all fronts whenever possible. The end result of the orientation towards production was that until very recent times other areas of management were ignored to a greater or lesser extent.

In the middle fifties this was realised and there was a sudden burst of enthusiasm for marketing and sales methods: this is also very laudable. There was however, one important trend which was not so desirable, from the point of view of transport and distribution anyway, which was too much specialisation. There is little doubt that specialisation can increase productivity in management just as it does in production, but it is important not to push the movement too far, and this is exactly what happened as far as transport and distribution goes.

This function was grouped in general terms under sales and/or marketing. As the size of the problem increased specialisation seemed the obvious answer (and so it is up to a point). But the pace of development in other fields of management activity was so fast that the essential unity of command in total distribution costs was lost in the attempt to keep up with advances in other more fashionable disciplines. As a result of these movements, we find that the function has been sub-divided for greater specialisation so often that the general direction has been lost, so much so that a significant proportion of companies do not even know how much the activity is costing them. The time has come for a re-marshalling of thought in this field; the time is now ripe to regroup.

This is not to say that all the specialisation that has taken place should be reversed. A higher level of manager must be inserted into the structure of transport and distribution, and he must be the coordinator. It will be remembered that we did not say that specialisation was bad, only that it had gone so far in this area that the overall picture had been confused. This is what must be mended.

It is quite possible to have a firm within which the inventory, warehousing and transport functions are all operating effectively, but because of the lack of overall policy the general level of efficiency from the total distribution cost viewpoint can be low. You can find a situation where the warehouse manager is running his warehousing network as it stands very efficiently, but the total system may be too large or too small. He may have been told to maintain service levels that are too high, or he could provide the same service level at a lower cost with cooperation from transport.

This set of circumstances could be repeated again and again. The point is that if an overall authority exists the policy of trade-off can be introduced. This simply implies accepting higher costs in one section of the operation because of the possibility of lower overall costs. Perhaps an identical service level could be provided at lower inventory levels by the use of a more expensive and faster form of transport. If the total savings are worthwhile then this would be a desirable step. However if the warehousing manager is not in control of transport and the two departments are run on a separate authority basis (a common situation), then the warehouse manager is going to have a difficult job persuading the transport manager to apply for higher budgets so that warehousing can reduce its costs.

This type of conflict can often be smoothed if both of these managers are aware of their part in the overall distribution function, and subject to a distribution coordinator who regards both departments as part of the same structure in the overall organisation of the firm — more will be said later.

On this point it is true to say that changes in the basic attitudes of the firm to transport and distribution with a different management structure are difficult to introduce. But there are forces in action which are making these changes easier day by day.

WHY TDC WILL RECEIVE MORE ATTENTION

It is not so long since the phrase 'total distribution costs' (TDC) required explaining on practically every occasion it was used. This has now altered and the idea is becoming more widely accepted, and while the theoretical structures and techniques often do not work as well in practice as we would like them to, they still exist as targets.

One of the greatest allies that TDC has is inflation. We are faced with the situation today where costs of production are spiralling, while at the same time competition is becoming more fierce both in character and extent. The days are long past when the UK could regard particular geographical or product areas as its preserve. Because of this competition, we tend to find that not only are we faced with rising costs but profit margins are remaining steady and in many cases even declining. This has but one result: management is more ready to listen to overtures concerning cost reductions, most especially in the distribution field where they can often mean greater competitiveness through better service or the same service at lower cost. Therefore increases in cost coupled with greater competition must work in favour of the acceptance of TDC.

Other management sciences are contributing their part as well. With the great deal of attention that has been lavished on them in the past, there are many areas within production and classical marketing that are fast approaching diminishing returns. On the other hand the total distribution cost area is more or less virgin territory for many firms, and as such can often produce impressive results for modest expenditure in terms of time, men and capital.

Management is beginning to apply the oldest maxim in management: do not apply capital and effort to one area if they can be used to achieve more benefit for the firm elsewhere. This set of conditions is likely to grow more favourable to transport and distribution as time goes on, at least up to the point where TDC itself falls into the same problem category *vis-à-vis* some other management area.

The final movement making for the change which can be discerned is, of course, legislative in origin. Until the passing of the 1968 Transport Act firms could continue to dig their heads in the sand and ignore the forces we have mentioned. But the 1968 Act changed that. We are not concerned at this point with the detailed provisions of the Act (these will be dealt with under road transport below) but the greatest service that the Act did for transport was to bring it to the attention of management further up the scale than it was normally dealt with.

By the projected introduction of quantity licensing (which may or may not be a good thing) the government ensured that firms had to ask themselves very important questions about the future trend of their policies and expenditure in the transport field. This cannot be done without first gathering information.

Transport managers who had been trying for years to get the importance of their job recognised were aided more or less overnight by the 1968 Act. By forcing this attention on the function, the government paved the way for a more realistic examination of the contribution that transport and distribution could make to the overall profitability of the firm.

TRANSPORTATION MODES

Before examining air, sea, rail and road individually it will be useful to look at the broad general characteristics of each of the modes so that their benefits can be seen overall.

Air has one basic advantage over other forms of transport and this is its speed. We must however take care when we speak of this advantage of air as it can have its importance negated by the now legendary 'ground barrier'.

The transit speed of air is always greater than that of any of the surface modes. The problem is not transit speed, however, but the total elapsed time between the order being placed by a customer and his receiving it in his warehouse. This being the case, very often the theoretical time savings by air are much reduced in practice by delays on the ground. It has been pointed out, for example, that the total speed between Paris and London by air is today slower than it was prewar, factory to customer that is.

This divergence in total elapsed times and transit times, however, declines as we move from short-haul to long-haul operations. The greater the distance then the more the pendulum swings in favour of air. This advantage in speed can in certain circumstances allow the firm to make economies in safety stock, warehousing and other important cost centres. Air does have very positive disadvantages, however, perhaps the most obvious of these being weight limitations. These have become less critical, although still important, since the introduction of all-freight jumbos.

The most outstanding characteristic of air freight over the last few years has been its rapid growth rate. It has been estimated that by 1980 the volume of cargo traffic handled by the world's airlines will equal the passenger traffic. Air freight is expected to grow by about 40 per cent over the next ten years.

Another problem in the use of air freight is that only a comparatively narrow range of products is suitable for regular movement by air. The range will become more obvious in the detailed discussion of air freight, but for the moment consider that the chief economies obtainable through the use of air freight rely on its superior speed. There are many products for which these savings through lead time economies are of insufficient magnitude to warrant the use of this mode. To give an extreme example, it would be doubtful if the increased service which it would be possible for a quarry to provide, would make it an economic proposition to freight slate by air.

The material to be shipped by air must have certain basic properties to allow it to benefit from the possible economies of this mode. If time is important either for the life of the product, such as fruit and flowers, or for its selling period as for fashion, then air can provide definite advantages.

The most suitable use for sea transport is the movement of large bulk over long distances. Water transport tends to have the lowest transport cost per unit per mile of the various modes under consideration. It also unfortunately tends to have the greatest elapsed time between placing of an order and receipt of it by the customer. Another disadvantage of sea transport is that in certain areas of the world it is subject to great interference from climatic variations.

The greatest single disadvantage of sea, however, is consolidation and distribution. The assembly of an economic sized cargo can take a great deal of time, both because of the volume dealt with and the methods used. Distribution from the port of destination to final customer can also cause problems, especially as the distance from the sea increases. The container is a successful attempt to overcome this problem of consolidation and distribution.

Rail is in essence very similar to sea transport. The chief problem with rail was also consolidation at the station of departure and distribution of the product at the destination. This was again solved by the use of containers, as in the service of Freightliners Limited.

The most suitable use for rail (other than Freightliners) is again for the movement of large volumes of material over long distances. Once a train of suitable load has been consolidated it is an extremely efficient form of transport between two points. Problems arise when the destination has been reached.

The major disadvantage of rail is that it tends to be inefficient on the short haul, too large a proportion of the total time being taken up with the consolidation of the load and its distribution. While Freightliner overcomes some of the problems here, it still leaves them for the movement which is smaller than the standard container used. If groupage is to take place to fill a container then we have once again raised time problems of consolidation and distribution.

Flexibility is another major disadvantage of rail, although this will not be important in certain situations. Railway stations are not all capable of the effective handling of freight. The really fast trunk trains do not stop at every station, therefore fast trains of the Freightliner variety are of use only if the customer resides within reasonable moving distance from a Freightliner terminal.

Another disadvantage follows from what has been said: railways are not really suitable for the movement of small units.

The principal advantage of road transport is its flexibility. It is quite possible, for example, to load a vehicle in Glasgow and have it make several drops on its way to say Birmingham. It can move with the greatest freedom of any of the surface transport modes mentioned here. The major disadvantage is that it is not suitable for the movement of large volumes of material and it is most economic on the short to medium haul.

Many authorities are of the opinion that the economic advantages of road transport taper very rapidly after the 100-mile trip is passed. This tapering as against rail is more apparent the greater the volume of material that is being moved. Against this, however, must be weighed the undoubted advantages that are possible through the greater flexibility of the road vehicle. It is also another advantage of road that there tends to be less damage to the products being moved compared to say general cargo by sea ferry or general freight by rail.

The real key to the success of road transport is that the problems of consolidation and distribution are reduced to a minimum. The movement of comparatively small shipments is probably most economically achieved by the use of road transport. Moreover the firm can easily operate its own road transport fleet. If the shipment is to move by rail then British Rail must be used, by air one of the airlines and if the sea is considered then almost certainly another firm.

There are many companies who feel that they would much prefer to use their own transport services whenever possible. It is because of this desire that the largest proportion of goods vehciles are owned by C licence operators.

From this brief consideration of the broad characteristics of the various transport modes certain points emerge. The first of these is that there is no such thing as the ideal transport mode. Under certain circumstances one method of transport will be the most suitable, a different set of conditions and another form of transport may then become the best. Bearing this in mind, any attempt to standardise the type of mode used within a large organisation with a variety of products and markets must naturally be a compromise.

As a result of this and the fact that business is dynamic in nature it follows that a once-and-for-all transport decision cannot be made. To exact a given set of statistics requires that the business be 'frozen'. Once this is done and the data obtained, we must be careful to remember that the firm moves on. Therefore just because at a particular time for a specific market it would seem that air freight is the best method, it does not mean that this will always be the case even for the same product and market.

It will also be evident that under certain circumstances there is little room for manoeuvre. The basic characteristics of the product and the market may decide for themselves which form of transport is best suited. The movement of large volumes of low value, bulky material over long land distances will obviously be best carried out by rail transport if a service is available. The movement of highly perishable foods (fruit and sea foods) over long distances will obviously demand a consideration of air freight.

The important point is that all the transport modes are not always in competition with each other. They compete only over easily observed ranges of products. This being the case the number of decisions that have to be made can be reduced by eliminating obviously unsuitable alternatives.

Finally, because of these well demarcated qualities of the forms of transport available certain implications for the rest of the total distribution cost triangle can usually be deduced. If we are going to use one of the slower modes, for example, we must be prepared to accept higher inventory levels for a given customer service level than would be required if we used a faster transportation method. Thus if the choice is between air and, say, road/sea ferry, then we must look for the advantages that might be reaped by the surface method to counteract the expected higher inventory levels, warehouse cost and so on.

To sum up, because of strong trends in the character of the modes of operation of the different transport methods a number of decisions can be recognised concerning the total distribution network before detailed examination need take place. This can often be a help in reducing the number of alternatives that must be examined.

2 Road transport— the legislative background

REASONS FOR GOVERNMENT CONTROL

Before looking in detail at the range of management methods available for the improvement of the road transport function it is essential that the legislative background be examined. This is so for two broad reasons: first, it is a good premise to have at least an overall view of any area's history before trying to tackle present-day problems, and secondly (and much more important) past history can help to forecast future trends in legislation, which can and does significantly effect operating costs.

Like so many other things it was the First World War that threw up the capacity for mass movement that road transport possessed. It is fair to say that since that time two broad threads can be seen in the attitudes of successive governments to the road transport industry.

In the first place they have seen the road vehicle as a very serious threat to that other form of transport which has held their attention for many long years – the railways.

The government of this country and many others have invested such vast amounts of time and money in rail transport that any other mode which showed signs of not only competing with the railways but beating them in the field of freight transport was bound to attract legislation. The problems of rail and its ability to capture a satisfactory share of the exanding freight business had been obvious right from the end of the First World War. The attempt by the 1921 Railways Act to improve the situation was not effective, and by 1929 it was felt that further action was needed and needless to say this was to take the form of greater regulation of road transport.

Secondly, governments have always tried to achieve 'greater utilisation' of rail transport and as well as regulation of entry into road transport industry they have tended to rely heavily on 'making road hauliers bear the full costs of their operations'. That is, they tend to see the road transport industry possessing an unfair disadvantage over rail in the form of a cross-subsidisation from other road users with respect to the provisions of track and also an escaping of true

costs inasmuch as congestion costs (and others) are not paid for by the hauliers.
In short it is felt the road transport has an advantage because of the fiscal
structure in the United Kingdom, and most especially because it is not yet
organised on a user cost basis for pricing decisions. More will be said on this
topic later, but first we will examine the way regulation has developed, its effect
and likely future direction.

THE ROAD AND RAIL TRAFFIC ACT, 1933

This Act gave form to the general proposals of the Slater Conference which had
been convened in 1932 to review the freight situation in the country. Their
report had included the following propositions:

1   There should be an increase in the levy on heavy goods vehicles. Indeed,
     the aim was to ensure that goods vehicles bore the full cost of their opera-
     tion. (It must be admitted that pricing policies were such at this time to
     make sure that this was no more than a pious hope.)
2   A distinction was made between hauliers for hire or reward, and those who
     were operating on their own account, i.e. carrying their own goods. The
     hauliers for hire or reward were to be made subject to government regula-
     tion with regard to safety conditions and wages. This concern with working
     conditions is, as we shall see, still a very important area for legislation. In
     fact it would be fair to say that this particular aspect of government control
     is today probably the most wide ranging of all.
3   After evidence from road haulage representatives with regard to the difficul-
     ties the industry was facing through cut-throat competition, it was decided
     to carry the distinction between hire and reward and own-account opera-
     tives to a logical conclusion and use it as a means of controlling entry into
     the industry.
   The 1933 Act introduced a four-tier licencing system. This lasted into the
1970s and illustrated the two broad trends in government attitudes already discussed. There was to be an attempt to introduce a more realistic cost structure
on the industry, and whilst the entry conditions would, in theory at least, reduce
to some extent the cut-throat competition, it also gave the government control
over entry into the industry and hence over capacity. The central authority was
henceforth able to influence the supply of road transport and this in turn gave a
potential power into their hands for the benefit of the railways.
   We now know, of course, that this did not in fact help the railways a great
deal, but this has most likely been due to an anti-railway bias which can be
detected in the government's advisers.
   The first type of licence was the A licence. This was granted for the general
carrying of goods anywhere for hire or reward. Next there was the Contract A
licence. These were for the exclusive carriage of a party's goods for a period of
not less than one year. Thirdly B licences: these were for the carriage of the
trader's own goods or subject to conditions for hire or reward. The usual condition was by destination, e.g. Glasgow and Birmingham. Finally we had C
licences. These were for own-account operators, e.g. manufacturers with their
own fleets. The C licence was granted automatically, but A and B licences were
subject to the Licensing Authority. To ensure coordination the licensing districts
corresponded to the Traffic Areas for road passenger traffic and the Licencing

Authority was the Chairman of the Traffic Commissioners for the area.

Until 1953 the Authority, when considering an application for the A or B licence, had to consider both the interests of existing hauliers and the market requirements, i.e. it had to be demonstrated that not only was there the need for a service but that already existing capacity was not adequate.

THE TRANSPORT ACT, 1953

The situation described above was slightly altered by *The Transport Act, 1953*. Under this Act, it became incumbent upon the objectors to the granting of a new licence that they prove there was no need for a new service. It also made the provision that prices charged was relevant information, thus introducing an element of price competition before there was any fleet on the road. It was also laid down that the major consideration to be examined by the authority was the requirement of the consumers of transport, rather than the interests of the providers.

At first glance this may seem an easing of the power of control of entry, a general liberalisation of conditions. The proviso or 'Normal User' went against this impression. The 'normal user' condition simply meant that all applications had to contain the statement of which traffic and what area the operator intended to carry on his business in. If the normal-user statement was narrow, such as 'Explosives — West of Scotland', then the objectors were likely to be few. On the other hand few transport companies would like to be so limited and the normal-user information usually covered much wider fields. 'General Goods — United Kingdom' was the kind of statement that most hauliers favoured. This general user condition involved problems. On the one hand there was the temptation to try and avoid objections and at the same time the desire to have as much operating freedom as possible. The sting was that an objection could be made to the renewal of a licence on the basis that the normal-user intent had been breached. The licensing system continued in this way until 1968.

The problems of the railways or, indeed, the problems of the road transport industry did not seem to be being solved, and in 1960 the Geddes Committee was set up to enquire into the state of the industry and make any recommendations it saw fit to bring about greater efficiency.

THE GEDDES COMMITTEE

Certainly there seemed to be cause for concern both on the efficiency side and also in another important area, public safety.

A note of caution, on an old theme, must be sounded. Statistics on the efficiency and safety aspects of hauliers and road transport are open to the same wide interpretations as those in any other field. Perhaps, in fact, they are even more apt to be misunderstood. This is a general problem, more about which will be said later.

At the present time I think it may be worth quoting a lecturer of mine who said that statistics are like the bikini, that which they reveal is interesting but that which they conceal is vital. This being as it may, the Geddes Committee felt that the major areas for concern were firstly public safety and secondly the fact that the licensing system might have been working against efficiency in the industry. The committee felt that the road transport industry was exceptionally open to concern on the major safety factors of:

1   Poor maintenance.
2   Overloading.
3   Excessive driving hours.

In 1964 spot checks were carried out on some 15,000 vehicles and 55 per cent had defects. This consisted of 10 per cent which were found to be outright unfit for the road and a further 45 per cent with various minor defects. The question of excessive hours is a difficult one. In this area there is great cause for concern since fatigue can be and is the major factor in accidents, but of course proof of the offence is difficult. There is also the very real problem of industrial relations. It is often the case that an industrial abuse is common, everybody knows it is common, but doing something about it is something else again. Suffice it to say that even a casual acquaintance with the operations of road vehicles from the 'waggon' side will show that the abuse is indeed widespread. Means of reducing the falsification of log books will be mentioned later when Common Market Regulations are looked at. Given the very slack enforcement of hours and the difficulty of proof it is a very enlightening fact that at the time of the Geddes Committee some 12,000 successful prosecutions were being brought per year.

It was obvious that a basic function of any government regulation — the safety of the public — was not being successfully controlled by the then-existing licensing methods. It is perhaps significant in this respect that although in 1962-63 there were 32,000 lack of road-worthiness notices on vehicles and 26,000 prosecutions for overloading and excessive hours offences, only eleven vehicles belonging to seven carriers were the subject of suspension notices.

The committee also felt that the existing licensing system had several adverse effects on the operating effectiveness of the industry. The most outstanding of these was the return load problem.

On the A contract licence and the C licence, especially, the conditions of operation often meant that vehicles were being used at 50 per cent operating capacity. In the A contract situation it will be remembered that the operator was carrying the goods of a single customer. All possible efforts were made to ensure that when a lorry was sent to a destination then the customer would have goods to be returned. This is obviously the ideal state of affairs. Unfortunately in practice it is not always the case that conditions fall out as we would like. In a great number of cases our A contract operator would find that having delivered his customer's product the vehicle had to return home empty. The conditions of the licence forbade him to carry other goods except those of his exclusive customer.

The C licence or own-account operators were in the same situation. The terms of their licence meant that they could carry only their own goods. Very often their vehicles would make a delivery of the product to one of their customers and find that there was the possibility of returning home carrying some other company's goods. This was impossible however and the lorry or van would have to return empty.

The fact that objections could be made in the licensing courts to new applications was also a problem inasmuch as it could hinder the entry of new firms. This in turn conferred a protected status on those firms already operating. To a certain extent at least they could continue along their way safe from the harsh winds of full and free competition. There was another aspect to this protection. If an already existing haulier wanted to expand his operations, say to move from a B or contract A licence to a full A licence, it was not just simply the case that he congratulated himself for being able to attract the extra business and proceed. He had to go through the usual licensing procedure, in other words flexibility and responsiveness to changes in demand were reduced.

There was, finally, a financial barrier to entry which the committee felt could also be traced to the licensing system. It is, of course, also true to say that the going market price was a measure of the 'restrictiveness' of the system. The rate was in fact about £350 per licensed ton for the top end of existing A-licensed fleets. This was in the middle part of the 1960s. This situation made the C licence seem attractive to many manufacturers and was the means whereby the structure of the industry became biased in favour of the C-licensed fleet.

The committee felt that the reasons discussed above and others were the causes of the then existing structure of the industry.

It is apposite at this point to look, however briefly, at just what the overall structure of road transport was; the nature of the Geddes Committee's dislike of this structure has just been examined, and before we discuss their recommendations and their results we must glance at the basis of the industry they examined. Many points worth bearing in mind under present and likely future operating conditions may emerge.

THE MARKET AND SIZE OF FIRM

As has already been mentioned, the basic characteristics of the major transport modes are such that they are not in competition with each other over the entire spectrum of products that they are in theory capable of carrying, i.e. assuming that the object of the transport decision is maximum performance of the firm in terms of profitability. It is for this reason that we pointed out that rail is under normal conditions best suited for large-bulk, long-distance movements. We would therefore expect such traffic to move chiefly by rail and indeed this is the case. In 1975, for example, well over 50 per cent of the tonnage of coke and coal was moved by rail within this country; the same holds true for iron ore and limestone.

It is obvious that whilst these first-option traffics do exist the vast majority of goods moved are not subject to such clear-cut conditions and in fact the greatest proportion of goods moved in the UK moved by road. Exhibit 2.1 shows the breakdown of the usual transport mode's share of total traffic. The dominance of road is obvious. The relative importance of long-distance and short-distance haulage is an area of interest, for it is here that we can begin to see the effect of haul length on the costs to firms and the influence of this on government thoughts on taxation.

· From Exhibit 2.2 it can be seen that, at first glance at least, the overwhelming proportion of traffic is on short-haul routes of 25 miles or less. This strong position of short haul has had important repercussions for governments, both here and on the Continent.

In general terms the trend in regulations has been to liberate short-haul movements and tighten up on the long-distance traffic. The governments concerned derive two major benefits from this approach. The first is that they can claim to be in fact encouraging market competition in the very area where most movements take place. They are therefore in an ideal position to refute any representation from the haulage industry that their attitude to the industry is too severe. They are always in the position to point out that the sector that accounts for most of the tonnage moved is the very one receiving the greatest considerations.

If we remember that one of the reasons why governments wish to regulate the road transport industry anyway is its ability to compete with the railways a further advantage emerges. By concentrating on the long-haul traffic, not only can the fiscal authority find arguments to back up its basically liberal stance, but it has greater freedom to help the railways stand up to their arch enemy. There are arguments against this line of reasoning, and these tend to centre around ton-milage rather than total volume moved. If ton-milage figures are calculated for short- and long-haul sectors it will be seen that there is nothing like the bias that the simple tonnage figures show. This is used by the champions of long-distance interests to underline their case that European governments in general and this country's government in particular are too heavily committed against that sector.

Exhibit 2.1 Modal share of movement

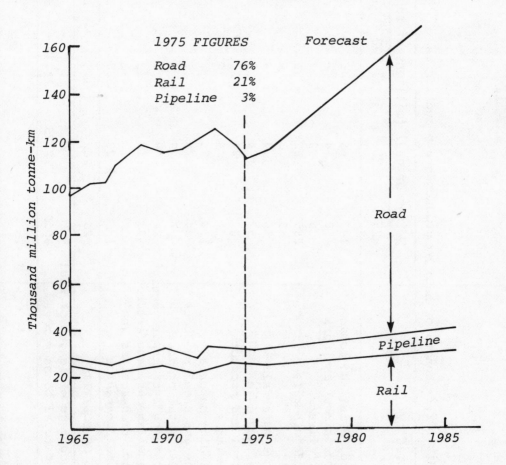

Exhibit 2.2 Length of haul by product group and tonnes

Commodity	Weight of haul (millions of tonnes) for length of (miles)						
	<25	26-50	51-100	101-150	151-200	201+	Total
Food, drink and tobacco	142	58	45	19	9	8	282
Wood, timber and cork	8	4	4	2	1	1	20
Fertilisers	5	2	2	1	1	1	11
Crude minerals	285	62	18	4	2	1	373
Ores	8	3	2	1	-	1	14
Crude materials	15	4	3	2	1	1	26
Coal and coke	52	8	5	2	1	-	67
Petrol and products	46	24	11	2	1	1	84
Chemicals	11	9	10	7	4	4	44
Building materials	114	25	18	6	3	2	168
Iron and steel products	44	10	11	9	5	5	84
Other metal products	7	3	2	1	1	1	15
Machinery & transport equipt	24	9	9	5	3	3	54
Miscellaneous manufactures	30	12	12	6	5	5	71
Misc. transactions and unallocatables	136	29	20	10	5	6	206
ALL COMMODITIES	926	262	173	77	42	39	1519
Percentage of length of haul of total tonnage moved	60.93	17.23	11.38	5.06	2.78	2.56	

To counter this argument, governments tend to make a great deal of play on the social costs of larger vehicles. This social cost will be dealt with later, but just now suffice it to say that the term encompasses those costs imposed by the road user on the community as a whole including, of course, other road users. There is a problem of interpretation here, and it is important inasmuch as the governments of most EEC members appear to favour a particular school of thought with its consequent influences on taxation thinking. On the one hand there is the group which maintains that the larger long-haul vehicles cause greater social costs and should thus be controlled more tightly, for the reasons already mentioned. On the other hand it is said that most social costs are imposed in urban areas, and the proportion of urban running will obviously be higher on short journeys. Against this it is pointed out that the typical vehicle on short journeys is of smaller size and therefore causes less congestion — a major social cost. Yet again it is held that vehicle size does not significantly effect congestion and other social costs. As can be appreciated the argument rages with little or no ultimate 'correct' solution — so much depends on the individual point of view. There is little doubt however that the government would seem to prefer the standpoint that short haul should be liberalised and long haul more closely controlled. This belief can be argued against but the important fact is that the EEC and the government in this country have enshrined this attitude in legislation, and if for this reason alone, might be said to be unlikely to change their minds.

The question of the size of operating units within the road transport industry is another area where a great deal of discussion is possible. This argument tends

Exhibit 2.3 Fleet size by number of licence holders

Number of vehicles	%	Number of operators, 000s
1	55	80
2	17	25.3
3	8	11.6
4	5	6.8
5	3	4.2
5 or less	88	127.9
6–10	6	9.1
11–20	3	4.9
21–30	1	1.5
31–40	0.5	0.7
41–50	0.3	0.4
51–100	0.5	0.7
101–200	0.1	0.2
Over 200	0.06	0.1
All fleets		145.5

Exhibit 2.4 Relative size of hire-or-reward and own-account fleets before the Transport Act of 1968

Number of vehicles	Hire-or-reward	Own-account
1	23,140	12,144
2-5	15,997	29,692
6-10	3,801	8,227
11-50	3,306	5,109
51-100	144	645
101-200	36	476
Over 200	18	178
TOTAL	46,442	56,471

to centre round the fact that the typical firm in the industry is small. In fact firms with five or less vehicles account for almost 90 per cent of firms (see Exhibit 2.3), and by far the most numerous size is two or less, i.e. effectively one and two goods vehicles. The top end of the fleet size is overwhelmingly dominated by the government-owned services. This is worthy of note because these two facts — small size and a dominant government undertaking — must have a profound effect on the nature of operations within the industry.

We have so far been talking about the public haulier but own-account operations are roughly the same. The major difference as one would expect are firstly a greater number of vehicles and significantly larger firms with fleets of more than five vehicles. The relative figures can be seen in Exhibit 2.4. In spite of what we have just said, however, it is interesting that for own-account as for public hauliers, firms with five or less lorries account for the greatest proportion of firms. It is therefore fair to say that the industry overall, both own-account and public, is dominated by the small firm.

ECONOMIES OF SCALE

Most recent government legislation has had as an element in its formation the hint that small firms might be less efficient than larger ones and therefore should be open to the full force of competition; if they continue to remain in business they are effective, if not then so much the better. This attitude is based on the position already mentioned, namely that if economies of scale exist then smaller firms cannot be good for the industry, and since the industry itself is so important for the national well being, the small firms cannot be good for the country. This is, as has been emphasised, an unresolved debate, but in my opinion (unfortunately at this time it is no more than that) too many conclusions have been drawn on the basis of too little investigation. Statistics relating to size and performance in the transport industry are extremely difficult to interpret. There has also been precious little work done in the field. In this country it is often the case that transport research does not attract the glamour of more 'academic' but less practical areas and as a result tends to find less finance for research. This is however another topic, but it is impossible to resist the following tale. I can remember not such a long time ago discussing the importance of logistics with a well known Professor of Marketing whose main point was that too much emphasis on profitability and operating costs detracted from the academic merit of the subject!

This is as it may be, but problems still exist. It is a normal supposition that for most industries economies of scale exist, that is to say that at least up to a point the unit cost of production decreases with increases in output, after which time diseconomies of scale set in and unit cost of output increases. This is a basic assumption, subject to a great many qualifications, even in those industries where there is a theoretically ideal case for their existence, but by and large they can be considered to exist.

Economies of scale are normally divided into two broad categories: technical and managerial. Technical economies rely on fundamental mathematical relationships. These would include, for example, the fact that the surface area of a ship increases in proportion to the dimensions squared, whereas the capacity increases in proportion to the dimensions cubed. After the usual considerations we can say that in most cases therefore the carrying capacity per unit will increase at a faster rate than the cost of materials used. Managerial economies are those advantages in management performance which accrue to larger firms. These will range from the simple fact that the bigger companies tend to attract the more able managers, although this is sometimes more potential than real, to financial, planning, personnel, and market and marketing economies.

Studies carried out in this country tend to come to the conclusion that economies of scale do not exist in the road transport industry. Therefore any government legislation which has as a main objective the basic reorganisation of the industry is starting from a false position, at least so the argument goes. This stance is further strengthened by the fact that research also would seem to indicate that there is no significant difference in the relative investment of large and small firms, indeed the smaller firms would appear to replace and modernise to a greater extent than the larger ones. The conclusion must be, therefore, that since there is no loss of economies of scale and since small firms invest as much proportionately as the large then a structure dominated by small firms is not detrimental either to the industry or the nation as a whole. Legislation directed at the structure must therefore seek a different justification.

This is the orthodox position, but perhaps there has not been enough attention paid to the managerial side of the economies of scale question. There is little doubt that technical economies are limited, but it is doubtful if the same applies to managerial economies. If this is true then studies undertaken in the past should still have shown returns to scale. In the firm there is no division between the two kinds of economies in the balance sheet. Why did they not show? There are probably two reasons for this. In fact the first instance there is the possibility of initial non-returns to scale, i.e. as a firm proceeds along the growth path it encounters in the first place not economies of scale but diseconomies of scale. This is shown in Exhibit 2.5. The research data for the actual (as opposed to deductive) existence of such a curve is very scarce indeed, being limited more or less to one study in a very narrow sector of the industry. More, much more work could be done (if funds were forthcoming) to see if it were a general situation.

Exhibit 2.5 Initial non-returns to scale

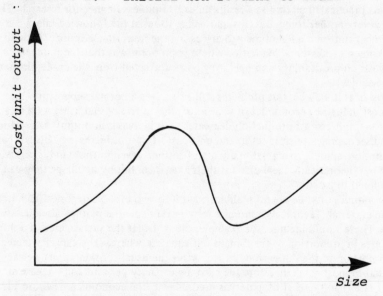

We will assume however for the sake of our argument, that it is general, at least for some sectors of the industry. If this were so then it would help to explain the dominance of the small firm, since there would be an efficiency barrier through which only the most effective firms could break. The argument would then be that these small firms cannot take advantage of the managerial economies of scale and therefore they do not show up in any studies. This is based on the premise that most of the managerial returns are not available to the small firm. This is true to a limited extent inasmuch as techniques like route selection, say, may involve unavoidable costs in implementing the basic study such that fleets of four or five vehicles would not be capable of generating sufficient savings to make the exercise worthwhile. This line of thought can be extended over numerous methods. To a certain extent this proposition must be agreed with. The chief objection is that many of the methods in question can be applied in some form by an individual without any capital investment beyond a good calculator. The benefits here rely on such a person being available to the firm.

The difficulty with this line of approach is that it would appear that the already existing larger firms are no more cost-effective than the smaller ones, leading us once again to the normal conclusions about economies of scale and legislation. The way around this problem is to come back to the definition of the economies we are discussing. They are, it will be remembered, managerial economies of scale. This in effect can be boiled down to the fact that without individual effort they are mere potential savings. To convert them into pounds and pence some form of executive action must take place. It has been apparent for some time now that, by and large (with some really outstanding exceptions), the level of applied management skill in the transport industry leaves much to be desired.

Therefore the point is put forward that economies of scale might still be found in the transport industry, but not without considerable effort being spent on the search. These economies will be (if they exist?) on the managerial side

and the reasons for their lack of appearance in studies in the past has been a combination of economic and managerial factors combining to ensure that potential
savings remained just that.

The argument about the existence or non-existence of these returns to scale
has not yet been settled although many wish it was. The importance of the debate
is that the answer will have an affect on government legislation and on the arguments that interested parties can present to the government and through these
ultimately on operating costs.

OWNERSHIP

Over the period we are discussing, i.e. up to 1968, the government always operated a stict separation of own-account and hire-or-reward firms as far as legislation
was concerned. The same consideration has, in fact, applied throughout Europe
as has the fact that the hire-or-reward sector has usually been the object of most
of the restrictive actions taken by the central authorities.

Own-account operations are those transport activities carried out by firms
whose main concern is not road transport for its own ends, i.e. the operations are
run solely for carrying the company's own goods.

Hire-or-reward operations, more often called the public sector, are transport
specialists. The chief activity this type of firm is engaged in is the carriage of
other people's goods.

Before we look at the relative strengths of the two sectors, and see what
developments are taking place, perhaps the best step is to look at the reasons
behind the existence of the two groups. The demand for freight transport is based
on the simple concept that manufactured goods and raw materials must be
moved to points of process and points of consumption. The split between transport modes and within modes will depend on the assessment of the ability of
each form of movement to satisfy the purchaser of the service. In the case of
goods movement the following factors will usually be considered.

FACTORS AFFECTING DEMAND

Speed and reliability   As we have mentioned already and will be discussing in
much greater depth later, speed can effect the levels of inventory within our
distribution network and, through these, costs. No less important is reliability.
Safety stock levels will obviously be smaller (all other things being equal) if we
have a reliable transport service. If a particular service builds a reputation for
delays, say through industrial action, then the buyers of this service will tend
either to look elsewhere, or hedge their bets by diversifying into more than one
form of transport. They may also place a premium on reliability and prefer to
keep their transport under their own control even if it means higher transport
costs.

Damage and theft are a second important consideration. It is true that the differing basic characteristics of the various transport modes mean that a variety of
handling situations occur, some of these will at least in the estimation of the
shipper carry a higher risk of damage or pilferage than others. In the past general

goods traffic by rail was thought to be especially susceptible to 'g' force damage in shunting. This has been largely removed by containerisation and other handling improvements. There is also a body of thought which believes that one's own drivers will treat your own product with greater care than disinterested strangers.

There is little doubt that the point where damage is most likely to occur is where a change of mode or of vehicle takes place. Many firms are therefore of the opinion that a thorough service is more desirable even if it might be a little slower in some cases. They would appear to have in mind here the situation where a fast rail delivery can be made station-to-station, but where transhipment is required, and prefer to go door-to-door by road.

Theft will always be with us. The operator who takes only small amounts of 'pruch' (as it is known in Scotland) seldom sees himself as a thief, and even less often considers the total throughout the system of the small thefts that take place daily. But such pilferage can amount to considerable sums over the year. Traditionally, own-account operations are thought of as being less open to this kind of theft than public operators, although this in many cases is a doubtful proposition.

The hijacker and large-scale thief makes little distinction between own-account or public vehicles. It must be mentioned, however, that security is usually easier to organise in your own depots.

Back-up services   Thirdly, there can be a wide range of back-up services that the public haulier may not be prepared to offer, or, if he is, will expect extra payment for. This includes such things as livery — the side of a road vehicle can and does provide a convenient advertising hoarding for the operator. Likewise drivers in smart uniform can convey a good public image — especially in such areas as hygiene, on which the public is likely to put a premium. The example that springs readily to mind is the food market where clean attractive uniforms can create a good selling image with the public at large. This consideration also applies to the vehicle itself. A public haulier is not likely to be so concerned with the cosmetic side of his vehicle as the own-account operator who is familiar with the problems of public image building.

The driver of the own-account operator is likely to be as unconcerned as the public haulier if he is expected to perform duties over and above what he is paid for. It is therefore important for the personnel officer of an own-account operator to negotiate any extra duties with drivers. These could include such things as the drivers carrying out some of the duties of salesmen, collecting and delivering subsidiary data (for example, computer print-outs or data files), collecting monies, cleaning his vehicle at the end of each trip and always presenting himself clean and tidy at delivery points.

Some premises are not generally accessible to the public and here again, to save double handling, it is probably preferable to make deliveries in one's own vehicles.

These and other considerations should be looked at by most transport managers before a decision is taken as to which form of transport would be used for a particular set of circumstances. It is not possible to generalise about which solution is best because to quantify the factors discussed would require a special knowledge of the individual problem.

Having said this, it is nonetheless true that individual transport managers carry out this task on a routine basis and it is important to try to assess their reaction to the question, own account or public?

The two best sources of information in this area are the Traders Road Transport Association (TRATA) survey of C-licensed fleets carried out in 1958 and the Transport for Industry survey carried out in 1966/67 for the Ministry of Transport by Edwards and Bayliss. The objective of both studies was to try and gauge the reasons behind the demand for own-account operations. The result of the TRATA survey is summarised in Exhibit 2.6. The basic statistics behind the survey are important inasmuch as the size of the sample and any inherent difficulties in interpretation will obviously affect the importance which we can give to the results of the study. In fact the number of vehicles surveyed was about 98,400 units — roughly 9 per cent of all C-licenced goods vehicles. The number of firms involved in the survey was approximately 4830. This sample was thought at the time to give a reasonably accurate result — this as we shall see was perhaps a little too optimistic. As can be seen from the exhibit the general points made in the discussion above tend, by and large, to be borne out by the responses of practitioners.

The most important reason given for preferring own-account operations was speed and reliability of delivery. This should not really be of any great surprise,

Exhibit 2.6 TRATA survey of C-licensed vehicles

	Percentage preferring C licence
Speed of delivery and certainty of timing	68
Cost	44
Premises beyond public access	32
Reduction in damage	33
Reduction in pilferage	21
Reduction in packaging cost	24
Prompt return of empties	30
Specialist vehicles	29
Services provided by driver	39
Advertising on vehicle	37

given the knowledge of the cost of inventory levels. It is perhaps though a small surprise that cost of movement comes so high in preference. The reason this is unexpected is that the vast majority of firms operating own-account transport services usually do not have as accurate data of the costs involved as the replies to this particular study suggest.

It is also unexpected that the delivery of goods to locations not normally accessible to the public looms so large in consideration. One cannot avoid feeling that there is a great deal of bias in this particular response.

It will be noticed too that the back-up service provided by the driver account for a significant proportion of respondents preferring own delivery.

Interesting though this survey might have been, there are objections which could have been, and were, raised to its scientific reliability. These centred around the fact that the sample was pre-committed. That is to say, only those firms which were already using the type of service under review were asked about its effectiveness. We would therefore in all reasonableness expect these individuals to be prejudiced in their replies. Self-justification might, in other words, provide the reason why many of the answers to the TRATA survey turned out the way they did.

There is, perhaps, an even more important objection to the study, and this would go right to the heart of it. No quantitative or monetary frame of reference was introduced. This is important because certain factors might be felt to be of major importance without there being any major financial repercussions if they in fact fail to live up to expectation. In other words, simply because a large number of the transport managers covered by this particular survey felt that quality was important (and this response appeared many times) is no indication that in efficiency terms the same aspect is anything like as crucial.

These problems of the TRATA survey were of course realised shortly after the work was published. This is not to say that the original exercise was a waste of time. Far from it — it helped to concentrate the attention of the powers that be on this area.

The end result was, as we have already mentioned, a further study of the same basic area undertaken by experts appointed by the Ministry. Their brief was to overcome the lack of quantification and the difficulty of bias, which were the main bugbears of the original effort.

THE MINISTRY OF TRANSPORT SURVEY

Five industries were selected by the Ministry of Transport for this next survey. Some 500 companies took part in the study and they were requested to provide details of movements during a particular week (in some cases this was up to 100 consignments). Firms were asked to explain their choice of form of transport according to the following yardsticks:

> Weight.
> Handling characteristics.
> Cost of mode and alternatives.
> Secondary services.
> Length of movement.

To produce a meaningful result within the terms of reference for the survey (which we will remember were the reasons why own-account or public transport were employed), the following factors were included in the analysis:

1   Load characteristics such as length of haul, weight, handling characteristics (if applicable), back-up services and degree of urgency.
2   Company size, location and presence of own transport facilities.
3   The transport manager's estimate of the situation, including costs, pilferage record and availability of service.

The study attempted to decide two major parameters: the relative importance of an individual element and the extent to which the existence of that property increased the likelihood of the mode concerned being used. The results indicated that length of haul was far and away the most important variable in deciding whether own or public transport was used. Of the other factors mentioned above only the weight of the shipment proved to be of importance; all the other considerations proved to be of only minimal importance when the transport manager made his selection.

It is thus obvious that a major difficulty has arisen in trying to reconcile the results of the two studies discussed. The second government survey tended to suggest that cost and back-up services were not a major force in determining by which method goods were to be moved. The main considerations would appear to be length of haul and weight of consignment. The same considerations apply between road and rail.

The problem that faces us is how we can explain these two apparently conflicting results? It has already been pointed out that the original TRATA survey basis was open to question. We can also say, perhaps with even greater justification, that the government survey, like most, was also open to bias. If any use is to be made of these two surveys then this conflict must be resolved.

The argument becomes even more involved however. Having looked at the wide disparity between the results mentioned, yet another survey was carried out for the Ministry by Sharp in 1970. This study was wider than the original MOT survey and tended to confirm the results of the earlier TRATA work. Two main problems were thought to account for the bias in the MOT data:

1   To prevent managers quoting prices for other modes which they were not fully familiar with, the survey asked them not to quote unless they had accurate estimates. This provision resulted in about 75 per cent of loads having no alternative price. Some of this proportion would be managers who knew from experience that other forms of movement were too costly to even consider asking for a quotation, but others would not state price as a major consideration because they did not know the cost.

2   Since in most cases short haul can usually be completed faster by own-account fleets than public vehicles a further confusion could have arisen. Most managers would fill in the answer sheet as the length of haul being important, when in fact it was speed. This might account for the fact that speed of delivery appeared as the most common factor for own-account movement in the TRATA survey, but is scarcely mentioned in the MOT 1967 results. On the other hand it again becomes the most important consideration in the 1970 study.

Given the problems mentioned concerning the 1967 survey and the apparent confirmation by Sharp in 1970 of the TRATA results then in all fairness these must be given greater weight in any explanation as to why manufacturers often prefer own-account operations.

Before pursuing this line of discussion further yet another digression intrudes. It will be noticed that in every case the studies mentioned above dealt with 'the transport manager'. There was no attempt to deal with the subject area as a part of the 'total distribution cost' concept. Since the whole point of writing this volume was to point out that it was incorrect to look at transport costs in isolation, then we would expect the interest shown in recent years in physical distribution management (PDM) to have some influence on the conclusions of such surveys. Alas as far as I am aware no research has been conducted on a similar scale which would inform us if this were the case. Speculation costs little, however, and it is likely that such a survey might be in general agreement with the above. In the first place, as will become apparent, speed of delivery and reliability are two of the most important factors in the PDM contect anyway. The most likely new influence would possibly be more direct control over fleet operations, thus allowing implementation of any realised managerial economies of scale, through the introduction of PDM. The conclusion must be reached that own-account operations do have advantages for the firms concerned which include those detailed in the TRATA and Sharp studies, even although there may be some variation in the relative importance attached to the factors listed.

EFFICIENCY OF OWN-ACCOUNT OPERATIONS

It will be noticed that at this stage there is very little evidence to confirm the Geddes Committee's belief that the licensing system prevented own-account operators from operating efficiently. Indeed, the evidence would seem to indicate that they were very happy with the cost and quality of their services. It might be said, of course, that the small firm was the real target of the committee but this has already been examined. Until the nature of the work utilisation data for the relevant period is looked at it is very difficult to avoid the conclusion that the committee were convinced that inefficiency was encouraged by the A, B and C licensing system in spite of the available data. After all, did these not show, as has been mentioned many times, that the C operators were happy with the situation as it stood. Nonetheless, Exhibit 2.7 would seem to indicate that own-account operators were less efficient than the hire-or-reward sector. Two approaches can be taken to the information. On the one hand it could be said to prove that the licensing system through the return-load problem was causing inefficiency, or, on the other, you could argue that C operators were obviously outside their field and that they should concentrate on production and leave movement to the professionals. It is interesting as far as the argument goes to look at the relative

Exhibit 2.7 Usage of fleets before the 1968 Transport Act

Public haulage, tons ULW	Average ton-miles per vehicle
3-5	82.0
5-8	206.8
8	362.5
Own account	
3-5	44.5
5-8	113.3
8	200.0

share of the freight market that the two sectors have been capturing over the past
eight years or so. Over this period the share of tonnage moved by own-account
fleets has fallen by roughly 10 per cent and their share of ton-mileage by about
12 per cent. Yet it will be noticed that many of the reasons given for own-account
operations in the surveys quoted have if anything become more important. We
are, however, jumping too far ahead and must return to the recommendations of
the Geddes Committee.

GEDDES' GENERAL RECOMMENDATIONS AND THE RAILWAYS

One aspect of the Geddes Committee's deliberations that we have not mentioned
so far is their attitude to the railways. The Committee felt that the licensing
system had in the past failed to protect the railways and, recognising the government's interest in this, recommended that other fiscal measures, such as taxes and
subsidies, should be used to protect rail freight markets. *The Transport of Freight*
(Command Paper 3470: 1967) set out the main proposals which were, it was to
be hoped, to become law over a transitional period. There were basically three
mainstays of government thinking at that time. These were:
1   No carrier licence for vehicles not exceeding 30 cwt ULW.
2   A series of enactments, applicable to all vehicles over 30 cwt ULW, basically
     designed to improve safety and efficiency.
3   A system designed to promote the fullest use of the railways through quantity
     licensing of vehicles of more than 16 tons gross weight on journeys of 100
     miles or more.
If the general feeling of the Geddes Committee's thinking is by now familiar, then
it will be obvious that the first concept was very much in line with it; indeed
most of the transport industry thought that the proposal made sense. At the
time there were some 900,000 vehicles in this category. They were employed
chiefly in very short haul delivery and had a much better than average safety
record. As a result of their capacity they did not on the whole present a threat to
the interest of the railways and, because of their safety record, did not pose a
threat to the public at large. Hence all sides welcomed this policy.

The second suggestion was not quite so straightforward. Permit plating of
lorries was to be introduced. All goods vehicles were to carry a plate setting out
safety requirements such as carrying capacity. No plate — no commercial operation.
Punitive penalties were recommended for non-compliance with plating legislation.

Drivers' hours were another major area affected. These had previously been
unchanged for 33 years and stood at 11 hours driving in a maximum of a 14-hour
working day. This was changed to 10 hours driving in 11 duty hours spread over
no more than 12½ hours, with a maximum working week of 60 hours. A compulsory rest day per week was also introduced. These might seem substantial
reductions and a great many problems were caused for numerous firms but as we
shall see later when we look at EEC requirements, the allowed hours in this
country must be reduced even further still.

This second proposal involved as well the removal of the old A, B and C
licensing structure. This was to be replaced by the introduction of the 'Operator's'
or O licence, application for which was to be made to the normal authority who
had to be convinced of the suitability of the applicant with regard to mainten-

ance facilities, adequate financial resources and (perhaps the most important) that he or the person responsible for the compliance with the Act held a Transport Manager's Licence. This latter requirement was a new one as far as this country was concerned. In most of the EEC member countries (and ultimately by regulation of all of them) not just anybody can call himself a transport manager, although this is the case in the United Kingdom. On the Continent a professional status similar to that of doctors or accountants is accorded the transport manager. The status is not as high as the professions we have just mentioned but nonetheless the transport manager has to satisfy the relevant authorities concerning his competence. This is usually done through professional examinations. These might include subjects such as road safety law, the legal requirements concerning maintenance, basic managerial skills, finance and transport practice. In the Netherlands, for example, the contents of these examinations are decided upon by a committee representing the government, the academic institutions dealing with transport studies and the industries themselves.

It was envisaged in this country at the time of the Committee's report that a similar board would be constituted (as indeed it was) to report on the viability and contents of this country's examinations.

The right of appeal against the granting of an O licence was available to employer's associations, the police, the relevant trade unions and some local authorities. In all cases the basis of the objection obviously has to be that the applicant had not met all or some of the criteria already mentioned.

From the point of view of the government perhaps the most interesting proposal was the third, or quantity licensing aspect. This intended that any vehicle over 16 tons gross weight used on journeys of more than 100 miles (or in traffic of special interest to the railways over shorter distances — coal, iron and steel) had to apply to their licensing authority for special authorisation to carry on the trade. In their application they had to specify not only the type of goods to be carried but also the nature of the service including, most significantly, price. Only two bodies were to be able to object to the granting of such special authorisations: British Rail and the Freightliner Company. It is of great interest to note that they could only object on the grounds that 'they could provide a service which overall is as satisfactory as that of the applicant, taking into account a combination of speed, reliability, and cost (to the consignor) in relation to the needs of the consignors and the nature of the particular traffic concerned. The test will, therefore, be on economic grounds; it is not the government's intention that the licensing system should be capable of being used as a means of diverting traffic to rail uneconomically. In short, the system is designed to promote carriage of the traffic by rail where this can be done without detriment to the consignor.' Pious thoughts indeed!

As was pointed out at the time, if traffic on the roads was uneconomic, why was it there? Obviously the consignors (who the government was so keen to protect) thought their goods were already travelling by the most effective means. If they had got out of touch with the new developments in the movement of freight by the railways, then surely what was required was a 're-education' campaign, not a forced march.

The most likely reasons behind this proposal were probably the ever-present government desire to see a greater utilisation of the railways, and also, perhaps the desire to seek market information through the appeals system with regard to the pricing policies of the road transport industry. More will be said on these subjects in the section dealing with the railways.

As was previously pointed out many of the propositions were not intended to have the full force of the law until later dates — some not until the early seventies. As we now know there was a change of government in the meantime and the Conservatives did not introduce some of the provisions, and subsequent Labour Governments have not changed that.

PRESENT POSITION

We must now look at those provisions of the Act which were not in fact passed into law. In the first instance the quantity aspect of the proposition received such a hostile reception from the transport industry at large that they were not introduced. The same fate befell the Transport Manager's Licence. In this case there is, however, a sting in the tail so to speak. By January 1978 it will become an EEC regulation that, in addition to the O licence, a Transport Manager's Licence must be held also. In fact the conditions attached to the granting of this TML are more or less the same as those originally proposed by the 1968 Transport Act. There are however slight alterations in origin and intention and perhaps a brief glance at these would be useful. The first point worth remembering is that the UK origin of the TML was based on an industry within which there was no legal distinction between own-account and hire-or-reward operators. This is the only company in Europe where such a system is in operation. The EEC countries, therefore, were asking the UK to put back the clock inasmuch as they see the TML requirement applying to professional hauliers only. Thus if the original proposals were to be accepted it would mean that those own-account operators who availed themselves of the chance to enter into competition with hire-or-reward firms for particular traffics would lose their right to do so. It is true to say that only a very small number took this line but some of those were large-scale operators.

It is interesting to note that the Road Haulage Association which can be said to represent the views of the hire-or-reward sector was in favour of the EEC approach. Perhaps it saw the chance to re-create a competition barrier between its members and those private operators who had entered the market. At the same time, the Freight Transport Association, representing own-account firms, were also broadly in favour, most likely because they see the TML as an expensive administrative procedure which was not really intended to apply to them in the first place. Those private operators carrying third-party goods, would, of course, have to have a TML.

The government felt that the cost of implementing a TML law where only a small proportion of goods vehicles would require enforcement would be high and the task very complicated. Thus the 1968 TML provisions were implemented after all.

Within the EEC the TML provisions will apply only to professional hauliers operating vehicles of 6 tonnes gross weight or over. Because of the original 1968 Act the TML will apply in the UK to operators of vehicles of 3½ tonnes or more.

Existing O licence holders, provided they have held their licence since December 1976, will receive the TML as of right, as will those responsible for the day-to-day management of a carrier's business since December 1974 even though they do not hold an O licence. The examination content will be as already mentioned and will be held twice a year by the Royal Society of Arts, in consultation with a committee comprising representatives of the unions, employers' organisations, the RTITB and the Department of Transport.

Those individuals who were nominated as managers or who obtained an O licence after December 1974 but before January 1978 will have two years to satisfy the RSA examiners and will be granted an interim TML.

It will be remembered that the 1968 Act saw the TML as centred in one 'home' depot. It is now likely that if he operates from more than one location then he will be required to take out a TML at least for every licensing authority he comes under. Once obtained, the TML is held for life unless the holder is convicted of specified offences or contributes by acts or omissions to a directive being made against the O licence of his employers. His TML could then be revoked or suspended. He might even be instructed to resit the RSA examinations. In other words, offences against traffic law could, after January 1978, result in the loss of both TML and O licence, the loss of either making it impossible to continue in business.

INFLATION

The situation is then that there will be two kinds of licence — General and Restricted. The restricted licence will allow the holder to operate as under the old 'C' licence. The general licence will require a Certificate of Competence (the official and strictly correct term rather than TML) and allows the holder to operate for hire and reward. In fact, of course, any transport operator who wishes to obtain a manager with a certificate of competence will be able to enter the market, but there are some own-fleet operations who have intimated that they will not in fact do this.

Given the extra burden of this and other legislation discussed below there is little doubt that the road transport industry must pass on higher costs in the form of higher prices and add to the general level of inflation throughout the economy.

Although individual legislation is reviewed in other parts of this book it might prove useful to bring together under this heading those major items which is felt will add most to the prices spiral — and at the same time to bring up to date specific changes in attitudes, since it is inevitable that these develop and change almost daily.

EEC regulations concerning drivers' hours are mentioned in the EEC overview, the basic effect being a reduction to an 8-hr day. As of January 1978 these will be introduced over a three-year period; the associated tachograph issue seems to have been accepted at the official level. The reduction in hours will prove a heavy burden on the industry and increase costs and hence prices will rise significantly. Indeed a figure of £100 million has been discussed as being the cost of the new hours. It really does not have to be repeated that such a cost increase must and indeed will be passed on in the form of higher prices. The tachograph problem will almost certainly cause disruption and probably strike action from the unions. In the modern transport industry such interruptions to 'normal service' inevitably have dramatic effects on the operators but also on the manufacturers, retailers and other organisations who make up their customers. Interruption will cause problems in stock levels and of course result in them providing a decreased service in turn to their customers.

But in reality these problems are merely additions to the central one, namely that a case can be made for saying that this country is in fact obtaining its road transport services 'cut price' and recent legislation has been moving in the wrong direction. At least, many professional hauliers feel this. They point to a lack of direction in minimum tariffs, EEC thinking is very much towards the forked tariff system. This consists of a brachet price being laid down for various services so that there is a minimum and maximum charge allowable. Whilst the EEC is certainly not pushing the adoption of the concept, it is fair to say that most hire and reward operators in this country would very much like to see the *minimum-rate* concept being introduced. They feel, perhaps, that entry into the industry is too easy now, and indeed the Foster Committee, recently set up to investigate 'O' licence procedures, is likely to hear the professionals calling for a reintroduction of restrictive licensing akin to the pre-1968 position!

The latest available figures show that on average haulage companies are obtaining something like an 11 per cent return on capital employed. There would seem to be little doubt that in times of inflation, where vehicle prices have increased by up to 200 per cent in the past six years, this is an insufficient return. Just what constitutes adequate return is difficult to say but many of the more influential firms talk of figures in the 20 per cent range — this must mean increases in average prices.

*   *   *

In practice, then, the United Kingdom system is now one of remarkably little restriction in terms of entry into the industry. This might be reasonably said to have been the base recommendation of the Geddes Committee, but as government objectives this could be difficult to prove. The end result, however, no matter what the government's intention was, has been the freest entry conditions in Europe.

3 The marginal social cost pricing concept

Whilst it is not the intention of this work to delve too deeply into the theoretical background to policy decisions in the transport field, the subject of marginal social cost pricing must be an exception to this rule.

Marginal social cost pricing (MSCP) in the road transport context is an attempt to ensure that each road user pays an amount for the use of road facilities equal, in theory (approximately equal in practice), to the use they make of the road infrastructure. At the present time the pricing policy used in this country is of the arbitrary type, where every road user pays a certain sum irrespective of the use they make of roads or, indeed, the total cost of roads.

It must be said, however (as discussed later), that some attempts are being made to change this situation. By 1979 the taxation system in this country will at least try and make some allowance for road use. By 1981, however, the EEC is committed to the introduction of a marginal social cost pricing system for roads. If this materialises as a regulation then the basic costs of transport will be substantially affected. Almost certainly they will move upward as firms are expected to take a more realistic share not only of the direct public costs of roads, but of the costs they impose on the community at large, in other words their social costs. As this happens the transport manager is going to be directly affected inasmuch as he will have to deal with greater costs for the same journeys and if the more extreme forms are to be introduced, with a price differential for various times of day, or even supplements for each journey to city centres, route planning will then become of even greater importance than at present.

As will be seen, however, MSCP is difficult to implement and at the time of writing (late 76), it is not known which system the Common Market will eventually adopt. There is therefore a case to be made for a brief examination of the chief trends of thinking with regard to MSCP — although it is not the intention to cover the subject in depth.

In general terms we can say that there are four major pricing policies that might be followed:

1 Arbitrary pricing Under this approach the roads would be financed from a general taxation fund. There is no attempt to relate the amount spent on road provision to the amounts collected from taxation. In some years, therefore, there may be a surplus of collected monies over road costs. It should be noted that 'road costs' will be defined later — assume pure construction costs for the present. The main advantage of this system is that administrative costs are low and there is always the possibility of surplus revenue for the government to use elsewhere in its programme. This is the policy pursued in this country.

In 1965-66, for example, the ratio of revenue from taxes to costs (track costs + accidents) for cars was 2.1:1; in 1970-71, 2.0:1; and in 1975-76, 2.0:1 (non-business) and 1.5:1 (business). In other words, for each of these years, this particular class of vehicle contributed nearly twice as much as it benefited. (Accident costs are not included in the 1975-76 data.) For buses and coaches in the same periods the ratios were 1.4:1, 1.4:1 and 0.8:1, i.e. by 1976 they were underpaying. The ratios for light vans (under 30 cwt ULW) were 3.3:1, 2.1:1 and 1.9:1 — again a class contributing more than its fair share. For lorries and vehicles over 30 cwt ULW the ratios were 1.8:1, 1.5:1 and 0.8:1 — these, like the buses, undercontributed in 1975-76.

The ratios for total traffic were 2.1:1, 1.9:1 and 1.5:1 — overall an oversubscription. We can now, of course, point to the major disadvantage of the arbitrary pricing system, namely that there is no relationship between the use that individual classes of vehicle make of the roads.

It was estimated by the government in 1976 that a 32-ton, 4-axle lorry imposed damage on the roads equivalent to about 10.760 cars, assuming average mileage all round. This is not the end because there is inequity within groups as well as between them. Vehicles in the same excise group pay the same taxes, but those vehicles covering substantially greater mileages impose more damage on the road networks and provide greater revenue for their owners without them paying proportionally higher track costs. They do pay higher fuel taxes but the imbalance remains. Indeed, from the figures already given, it is obvious that in 1975-76 operators of the higher weight category vehicles received a subsidy from other road users — especially private car owners. It is interesting to note that in the heaviest lorry groups it was estimated that they fell short on average by about 40 per cent — or, to put it another way, the ratio of revenue raised to cost was about 0.6:1.

There is, then, an argument against the arbitrary pricing concept, no matter how attractive governments may find it. The question then is: Are there any more equitable methods available? If there are alternatives then we must assume them to be more desirable only if their use would bring about a net benefit. That is to say, they would be worthwhile if the advantages of their introduction outweighed the costs of their administration. It is this net benefit that argument rages around on the alternative systems, including marginal cost pricing.

2 Average cost pricing This method has some attractions. The process is simple and should not involve too much increase in administration costs.

Instead of arbitrary tax costs, the previous year's total expenditure is calculated. This is already available from standard government sources. The total
numbers of vehicles using the roads network is also known. The charge to be
levied is simply total costs divided by total numbers of vehicles. The case can be
made that this is desirable since the cost taken into account is the actual expenditure on the infrastructure the previous year. The major objection to this is
that this very cost is more than likely to vary from year to year. Thus nobody
will know exactly, in advance, what their next year's taxation bill would be. It is
argued that the most private individuals would find this undesirable — probably
correct.

There is, of course, the more basic objection that there is as yet no attempt
to relate the use made of the roads to the costs paid by individual vehicles.

3   Monopoly pricing   This system is unlikely ever to find favour in this country.
The basis is to allow the suppliers of the service to charge the users whatever the
traffic will bear. Thus revenue bears no relationship to costs or to the use which
is made of the roads, simply to the ability of the users to pay. The availability of
supply services is restricted. The point is that revenue maximisation becomes the
objective, whereas what we would like to see would be a self-financing system,
with revenue related to cost and use.

4   User cost pricing   In its simplest terms this approach seeks to raise in revenue
from those who use the roads the costs imposed by them on other road users,
the suppliers, and the community at large. Under this system those who use the
roads most often would pay the most. In those areas where road use implied
higher than usual costs, such as city centres at peak travel times, then further
costs would be incurred. The whole concept is based on making sure that those
making journeys bear the true cost of those journeys. Many maintain that this is
the only equitable policy, not only in social terms but in economic terms as well
since they are of the opinion that this approach would bring increased efficiency
in the use and provision of roads.

These arguments are certainly attractive and, at first glance, sound. There are,
however, many objections to the practical formulation of such a policy. This is
especially so when we look at the implications behind marginal social cost princi-
ples, which are the mainstay for the most favoured implementations of user cost
pricing.

It will be obvious that two steps must now be taken. First, we must define the
costs which we have been talking about more fully; secondly, we must outline
the ideas behind marginal social cost concepts and discuss how they might be
applied in practice. Once this has been done then the objections to the approach
must be dealt with.

INFRASTRUCTURE COSTS

It is possible to break up the total costs incurred in providing and using roads into
two broad categories, each with various sub-divisions:

(a)   Land   This is one of the most obvious costs associated with the construction of roads and at the same time a topic that can cause a great deal of discussion. The main point is that road users should be charged an amount to cover the economic rent that land in use for roads would command. The economic rent concept is a payment made to a resource to cover its scarcity value. If, for example, an individual owned a supply of water in Scotland, say, then the price that he could charge for it under normal circumstances would be determined by the fact (to a great extent) that water is usually not in short supply. If, on the other hand, a great drought hit the country leaving only his supply then the price he could charge would increase — even though the only characteristic that has changed has been scarcity. To look at it another way, building land will vary in cost a great deal. Within Greater London land is limited, sites on prize locations even more so. The variation in price is a result of the economic rent concept, namely that extra is paid because of short supply. Likewise with land used for road construction. It could be argued that a price was paid when the land was bought in the first place and any difference between the price paid originally and the current price (the rent concept — increased demand but fixed supply) should be ignored. There is a certain attraction to this view, but it must be kept in mind that we would like to see the most efficient use of resources possible. If, therefore, road users are not prepared to pay an annual sum at least equal to the economic rent, and somebody else is, then the value they are deriving from the road's use is greater than they see the need for paying. Thus the resource would be better turned to another use where the full rent could be obtained. The charge to be made is, of course, the alternative use rent. Some argue that no payment should be made on comparisons with alternative uses in the same area since in many cases the value increased because of the presence of the road. The counter-argument is usually to point out that the presence of water, gas and electricity supplies enhances the value of city properties, yet we expect those utilities to pay the going costs of land in the area.

(b)   Construction costs   These costs are straightforward, being labour and materials (excluding land) costs.

(c)   Maintenance and deterioration   These are not the costs under this heading associated with traffic use, but those which would be incurred even if there was no traffic on the road at all. Certain administration costs would still be incurred even if they were only those associated with controlling the workforce employed to deal with climatic and vegetation effects.

(d)   Interest charges   This is again a topic which would seem to present no problems but which in practice does. In theory it is claimed that the interest charges should at least be equal to the opportunity cost of the capital employed, i.e. equal to the next best return that could be obtained by investing the monies concerned in the next most profitable project.

In practice, of course, interest has to be paid on the finance used to pay for the construction of the various road projects. The argument is whether road users should be expected to meet such a cost element, if and when they pay on a user cost method. The general opinion of the authorities would seem to be not. In the first instance it is felt that since all road users have over the years paid more than the construction costs anyway no further capital charge could be justified.

As far as the argument that the railways have to raise monies to pay for track costs is concerned it is pointed out that the railways have had large capital debts written off by successive governments and, therefore, it cannot be argued that current railway costs are related to the replacement costs of renewable assets.

2 Costs arising out of journeys

(a) Private costs   These are costs that fall directly on those making journeys. This would include items such as fuel, oil, tyres and maintenance costs.

(b) Road usage costs   These are the costs incurred through the use of the roads by the various categories of vehicle. Some mention has already been made of the relationship of revenue to costs for some classes of users. The main area of interest here is, of course, goods vehicles. In the period 1975-76 estimates are given for this class in Volume 2 of the *Transport Policy Consultative Document.* Allocation is between rigid body and articulated vehicles on the basis of number of axles and gross vehicle weight:

Rigid-bodied vehicles
2 axles:
    5 tons GVW   1.7:1
    12 tons GVW   1.2:1
    16 tons GVW   0.7:1
3 axles:
    16 tons GVW   1.2:1
    24 tons GVW   0.7:1
4 axles:
    24 tons GVW   0.9:1
    30 tons GVW   0.6:1

Articulated vehicles, not surprisingly, turned in results of a different pattern.

Articulated vehicles:
3 axles:
    12 tons GVW   1.4:1
    16 tons GVW   1.2:1
    24 tons GVW   0.6:1
4 axles:
    24 tons GVW   0.9:1
    32 tons GVW   0.6:1
5 axles:
    32 tons GVW   0.7:1

It will be noted that as the number of axles increases, wear and tear on the roads decreases and the ratio of revenue to cost thus improves. These figures refer to road track costs only. If the entire range of costs involved had been included then the ratios would, of course, have been less favourable.

(c) Congestion costs These are costs imposed on motor vehicles by one another; these cause some problems in treatment. The government have chosen to include congestion costs in user or private costs since it is felt that they fall directly on those making the journeys. These elements include those which could be tied to a time factor. The basic manifestation of congestion is decreased traffic speeds or increased journey times. Thus working time, higher fuel and maintenance costs, a drop in the utilisation of vehicles, loss in leisure time and so on are considered to be reasonable cost centres attributable to congestion. The official view is that if a particular vehicle class imposes more congestion than it suffers then a transfer payment should be made by the government to the class suffering. However, it is considered that the procedures involved would be too complicated for practical purposes. There is some argument against this treatment. First, it is said, not all the congestion costs fall on the individuals making the journeys. Employers lose production or pay in some other form for increased journey times. This increase in costs is not recouped from the journey makers but is a higher cost element which finds its way indirectly in the form of higher prices to the consumers — who may themselves make no use of the type of transport in question. This same argument applies to the time lost in the transport of materials. Since service levels are an important cost consideration for many companies, time is a major cost factor. If congestion throughout the country is causing more products to be in the 'pipeline' at any one time, these represent finance tied up, extra costs for the manufacturer and, thus, higher prices for the consumer. The other main argument against the government point of view is that if all the different categories of road user were paying the true economic cost of their journey there may be many who would not make the journey or would go by some other means such as public transport or they might double up on car use. This might reduce overall congestion. In the case of goods vehicles, however, such extra cost sharing could induce more effective route planning, load consolidation, or vehicle scheduling, all leading to a more effective use of the road infrastructure.

(d) Community costs These are the costs imposed on the community at large by road users. These are usually regarded as those expenses generated by accidents, noise, fumes, vibrations and decreases in the quality of the environment. The government attitude to these is again ambivalent. They admit that a case can be made for road users paying for the costs imposed on the community in this way. They even go so far as to agree that if such charges were made there might be a reduction in the number of occasions when they arise, but they consider that the method of assessing and gathering such costs would be too imprecise for practical use. However, it is considered that the existence of such a situation can be used to justify collecting more from road users than simply road construction costs. Fair enough — but who says how much more; surely a less than perfect road pricing system is better than arbitrary sums.

These then are the total costs involved in the provision, maintenance and use of a road system. It will be obvious that the use of simple track costs as a measure of how much each vehicle class is contributing (or indeed each vehicle) to total cost is less than fully accurate. If we are to achieve a more optimum use of resources within the country at large, substantial changes must take place.

We must now address ourselves to the discussion of marginal costs, social costs and the ideas behind a marginal social cost pricing approach.

The entire intention of MSCP is to achieve the best allocation of the available resources within the country. The concept was economic in origin and is subject to the very real limitations of any such principle. However, no matter how much we qualify the economic theory, enough can usually be salvaged to make a reasonable basis for a practical approach.

The true effective cost of anything is its *opportunity cost*, i.e. the giving up of whatever we could have had if the resources used had produced something else. In other words, if we have only £1 and the choice in spending it is between, say, three pints of beer and a salad, then if we choose the beer the true cost is the salad, or if we chose the salad then the true cost is the beer. The *marginal cost* is the true cost of producing just one extra unit of the product in question. Therefore if we are considering producing one extra unit of a product, the consumer of that product must be willing to pay at least the cost of the resources required for its manufacture. This is simply saying that the output of a product should be extended to the point where its marginal cost equals price. At that point the output is just equal to what value the consumers put upon that combination of product and quantity. This applies, of course, only in ideal circumstances — where there are no institutions bending the pattern of costs and prices through their power, where everybody is perfectly aware of the state of supply and demand and prices in the market, and where anybody can enter the market if he sees an opportunity for him to do so. A smaller output would fetch a higher price, indicating that some factors are present ensuring that a product is being produced which is regarded as less valuable than our material in question. A higher output could not be sold, except at a price lower than the marginal cost of making it, thus indicating that forces are ensuring that our product is being manufactured rather than something else which consumers would value more. There is a further situation which might arise and this is where consumers are not aware of the true costs of the product and demand a greater supply than they would because they receive an outside or unperceived subsidy.

Whilst this objective of achieving the best allocation of resources through setting the price equal to marginal cost is true only in the ideal conditions outlined above, a school of thought exists which says that for certain activities, especially those undertaken 'for the public good', it is as good a target for operation as any other. Indeed, it is better than most since the objective is the optimum allocation of available resources. Whilst it is recognised that it will operate 100 per cent only in specific circumstances, it is more desirable than other rules not fully effective aiming at individual gain. As far as its application to government services and/or industry is concerned then a great deal depends on what view is taken as to what the objectives of these activities should be — commercial profit or self-financing efficient allocation of resources.

The upshot of this is that if the demand for a service or product can be said to be an accurate measure of the benefits that the consumer receives from the product and/or service, then the optimum production point will be where the marginal cost curve cuts the demand curve, or (to be more correct) if the demand curve accurately measures the benefit consumers receive from additional units of supply, and the marginal cost curve accurately measures the additional costs imposed on society for producing the additional units then society will gain maximum benefits if the marginal cost of producing extra units equals the marginal benefits of consumers.

In respect of transport the argument runs thus: to maximise social benefits, the road tax system should be such as to ensure that each user pays a price equal to the marginal cost of the road usage he consumes. There are many problems associated not only with the translation of this 'rule' into a workable policy, but also with the theoretical concept behind it. The first problem is that the demand curve for the product or service must accurately reflect the true benefits that consumers receive. How effectively can the market mechanism measure the benefit that consumers derive from a product? Simply because a rich consumer is prepared to pay a higher price than a poor one is no guarantee that his satisfaction and/or level of consumption is greater or more desirable. If the market does not accurately measure the benefits arising from consumption then it might not be a suitable method of allocating resources. In other words, setting prices equal to marginal costs might result instead in undesirable distribution of resources. It is argued, however, that it is not the marginal concept that is the cause of this problem but the inequality of income. There are ways of treating this, such as through the tax system or by subsidies for certain categories, but we are interested in the marginal theory's application to transport infrastructure, and taking income distribution into account is usually an inherent part of investment appraisal procedures. It is usual therefore to assume that in transport considerations the demand curve reflects benefit received — always with the proviso that certain low-income groups might require subsidy in specific cases. As far as goods transport is concerned this qualification would be as follows. There might be certain small operators who could find the application of MSCP prohibitive for their business. One is thinking here of the rural market especially. In this case government exemption from full payment, or direct subsidy for social considerations would be the rule. This in fact already takes place in, for example, the Highlands and Islands, although naturally not under marginal pricing policies. Under marginal pricing, losses are likely to be incurred in certain sectors, as shown in Exhibit 3.1. This might be overcome by charging a fixed cost to cover the loss whilst recovering marginal costs through a price based on consumption, such as is done on, say, the telephone system. This approach is objected to on the grounds that some consumers may be unwilling to pay the fixed charge even although they are willing to pay their marginal costs. This is unlikely to be a deterrent in practice since consumers are already used to paying fixed charges for vehicles. On the other hand some form of price discrimination might be used. Those consumers whose demand is less likely to be affected by price will pay a greater share of the deficit than those whose consumption is easily affected by price changes. This system is already widely used by British Rail such as in allowing day returns only after 9.30 a.m. Since we are to accept losses so readily it follows that profit ceases to be the ultimate measure of effectiveness, of deciding whether a project will continue or be abandoned. This is usually a stumbling block, since the measure of social benefit, which is the new criterion, is so difficult to quantify. It is also pointed out that internal control and appraisal would be much more difficult without the profit measure.

It is sometimes pointed out that any attempt at MSCP must take place throughout the entire economy. If some areas continue as before then there will still be an overall poor distribution of resources. Whilst this is true, it is also argued that if marginal prices are applied throughout an individual sector, then although the allocation of resources to that sector might have been poor, then at least distribution within the sector will be good.

Most important as far as transport is concerned is that any divergence between

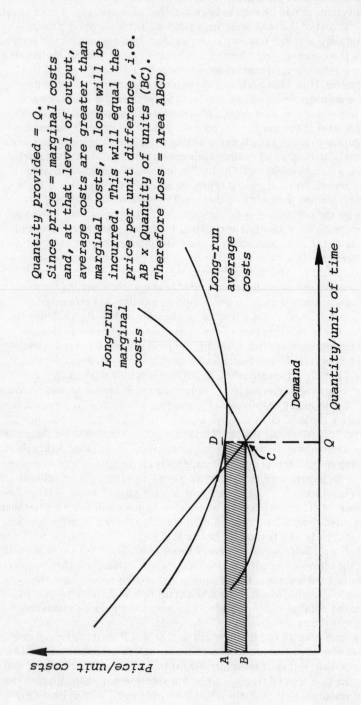

Quantity provided = Q.
Since price = marginal costs
and, at that level of output,
average costs are greater than
marginal costs, a loss will be
incurred. This will equal the
price per unit difference, i.e.
AB x Quantity of units (BC).
Therefore Loss = Area ABCD

Long-run marginal costs

Long-run average costs

Demand

Quantity/unit of time

Price/unit costs

Exhibit 3.1 How losses might arise under MSCP

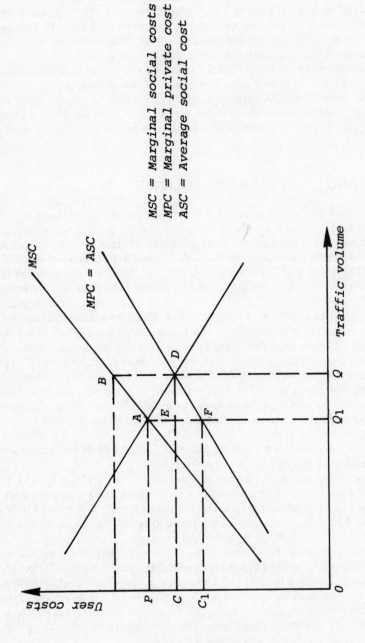

MSC = Marginal social costs
MPC = Marginal private cost
ASC = Average social cost

Exhibit 3.2 The effect of MSCP policies

private and social costs must be taken account of. We have assumed so far that the costs borne by transport users reflect social costs. This is not so and the problem arises out of the perceived costs issue. If we look at the situation on a congested road this will become clear. The individual road user perceives the costs that are being imposed on him by other road users. He takes these into account when deciding whether to make a particular trip by road or some other means. He does not consider the costs he is imposing on other road users. He imposes costs on other road users but does not have to pay them, hence the difference between perceived costs, or private costs, and social costs.

This is the entire objective of MSCP policies, i.e. to try and maximise the social benefits not just the private ones. This means that the individual road users must be made aware of the true costs they impose rather than just the perceived ones. To achieve this all the costs imposed on society must be included in our calculation of cost and a price charged that will equate marginal benefits with marginal social cost.

MSCP AND ROAD TAXATION POLICIES

The result of this in an ideal situation is shown in Exhibit 3.2. Assume in the first instance that the road is congested but no tax is levied to bring home the true social costs. The amount of traffic using the road will then be Q, i.e. the amount that considers its marginal private cost (MCP) equal to its benefits at cost C. If we extend the quantity Q to the marginal social cost curve (MSC) then we can say that a marginal social cost of QB is imposed; this obviously exceeds the average social benefits as measured by QD. Since we wish to maximise social benefits then we need a traffic flow of AQ_1, i.e. a flow where marginal social benefits greatest consistent with cost. To achieve this we would have to impose a congestion tax of C_1P per unit. This would raise the total cost paid by the users to OP. The costs of using the road (net of tax) has been reduced from OC to OC_1. This is the benefit obtained from MSCP. The users who continue consumption of the road will now of course pay OP. This consists of two elements: the cost of using the road and the cost imposed on society as a whole by that use, in other words the private and social marginal costs. Society as a whole will therefore receive a surplus represented by the area C_1PAF, although in strict terms it is neither a benefit nor otherwise; it is a transfer payment, collected from one class of society and available for distribution to another.

Those consumers who have been removed from the road ($OQ-OQ_1$) have suffered a loss in benefit represented by the area AED. These were road users who only used the road because they were not paying the full social costs of their journeys. From the above discussion, it is fair to say that in the theoretical situation, at least, the MSCP policy has some attractions.

As already pointed out, the next stage of our review must be to see how such a method could be applied in practice. The basis is simple: we merely take all the costs involved in the provision and use of the road network and apply these in such a way that each user pays the marginal incremental cost he imposes. Needless to say, translating this into a practical method of working is not so simple. At the root of any form of pricing approach must, of course, be charging techniques and we will now briefly review these.

In the first case we have the many indirect methods. First, fuel tax. This was first introduced in 1909. It was felt that since new road schemes were being initiated for the benefit of car users then they should pay a special tax. Originally it was intended that this revenue be committed totally to road construction. This, as we now well know, was and indeed is not the case. The main advantage of this type of tax is ease of collection. There is also the possibility of discriminating against, or in favour of, different fuel types, i.e. diesel as against petrol. Secondly, there are tyre taxes. These are intended to be a tax on vehicle usage. Thus the vehicle that does the greatest mileage per year will pay more in tax because it will use more tyres. There is an attempt here to relate road use to some form of payment for that use. The main objection here is that, in the absence of any tyre safety legislation, there would be a strong temptation to keep tyres on vehicles as long as possible, possibly beyond the safe time.

Then there is the annual licence. Every vehicle must have a currently valid excise licence. Until 1948 the cost of this varied with the capacity of the vehicle — an attempt to relate wear and tear costs to use. The original assumption was that the higher horse-power vehicles caused more damage and were likely to be owned by individuals more capable of meeting the costs so incurred.

Then there is purchase or car tax, this being a tax on the purchase of a vehicle. In theory this type of tax could be used to encourage or discourage the purchase of any selected type of vehicle. Past experience has tended, however, to indicate that such a tax is regarded by the government as a regulator on consumption, and as such follows the normal trend in taxation policies. As such it is not very likely to hold much attraction as a means of affecting road use, at least in terms of journey cost.

Parking charges of one kind or another are yet a further method of indirect charge. The aim here is to make a charge related to the cost of bringing the vehicle into a particular area. This might have some attractions when regarded with respect to private cars in city centre areas, but has much less relevance when looked at with regard to goods vehicles.

The next general category is direct collecting methods. One of the oldest of these is tolls. As a general method these were abolished in the UK in 1871, but they are still used on a variety of bridges and tunnels. On the Continent and in the USA they are still used on road networks. They are not usually employed as a method of marginal cost pricing but as a method of recouping original capital cost. After this has been repaid, the facility in question loses its toll — in theory. This can lead to problems. In the USA, bridges that have recouped their costs often become more congested than those new ones still charging tolls, thus destroying the whole basis of the concept.

All of the methods mentioned above suffer from a basic and essential failing — they are inflexible. The aim of all of them is to gather additional revenue. They were not conceived as a means of varying the price paid in relation to the use made of any particular facility. If we are to introduce an MSCP system (and the case for so doing is open to question, irrespective of EEC decisions), then we must have a method that fulfills as a minimum the following conditions:

1 *Flexibility* Charges must be capable of being related to road use. Since we would expect charges to vary with mileage, time of day (perhaps) and type of vehicle, then the second basic criterion must be certainty.

2   *Users*, or potential users, must be certain of the likely charges in advance. The whole idea of the system is to ensure that journeys and modes will be consumed only if the benefit from so doing is at least equal to the cost. If the consumer does not know, at least roughly, in advance what that cost is to be then the technique would achieve nothing.

There are two devices available which would satisfy these conditions. The first is on-vehicle metres. These would be in effect similar to a taxi meter — although the mechanism would be quite different. The on-vehicle meter (OVM) would be of the solid-state device type with practically no moving parts. It would be located on the vehicle close to the ground, but would have some form of mechanical connection to a visible device to indicate when the meter capacity was used up. The various traffic zones in the country would be divided up into individual areas in order of increasing congestion. A charge per type of vehicle would be decided for each of these zones, the higher the charge the faster would the capacity of the OVM be used up — when finished the visible sign would be triggered. Each OVM would have a fixed capacity of 'points'. Thus, for a given vehicle in a low-cost area, capacity would be consumed more slowly than if the same vehicle were always used in higher cost areas. We have assumed that the OVM used would be a solid-state device but plans are also available for clockwork meters. These would be of given points capacity and they would have to be taken at predecided intervals to the equivalent of present day taxation offices to be 'rewound' once they were exhausted. Likewise our solid state models. It has also been suggested that OVM acting as pure recorders could be introduced. These would be taken to the taxation offices at intervals and the used units paid for.

This particular pricing method has been under appraisal by the government in the past and has had some objections raised to it. The most important from our point of view was cost, coupled with inconvenience. A network of pay stations would have to be instituted. Even if these were reorganised tax offices, outlays would still be incurred and there would be extra costs involved in enforcement since the clockwork devices might be open to tampering.

The alternative is the off-vehicle meter (FVM). The FVM operates by having a solid-state 'black box' fitted to each vehicle. This identifies that particular vehicle and no other. Under the FVM system time spent in the various zones would be recorded in much the same way as telephone costs are monitored. A central complex would note when and for how long and in which price zones a vehicle was moving. At discrete intervals a bill would be sent to the registered owner of the vehicle.

Both systems would rely on wire loops placed under the road at strategic junctions. Different charges could be made for different zones depending on location, time of day, traffic flow and various other considerations.

It is worth remembering that the National Board for Prices and Incomes recommended in November 1970 that road pricing experiments should be carried out. Trials were implemented in Southport a few months later. In these experiments the FVM device was favoured, and some 5000 road users took part on a voluntary basis. The movement however lost momentum and no recommendations for general application were made.

The technical expertise to introduce a form of road pricing based on the use of FVMs has been with us for some time and such techniques would allow the mechanical side of an MSCP programme to be completed at any time assuming government desire. Why then has there been no positive move in this direction?

There are probably two main reasons to be examined to explain this lack of action. In the first case there is cost. A wide-ranging study would have to be in-itiated to examine, evaluate and quantify the total costs involved in road infra-structure and use. At the same time, just exactly how these costs could be divided between vehicle classes, geographical locations and times of day of travel would also have to be decided. There would also have to be a parallel scheme to lay the necessary control wires and central computing devices. In other words, a rather large capital investment scheme would be involved.

PROBLEMS FOR MSCP

There are still some practical objections to the entire approach which have not yet been reviewed. The first and most important of these is the technical ability to calculate on an equitable basis what the price to be charged for each mile for each vehicle category should be. This is a task of monumental proportions and there is a school of thought that maintains that the cost of so doing would in reality outweigh the benefits likely to be achieved by introducing MSCP. Studies have already been completed for the EEC on exactly this basis, but not for this country.

Then there is the problem that the transport sector has private and public components. If a system of MSCP were to be introduced, then it is likely that the higher costs that government-directed vehicles had to face would be regarded in the real fashion, i.e. true costs which had to be borne without being passed onto the consumer. This is fine for nationalised concerns where the attitude to 'profit' is already confused. On the other hand private firms would most likely pass the increase on to the consumer since past profit levels (under conditions of cross-subsidy) would be taken as performance targets. In the political sense, then, it would be very difficult to sell MSCP as an advance when consumers might very well have to pay higher prices in the shops for most of their purchases.

At the same time, for the very reason just mentioned, it would be very difficult indeed to sell the idea to industry. It must be remembered that industry, both transport and general, has some very powerful legitimate pressure groups.

It is unlikely then that the UK will willingly introduce MSCP.

4 The EEC and road transport policy

On 1 January 1973 the UK joined the EEC. At the time there was a great deal of talk about the 'new terms' under which entry was made. It must be pointed out that as far as transport policy within the community was concerned, no objections, suggestions or alterations were put forward by this country. In fact we were to be faced with a transport policy virtually unchanged since the community was first brought into being, although (as we shall see later) it is probably fair to say that a new emphasis has emerged in the last two or three years.

EEC POWERS

Before we attempt a brief survey of the EEC position on transport it might be as well to mention that we must be clear about the meaning of the various terms used when discussing the statements issued by the Community.

In the first place we have Opinions and Recommendations. These have no binding power whatever and are intended solely to indicate to member governments the general direction that Community thought is likely to take.

Secondly, there are Directives. These are more important in the fiscal sense as they are intended to be binding in terms of the ultimate objectives. The EEC, however, does not lay down detailed steps as to how the desired end is to be achieved, simply what it is. The member states then move towards this in their own ways.

Finally there are Regulations. These are binding both in general and in detail. They are considered to supersede the local law of member states, although in practice a great deal of haggling can and does take place.

General policy starts with the Commission who deal with general proposals and conceive, prepare and draft the relevant instruments. However, the actual legislation can only be passed by the Council of Ministers and, naturally, there is the possibility that much will be changed in the process. In the future it is likely that the European Parliament may take a greater and greater share of the actual legislative process; indeed this is the avowed intention of many of its members.

It is not our place here to discuss the politics of the EEC, however, and with this very basic introduction we must return to the transport element.

HISTORICAL BACKGROUND TO EEC TRANSPORT POLICY

The ground rules of the Community were laid down in the Treaty of Rome. Article 3(e) of the Treaty declared that a basic long-term aim of the Community should be the introduction of a common transport policy. It was also recognised from the outset that many difficulties lay in the way of the achievement of such an aim. In other parts of the Treaty (notably Article 61), there were sufficient indications that it was not the intention simply to remove the national transport structures of member states, but eventually to introduce a wide-ranging and comprehensive new policy. This is without doubt a laudable objective but as was to be expected the very great differences between the member states' national frameworks, to say nothing of the addition of another three members, has meant that in practice this aim of overall policy has moved forward very little indeed.

To see just how little progress has been made we need only look at the aims set out in the Transport Title of the Treaty, and compare this to the actual situation. We can then examine in more detail the proposed course of action for the future.

In the first instance the Council of Ministers is empowered to lay down provisions for achieving the general transport policy of the Community. The common policy was initially restricted to road, rail and waterway networks. There was power reserved to include maritime shipping and aviation at a later date.

By far the greatest attention was paid to the problem of discrimination -- indeed, most of the specific statement in the transport articles concerned this. Member states were required not to extend discrimination against the carriers of other members. Compare this with the situation today, some eighteen years later, say between the UK and West Germany. Only about 9000 permits are issued by the Germans for UK carriers. Supply is always exceeded by demand. The only alternatives are those which would greatly benefit other German transport modes. UK hauliers without transit permits can go via German Railways on a piggy-back system, or move through Hamburg which allows a special permit to the East.

Discrimination between particular undertakings was outlawed. Think of rail subsidies. So too was favouritism between different nationalities where operating costs and conditions were similar, particularly in cross-frontier levies. This probably had in mind the practice of both the German and French rail networks in offering attractive discounts to native coal, coke and steel movements and discrimination against non-national movements. Many other similar provisions were covered, although because of special national interests exceptions were allowed for. State subsidies were allowed for the co-ordination of transport or for public service obligations. Thus in cases where government support was given to a transport sector for, say, regional policy objectives (common on the Continent), then support tariffs were acceptable. By and large there is little in the general outlook so far described to cause concern for the UK, although it must be said that certain aspects of the government's financial arrangements for the railways might give some concern if a fine tooth comb were to be taken to them, but this is to say the least most unlikely.

When we move from the general to the particular the situation changes. This is especially so when we bear in mind that in many ways national policy in the UK has run ahead of EEC regulations and in others has diverged. The immediate problem facing this country is basically that our transport requirements differ in many fundamental ways from our partners in the EEC but as a member we are expected to conform with overall wishes. Until 1973 the transport situation in the EEC remained pretty much as it was under the various national policies. This was not due to a lack of pronouncements on the part of the Commission but simply because most members of the Community for whatever reasons did not implement opinions and directives.

At the centre of any movement towards the implementation of the common transport policy was the question of control of entry to the road transport sector. All the member states with the exception of Belgium operated some form of government restriction on entry. This varied from the reasonably open Dutch methods to the more restrictive German and perhaps even constrictive French systems. All cross-frontier movements were subject to permit quotas usually on a two-tier system of border areas and the rest of the country. The Commission saw the obstacle this system presented to free movement of goods and in 1963 proposed the establishment of a Community Permit. The intention was that this would eventually replace all bilateral quota arrangements. These permits were eventually issued in 1969 and have shown up the problems of the transport policy becoming a practical proposition.

In 1975-76 the UK industry, consisting of around 600,000 vehicles, received only 272 such permits, the Germans 427 and the French around 400. Proposals were made to double the total number of permits. This was vetoed by the Germans who suggested a 30 per cent increase and this in turn did not receive support. It is in cases like this that the true nature of the EEC is seen. On one level the policy-makers decide upon very laudable courses of action. General transport permits allowing cross-frontier trading would have been a positive step towards the removal of any problems that transport might present to the free movement of goods between Community members. National transport interests, however, were and are too strong to allow such a development to receive anything more than token support. Think of the already-mentioned German reluctance to increase bilateral quotas with the UK, let alone trans-European permits.

From the German point of view, of course, this is a very reasonable standpoint. In the first case, as we will see, the UK just ignores EEC directives and even Regulations that do not suit her and, in the second, whilst UK demand for German permits always exceeds supply the opposite is not the case. The German transport industry usually demands only about 20 per cent of the UK permits, so why should they increase their supply. The Commission's attitude to this particular aspect of the nature of the structure of the transport industry was further complicated as far as this country was concerned by draft regulations to control entry into road transport, as described in the next section.

CONTROL OF ENTRY TO ROAD TRANSPORT

In an attempt to move further away from the various national regulations towards

a Community-wide structure, draft regulations were submitted in 1971 concerning the basic right of control of entry into road transport. Each member state
would have the distinction between own-account operators and hire-and-reward
hauliers. For hire-and-reward licences the individual countries would divide their
territory into two zones. The A zone would cover a 200-km radius from the home
depot. All vehicles of more than 3 tonnes carrying capacity would receive permits
for domestic operations provided they could show the licensing authority that
their costs were not abnormal and that sufficient traffic could be obtained to
allow the firm to make a reasonable profit. The rest of the national territory was
to be known as the B zone and permits for this were to be available on the same
basis as for the A zone except that national governments were to limit the number
of B zone permits in such a way as to ensure that an over-capacity situation and its
attendant destructive competition did not occur. For vehicles of less than 3
tonnes carrying capacity operating within 50 km of the home depot licences were
to be available as of right. The final control was, of course, to have been the in-
tercommunity permit.

Notice that even at this early stage, before the UK had become a fully paid-up
member so to speak, Community policy was seen by the Commission to be heading in a more liberal direction but as far as this country was concerned it was
moving backwards. It is this kind of situation which contains problems for the
UK transport industry. Given the very restrictive Continental policies, these
suggestions by the Commission were undoubtedly forward thinking, but the 1968
Transport Act had already gone beyond the frontiers of freedom so proposed.

The key factor as far as we are concerned is that if we were to fully comply
with the proposed regulations as they then stood then this country would be
stepping back to restriction of freedom of entry in the domestic market without
any real compensation in the form of easier access to the international market.

OPERATING CONDITIONS

There have been a great many Regulations passed concerning conditions of operation. These have caused a good few headaches in this country.

By 1970 all member states were expected to comply with Regulation 534
which laid down general labour conditions. These included rest and driving
periods, size of crew and minimum ages for drivers. When the UK joined the
Community it was agreed that these hours would be adopted by 1976 and the
even more controversial tachographs by the end of 1977. Neither of these courses
of action has taken place at the time of writing (May 1977). Both seem likely by
1978. The reasons from the UK point of view are obvious, but remember that
EEC Regulations are supposed to supersede national law. As far as drivers' hours
are concerned, cost and the attitude of the trade unions would seem to be the
most important factors. The reduction in drivers' hours is a major cost problem.
In the EEC most transport drivers are allowed a maximum of 8 hr/day driving,
subject to a maximum of 48 hr/week. In this country, we have 10 hr/day driving
and a maximum of 60 hr/week, this consisting of 11 hr duty spread over not
more than 12½ hr and a compulsory day off per week.

It was estimated by government officers that the implementation of just the
drivers' hours requirement would cost the UK industry about £100 million a year.

The unions present another major obstacle. In the first instance it would be unjust and,, more important, unrealistic to expect the unions to accept such wide ranging alterations to the working methods and hence wages without a package of some kind concerning the protection of earnings. If the TUC and the government is to be believed, and the 10 per cent rule with regard to wage increases is to be held, then there is quite simply no chance of the hours regulation being introduced.

Tachographs are even more difficult. The official trade union attitude is that they are 'spies in the cab' and to a certain degree they are correct. The tachograph is a fairly simple attachment that will record running time, speeds and stops. On the Continent, especially in Germany, they are used frequently for the enforcement of safety regulations and also in court to help determine responsibility in accidents involving goods vehicles. A recent case in this country springs to mind where, after a collision involving a lorry, the log book was alleged by the police to have shown that the vehicle had travelled some 60 miles in under three-quarters of an hour. The hope is that such cases would be reduced by the fact that a permanent record was being kept. From the point of view of management tachographs have many attractions. As we will see, one of the greatest difficulties in fleet planning is the collection of basic traffic information concerning speeds and times. With tachographs fitted this problem would be significantly reduced. There is, however, little likelihood of the trade union attitude altering on this subject. It is interesting to note, however, that the Royal Society for the Prevention of Accidents has recently approached the Department of Transport with a paper in favour of tachographs. The present situation is that the government is unlikely to do anything before 1980 (the next final date for introduction) in the hope that changes might be introduced since not all Community members are happy with tachographs anyway, even though 1978 is the target.

Another area where attempts at harmonisation have caused problems and generated a great deal of discussion is in the field of vehicle weights. In 1972 proposals were formulated that would have resulted in the vehicle length, single axle load and gross vehicle weight acceptable among the Six being substantially greater than those already approved in the UK.

Two main possible trouble points were seen in this series of regulations. First, the movement of heavier lorries through the UK was seen to be a potential environmental hazard. In combatting this hazard and bringing bridges, etc., up to new capacities a cost of about £250 million over a ten-to-fifteen year period would have to be met. Secondly, by specifying greater weights and a higher power-to-weight ratio than was then in force in this country, it was felt that a blow was being struck against UK commercial vehicle manufacturers.

With these few examples we can see that progress towards a common transport policy through regulation is to put it mildly a very difficult task -- more so when we remember that the ultimate objective must include fiscal harmonisation. There has been very little progress in this field probably because the Commission are well aware of the great difficulties in store. These centre around the problem of a common infrastructure policy.

This policy has long been a central aim of the Community and as early as 1955, even before the Treaty of Rome, a network of trunk roads throughout the Community territory was put forward as a target the Community should work towards developing. After the Treaty the Commission made recommendations concerning the definition of routes and investment priorities for just such a network. This is as far as the project got, except that member states were required to consult with the Commission on individual projects which might be of general Community interest. The problems behind such a scheme and the reasons why member states were reluctant to become involved were, and are still, obvious and reasonable. In the first instance, then as now, not all member's infrastructures were at the same level of development, and in the absence of a separate Community budget for general interest projects, then one member might have been in the position of receiving large benefits without contributing anything to the project. It could be argued of course, that this type of situation was the basic point of the Community anyway — with community spirit all members helping each other, not always getting the same share, just a fair share. This might be the ideal, but then ideals seldom survive in practice. It was also argued that if a different set of investment criteria were to be applied to international projects than were applied to internal ones then individual cases of misallocation of resources could arise, and this was most certainly not an objective of the Community.

It can be seen then that some form of fiscal harmonisation must be reached on two fronts if there is to be any acceptable attempt at common infrastructure planning. In the first place all schemes, both domestic and international, must be judged with the same investment techniques. And to prevent any accusations of unfair advantage it would be desirable to develop a method whereby costs could be allocated to users. To prevent national governments using investment funds to favour one particular mode of transport to the detriment of another then the investment criteria mentioned must apply to all modes.

The mind has a tendency, if not to boggle then at least to blink, at the scope of this undertaking, but reasonable progress is taking place. All Community members have been undertaking individual studies to try and determine the best form of common accounting procedure for infrastructure costs.

PRICING POLICIES

The most important side of the entire project is, however, the formation of a common pricing system, and by 1981 it is expected that such a system — almost certainly MSCP — will be in operation within the Community. The thinking behind this kind of proposal has already been dealt with, and it must be remembered that charging methods have already been tested in this country. In other words, the actual introduction of such a scheme could not be resisted by this country on grounds other than political ones, and this would be yet another Regulation that this country refuses to implement — perhaps the rule that will break the Commission's back.

Whilst pricing policies are well advanced, little progress has been made towards a common investment appraisal scheme. At the present time individual practice among members varies considerably, but the general opinion seems to be in favour of some form of user cost-benefit scheme. This is basically the method used in this country at the present time so if it is adopted by the Community then very little change will probably be involved for the UK.

In 1973, after the UK joined the Community, the Commission issued a policy statement pointing out that progress towards the common policy on transport had not proceeded as rapidly as might be wished. The Commission seemed to recognise that Regulations, which it will be remembered supersede local law, might not be the easiest way to advance. It agreed that the time had come to give a new impetus to the movement towards the Common Policy, and since then it is fair to say that greater emphasis has been laid on harmonisation rather than regimentation. After all, is it really important that vehicles in Bavaria say operate in identical conditions to those in Scotland, so long as the general environment and objectives are the same?

The 1973 statement set itself two aims. First, it set out anew the desirability and requirements of a Common Transport Policy and described the components of a transport policy that would provide the needs of an economic union. Secondly, it set itself the task of laying out a programme of action. The Commission realised that there had been little progress in the attempt to liberalise the transport market (that is, with the exception of the United Kingdom). It saw as the main factor behind this failure the continuance of restrictive national policies, and since harmonising of national regulations had been a target right from the start of the Community's push for a Common Transport Policy, then it followed that the initial drive had failed. This side of the problem is accentuated by the permit quota situation already described.

It was felt by the Commission that at the root of any attempt at co-ordination of a system of transport originating in different national transport regulations was a common approach to infrastructure. Great emphasis was placed on this in the 'new impetus'. The statement again pointed out that the ultimate consideration was an effective pricing policy and reiterated the determination of the Commission to achieve this. It is fair to say that the 'new impetus' was not such a new determination, but perhaps, a reaffirmation of an attempt to reach the same objective by more liberal means.

At the same time that these general suggestions were made it was clear that EEC transport policy must cover all forms of transport including ports and air transport, although no time limit was set. As can be guessed there originated from this general statement a wide-ranging list of actions that the Community was expected to carry out. There was, for example, a desire that there should be an improvement in the data base for transport within the Community. This included as aims the improvement of forecasts of freight requirements, transport statistics in general, and the improvement of the professional standards of transport management — a subject already dealt with. A much wider area for action was the desire to accelerate the Community-wide adoption of various directives and regulations which the Commission had already introduced but which member states, for whatever reasons, had not fully implemented. These included Community Permit suggestions, directives on goods vehicle dimensions, weights and tax systems, the general liberalisation of the transport market (which does not apply in reality to the UK) and the introduction of a common charging method for the use of infrastructure.

Finally, there was a generalised wish expressed that the member states of the Community would pay more attention in deed rather than political niceties to the statements that the Commission had been making for the past eighteen years or so.

NATIONAL INTEREST

To conclude this very brief discussion of the EEC we can, perhaps, say this. The original aims laid down were desirable and forward-thinking, but perhaps too wishful. They ignored the fact that in spite of what was expressed in public, national interest was, and still is, the major consideration in Europe. Indeed it must be, so long as the governments concerned pay any real attention to the power groups within their bou.idaries. Those concerned with the original organisation of the Community were carried away by their enthusiasm in assuming that each member state had had enough of pursuing national interest to the negation of community interests. This unfortunately is just not the case.

This attitude does not only spring from a narrow nationalism, but also from a wide-based democratic desire to see improvement for the majority of people. The problem is that this majority usually means the majority of *our* people — whoever *our* happens to be. The European concept just does not exist in many of the members of the Community, and in all fairness perhaps less in the UK than almost anywhere else. Perhaps at the root of this is the fact that not all members started off from the same economic base, nor have they all progressed at the same rate. Many people in the member states do not like these truths — no matter what they might say in public. The end result is that many members are prepared to accept that which suits them and their image of themselves, but not that which pleases neither.

Thus we can have reasonable objectives set down by the Commission — even for long-term implementation — which are regarded as an insult on the honour which some members just might have had X number of years ago, and because of this perfectly fair long-term objectives are weighed down with past short-term albatrosses.

The future bodes no better, for co-operation on matters of basic economic importance is probably only possible on the Commission's level between partners of at least almost equal economic strength, and at the present time this all important condition is just not present. To illustrate the point one recalls the statement which was attributed to a union leader when the subject of tachometers was raised: 'Who cares about the Germans, they lost the War'.

5 The 1977 Transport Policy White Paper: road section

TERMS OF REFERENCE

After many promises, consultations and postponements, the government eventually published its *Transport Policy White Paper* in July 1977. This was as a result of consultations between the government and interested parties initiated in 1976 through *Transport Policy: a consultation document.* Therefore before we look at the latest propositions from the government concerning the long-term future of transport in this country it is probably as well that we examine, however briefly, the consultative document. Briefly is said with deliberation for this would appear to be yet another government report where the greatest weight is put on passenger transport. I am not saying – nor even suggesting that passenger transport is unimportant, but perhaps at some future date some government official might consider that the use of transport infrastructure by commercial traffic might be important enough for the national well being to justify trip generation data and investment criteria including goods vehicle considerations other than side issues.

The document consisted of two volumes: a general statement of ideas and a more statistical back-up. As far as the transport of goods was concerned the document recognised the growing preponderance of road. Over the period 1964-74 road transport freight traffic increased by over one third but that on all other modes dropped. Road accounted for 85 per cent of the total tonnage moved, even although over 66 per cent was carried on journeys of 25 miles or less. This large percentage of short journeys accounts for the fact the road's share of ton-miles was only about 65 per cent. It is also interesting to note that whilst the total volume of goods carried by road has grown sharply in the last ten years or so, there has been a much smaller increase in the total number of miles covered. This has been due to a tendency to increase the carrying capacity of the vehicle. This is interesting in the light of past and present trends in EEC legislation on the subject of vehicle size, even though we are trying to get agreement on a compromise weight of 40 tons spread over five axles.

The paper points out that the interests of transport workers must be remembered — but not to the extent, it is assumed, of preventing the introduction of Community Regulations. The ultimate constraint as pointed out is limits on public expenditure — more will be said on this point later.

The document rejects a TUC suggestion that a new transport authority be set up, independent of the government, and sums up the essence of the report as 'the government therefore reject the notion that our transport problems can be solved by major organisational changes, or the hiving-off of decision-taking to an outside body. This does not mean that everything in the garden is lovely. There has been too little coordination and coherence in transport policy in recent years. The answer lies partly in revising and clarifying the aims of transport policy (which is precisely the aim of this review); partly in changes within the government to strengthen the capacity to co-ordinate and monitor transport; and partly in establishing an outside forum, not for the execution of policy but for its continued scrutiny and supervision.' The existence of a body independent of the government concerned with transport policy is, of course, ridiculous, at least for EEC members. If the reader feels that the government have more or less ignored our entry into the EEC then I can but only agree.

PROPOSED PRICING POLICIES

Chapter 5 of the consultative document goes on to discuss the problems of pricing policies with regard to roads. It might be felt that this is a little belated. We did after all enter the Community in 1973, raised no objection to transport policy, and the Commission is almost certainly going to pass a directive for effect in 1981 for implementing MSCP. The government, however, would seem to have ignored this fact, at least in 1977. To quote from Section 5.2: 'The strict economic approach to pricing would be to ensure that the user pays at least the full marginal resource costs of his transport; then there would (in theory) be no miscalculation of resources. But it was argued that we cannot conceivably leave the provision of transport solely to market forces; the user does not always pay the costs he imposes on other people; and there will always be situations where, for social or environmental reasons, part of the total resource cost should be met by the community. So the central issue is first to define the resource costs, then to identify the exceptions to the general rule that the user should pay these costs in full.'

The document then proceeds to discuss the inherent problems in an MSCP system. At no point is there a statement that such a pricing system will most likely become a Community Regulation by 1981. Indeed the document goes too far; it points out that substantial changes might be required on taxation policy, but then says that before such changes would be introduced consultation with the affected industries would first take place. Fine. But what about the EEC Regulations? Is this country a member state or do we only accept those Regulations which suit us and ignore — even in government publications — whose which do not? Indeed, are we members of the EEC or are we not? If this was to be answered on the basis of those regulations or even directives aimed at transport then the final conclusion would be obscure indeed. The document then proceeds to discuss revenue and expenditure, but only in the most superficial way. It is pointed out that until recent years goods vehicles contributed more in fuel and licence taxes than the road provisions and repair costs that could reasonably be attributed to them. This, of course, ignores the section which went before dealing with MSCP — since this has never been applied, how can anyone say that goods vehicles have met their total costs?

The document does recognise the fact that some categories of goods vehicle have not been paying their way recently even if the very narrow road maintenance costs alone are taken. In fact, in 1976 a 32-tonne four-axle vehicle with an average mileage was paying in road and fuel tax about £1600 a year less than its road maintenance costs. For the same vehicle travelling 100,000 miles a year the underpayment is around £4500. In 1976 the government indicated that some form of taxation dependent on road use might be introduced. This must be taken as a thought on the way to some form of MSCP, but no more has been heard on the subject. In the consultative document it is recognised that any form of new taxation system must involve increased costs for the industry, but it was felt 'desirable to restore a sounder relationship between the taxation contribution made by the road transport industry and the costs it imposes on the community'. It was considered that the average increase would be in the region of 5 per cent with a likely maximum of 15 per cent. No indication was given as to how these figures were arrived at, presumably by some form of splitting up the underpayments of the various vehicle categories where appropriate. The government's intention would be to phase such increases over a period of time. Powers were taken however, in *The Finance Bill, 1977,* to start collecting data concerning laden weights and axle numbers to allow a more reasonable approach to taxes. It is sorely tempting to point out that this should have been undertaken some time ago if we are to attempt to keep up with EEC regulations.

Whilst on the subject of heavy vehicles it must be mentioned that a great deal of attention was paid to the environmental effects of goods vehicles. Indeed, the government sees as a basic task the 'civilising of heavy lorries'. Emphasis was placed on the carrying forward of particular by-pass schemes, and mention was made of a national system of lorry routes. This would have been designed to make maximum use of the country's best roads. It should be pointed out, however, that these particular proposals were dropped from the White Paper. There was, however, encouragement for local authorities to implement powers given to them under *The Heavy Commercial Vehicles Act, 1973,* and other legislation to exert some control over lorry flows within their areas where environmental issues are affected.

Finally the government stated its intention to tighten up the enforcement of already existing safety regulations and to pursue even more effective legislation.

The Transport Policy White Paper was presented to Parliament in June 1977 and it must be admitted was probably the greatest non-event of the year. As far as road transport is concerned (rail in both the Consultative Document and the White Paper is dealt with in the chapter on rail), very little changed from the Consultative Document to the White Paper. It is recognised that road transport will continue to provide the lion's share of goods movement into the foreseeable future. Because of this the government reaffirms its desire to relieve the problems that lorries cause. It is emphasised that these controls will mean higher costs which will ultimately fall on consumers but 'a less noisy, less polluted environment is as much a part of the standard of living in its broadest sense as lower prices in the shops'.

The government points out that by-passes and new roads will not solve the problem of goods vehicles in towns as drops have to be made to premises in the towns, but a plea is made for better traffic management to keep heavy lorries out of residential streets. Local authorities are again asked to implement the powers they already have to facilitate this aim. After consultations with interested parties the direction of lorries through a national network of lorry routes has been dropped for the near future — at least. It was found that lorries already use the more desirable routes, and again local authorities were encouraged to use their powers to redirect traffic if any local problems arose.

Further government support is promised for projects such as those proposed by the independent Lorries and the Environment Committee designed to reduce traffic problems through better management.

The aim of reducing noise pollution through greater attention being paid to this aspect at the manufacturing stage is encouraged. Lorry design will be improved by further legislation requiring higher braking standards and anti-jack-knifing gear.

The operation of the O licence system of the 1968 Act is to be reviewed. Particular attention will be paid to tightening enforcement and the uniform licensing arrangements for goods vehicles of 3½ tonnes upwards. This would seem to be an indication that the government may be considering some form of restriction of entry into the market, perhaps a return to some form of two-tier system — even the EEC one.

Early legislation is promised to deal with overloading and bad maintenance, and to provide for better spot checks on vehicles, and for ensuring defects are put right. Powers will be taken to increase the limit of one mile which lorries can at present be diverted to a weighbridge without compensation.

It might also be the case that a supplementary licence for the carriage of dangerous goods will be introduced. The granting of such a licence would be dependent on the applicant demonstrating that he is fully qualified in this field and that his drivers were trained to deal with any emergencies that might arise.

There is again affirmation that the UK will introduce the Transport Managers Licence requirements in 1978.

FAIR COMPETITION BETWEEN MODES

'The aim of the government should be to ensure that there is fair competition between road and rail and that the railways cannot only retain a significant share of freight business but also expand it in line with their capacity to improve the reliability and reduce the unit costs of their service.' To achieve this aim the government is determined to remove any subsidies payable to freight movements on either road or rail. They intend, therefore, to remove any further support to rail freight services after 1977. To ensure that there is a reduction in the hidden subsidy that road transport receives, new vehicle taxation measures are proposed. It is intended that goods vehicles will bear the true costs of the roads including the costs of policing them and of accidents. Tax changes in the 1977 budget were such as to ensure that lorries of over 1½ tonnes will cover their road costs in 1977-78. There is still the problem, however, that there is still no equity between various groups. Thus some lighter vehicles will more than cover their costs whilst the really heavy vehicles will not. In 1976-77, for example, taxes on the heaviest groups fell short in total by about 40 per cent of their costs. The government therefore intends to modify the present system to allow higher charges for vehicles with the greatest fully laden weights. The system now bases its charges on unladen weights. Since vehicles of the same weight but different axle numbers impose different costs it is hoped that this may also be recognised in the future. The greater the number of axles, the lower the surface wear and tear.

These changes will not be fully introduced until 1979 — interestingly just 2 years before the Community is expected to introduce MSCP.

In Paragraph 183 the White Paper states that the government has no intention of adopting the MSCP approach. It bases this on the statement that costs cannot be measured in an objective way. In Volume 2 of the Consultative Document (Page 114, Table 4) just such estimates are given for social costs. It must be stressed right away, however, that the authors of the report qualify their figures very strongly indeed. This is not the point, however. Figures were produced and there is little doubt that more research expenditure could substantially improve the reliability of such studies. The study quoted was carried out for 1972/73. It is interesting to note that if the social cost figures suggested (and the authors feel some were very much underestimated) are included in the costs of goods vehicles of 30 cwt and over, the ratio of revenue to costs is 0.7:1.

In the second part of Paragraph 183 the government goes on to say that social costs will be taken into account when deciding how much 'road taxation should exceed the directly ascertainable public costs of the roads'. If social costs cannot be calculated accurately, why bother? It would seem that this statement is giving the government *carte blanche* to raise extra revenue. It would appear that they prefer to guess what costs (which they say cannot be measured) should be for taxation purposes.

As far as road pricing is concerned the, there would seem to be little chance of the UK taxation system introducing a regulated social cost method. There has been, however, a statement of intent that the social and economic costs imposed by goods vehicles be recovered in some measure through taxation. In practical terms this must mean — as the government says in all its transport documents — an increase in the operating costs of the industry. This in its turn will be reflected by increasing prices in the shops and for industry. The ultimate justification for this is that in the past the industry was not paying its full share of the costs, especially if social costs are added to the total. The whole exercise is probably symptomatic of the fact that this country must now take a realistic stock of its true economic position. Practices that have been accepted as normal must now be reviewed in an individual, more self-financing, way.

6 Road transport effectiveness

TRANSPORT MANAGEMENT

Irrespective of the general legal framework within which a particular manager must operate there are certain techniques which may be of some use. These are the subject of our next discussion.

In the transport of goods by road there are two broad divisions into which possible economies may be placed. The first of these covers the actual operation of the road fleet, its maintenance and general road-worthiness. This is the field of the specialist; besides with the new regulations in force there are standards laid down which must be adhered to, no matter what the cost. The other area is in the planning of the movement of the vehicles themselves and it is this that we are most interested in.

There is an even more basic division than the main one mentioned above, and this is into those costs which are imposed by the State and are more or less inevitable as far as the firm is concerned and those which can be reduced and have their whole function made more effective. In this second division management concepts are by far the more important rather than the mechanical side. There is indeed even a degree of overlap when such things as programmed maintenance and so on are considered.

INFORMATION COLLECTION AND INTERPRETATION

The application of methodical investigations to the transport field is really little different from their application in any other field. There are a limited number of mathematical tehcniques which help to maximise profit or minimise costs. The real problem is deciding which to use, when to use them and how to interpret their results.

As always, no method will allow the manager to sit down with a slide rule and a collection of statistics and, after some reasonably simple calculating, come out with the plan which the firm must follow religiously if it wants to quadruple its profits. Indeed we all wish there was. We will limit ourselves here to a discussion of the more basic useful techniques, but we must remember their weaknesses at all times. If we do not then the projects undertaken will give disappointing returns.

There are three broad areas within which the possibility of error will occur. The first of these is simply the mechanics of the particular method. There is really very little that can be done about this except to advise care at all times and to check each step carefully. One problem can have something said about this though and that is to beware of the 'short cut' methods. These are good when dealing with the simple illustrations that must inevitably be used in a short introductory work of this kind, but they have their dangers. These seem to come from the reliance of many of these 'short cuts' on mental jumps. While this is fine for illustrations, say in linear programming, I have found that in practice the slower methods, where most of the simple calculations are written out, are easier to check: more will be said on this later.

The second area where error may originate is more important: this is in the collection of the original information. If the information is incorrect in the first place then no matter how well the method is carried out the answer will be wrong. This is again a matter for attention to detail.

The real danger is not in the accuracy of the material (it is assumed that everybody will attempt to keep this as high as possible); the most dangerous area is interpretation of the information. It is far too easy to jump to conclusions regarding certain apparently true facts. We must be careful to ensure that there are no known forces affecting our information. It would be easy to get the wrong impression of demand, for example, in studying data covering six months if there is a marked seasonal fluctuation for the product, or in inventory levels where there is a strike at the customer's plant and so on.

We must also always be sure that we know what the aim of the survey is and what results it might have, say, on wage demands. This might seriously affect our expectations of return and it would not be the first time that confusion has arisen over the final target of a particular management exercise. The same type of dangers are present after the mechanics of the project have been completed and the time comes for the implementation of the results.

There are two divisions here: those inherent in the method and those in the actual implementation of the result. We must understand right from the start that many of the methods we will be looking at, particularly those dealing with routing decisions, will not give the best possible answer. They will give a good answer but not the optimum one.

There are methods available which will give the optimum answer to many of these problems, but almost without exception they require the use of expensive data processing equipment and even then the optimum results depend on the continuance of conditions which in the real world can only be described as unrealistic. Some of the methods discussed will give as good an answer as matters, and as we go along the relative accuracy of each of the methods will be mentioned.

Then there are the problems that arise out of the conditions that must exist if the methods are to work; these are often divorced from real life and this must be remembered. There are no magic solutions to management's problems in transport any more than in any other branch of business. The best procedure to adopt is to first realise there will never be an ideal answer and even if there was the practical difficulties in actually operating it would reduce its effectiveness — a linear programming matrix has never heard of traffic jams. But it is better to have some

idea of what might be achieved than to just guess. The best results will depend on
flexibility of interpretation. Look at the conditions laid down in the problematic
solution, pinpoint their divergence from realities and change the thing; it is better
to increase profit by half the theoretical amount than by none at all.

BASIC COLLECTION

Bearing these facts in mind how do we improve the effectiveness of our transport?
This depends on various factors, not the least being the budget available.

We must keep things in perspective. In a very small organisation transport is
only one of the functions in the total distribution cost. It might very well be the
case that little can be done profitably in the way of improving routing arrangements and which customers are served from where. The cost of the study may be
greater than the improvements in operating effectiveness. In this situation it will
probably not prove necessary to proceed beyond the original information survey.
This survey is nearly always worthwhile because it will throw up basic information regarding the depot. It may, for example, show that loading arrangements are
poor and so on. It may show that the depot is the most fruitful place for reorganisation. Some firms find it a shock when the original survey shows a large
proportion of their drivers' time is spent loading and on paperwork in the depot.

This is not really the area for discussion here. However it may be worth
pointing out that a work sampling study such as described in the section on warehouses can help considerably in reorganising depot operations.

The first step we must take in our original collection survey is to define the
objective. Is it, for example, simply to find out what's going on? Is it to allow us
to arrange more acceptable work targets? Or is it a basis for the entire review of
our transport network? Whichever is finally decided upon will involve more or less
money and effort so it is as well to start off properly.

There is one problem, however, which must be dealt with, no matter what the
final objective is and this is the problem of the employees. If we are to keep the
costs at all reasonable, we must rely in the last analysis on the drivers for some of
the most basic information. Nobody is under any illusions about the difficulties
involved in persuading the unions to participate in such tasks, but they still must
be done. The first rule must then be to try to explain the aim of the entire exercise to the personnel involved. We have already said that the particular methods
used will ultimately depend for their accuracy on the accuracy of the input data.
Therefore it is of the utmost importance that every effort is made to obtain the
full cooperation of the drivers. There is of course always the possibility that some
part of the economies made will be passed on to the workers in the form of extra
wages. The advisability of making this clear at the outset will depend on the
personalities involved, remembering always that there just might not be sufficiently large immediate savings to allow wage increases.

The alternative is to use one of the many types of recording device, but this is
likely to arouse more opposition if recent examples are typical. The only other
possibility is to include study personnel in selected journeys to try to build up a
picture of the situation. These are problems which must be solved by the manager
on the spot; no amount of discussion in this book is going to make the problem
more simple.

After the preliminary discussions concerning the implementation of the study,

Vehicle number	Route number	Driver's name (optional)	
Times	Drop number	Distances	Comments

Exhibit 6.1 Initial survey form layout

the mechanics of collection must be decided. The cheapest, easiest and most useful way of doing this is to design a report sheet (see Exhibit 6.1) to be filled in by every driver on every route (possibly assisted by a tachometer?). The more simple the entries to be made then the greater will be the chances of the information being accurate and the degree of cooperation high. We must therefore try to reduce the content to the essentials.

Firstly there must be some reference to the vehicle, route and the driver (although the last may be dropped); then the important categories are decided. These will depend to some extent on the final aim of the survey, although there will always be some common entries.

Times are important; therefore we must allow a column on the report sheet for these. This information is simple but important. It will tell us when the driver starts at the depot, when he leaves and when he reaches key points along his routes. There will also be provision for the drops he makes, how long he stays, what his time is taken up with and how many pallets or cartons are unloaded.

The next column we must have is for distance. This will record the distance
moved between each of the drop points. In this way we will be able to see if
there are any special slack zones, i.e., if there are any particular segments of the
overall journey which would seem to require particular attention. These will
show up by simple cross-reference between the time columns and the distance
columns. Any really great discrepancies must be investigated. To help in this
investigation we have our final space, which is for observations. This will allow the
driver to explain the factors affecting the various distances and times. There may
arise the situation when, for example, it is noticed from the time and distance
columns that a very short distance has taken an inordinate amount of time, and
the comments column may show that this has in fact been caused by a traffic
jam and so on.

Having initiated the survey and carried it out, the next step is to analyse the
results. There are several ways of tackling this, depending on the object of the
exercise. In our case we assume we are using it as the first step in an overall investigation and consequently should attempt to gain as much information from
it as possible. The usual method when trying to gain knowledge from this type of
information source is compression, which is done by summary.

An examination of the various report sheets is first made to see if there are any
outstanding features. Does a particular route consistently take longer than appears
necessary and if so why? Check the comments columns for common explanations.
If they turn out to be inherent in the route, would it be possible to change it?

An outstanding factor might be the amount of time spent before a driver takes
the vehicle from the depot. Is this caused by loading problems, or perhaps last-
minute maintenance? If so, could a shift system using, say, articulated vehicles
help to reduce turnaround time. Could a night shift be introduced for maintenance
and so on? Is there a habit of going to a particular customer first and having to
wait; if so, can we reschedule the order of delivery? In other words, a careful
examination of the data thrown up by the record sheets should be available for
immediate use to improve the effectiveness of the fleet.

The greatest use might be, however, in building up a picture of our network of
operations from which it may be possible to see ways of improving the organisation.
Exhibit 6.2 shows a simple network; the data shows the amount of time or distances between the points. This could be a section of a much larger delivery
pattern on a local basis or it might illustrate a wide geographical area indicating
the main trunk routes between the firm's major depots. The data might be either
times or distances; the choice will depend on what the individual firm considers
the most important. As a general statement it could be said that, in the local
delivery situation, times might be the most important, whereas on the movement
between depots, distances sometimes warrant more consideration. The important
point is that reasonably accurate data can be extracted for either, or a combination of both, from the original record sheets. Let us assume that Exhibit 6.2
represents the network of operation for our company and that our desire is to
find out the cheapest routes between all the points on the network; let us further
assume that cost is proportional to the data in the network, be it time or distance. As always there are a great many ways of tackling this problem. We will
continue with one, the one which is the easiest to apply and which gives a good
answer, although it might not be the best theoretically possible.

We adopt an iterative procedure, i.e. we start off from what we know and

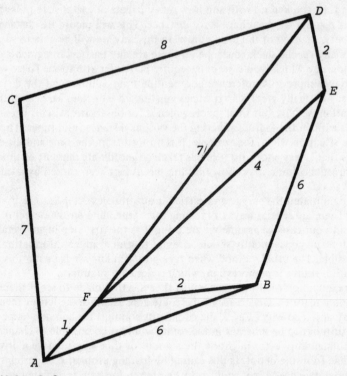

Exhibit 6.2 Network of depots. Movement costs are proportional to the figures given

attempt to continuously improve the situation until we can no longer do so. First we set up the basic information that we have assembled from the original driver's record sheets as in Matrix 1 (see Exhibit 6.3). This sets out all we know from our original network. In drawing up this matrix we only include data in direct line, i.e. wherever we must pass through more than one point to move from one location to another we allocate the symbol X to that data. Thus from A to B is direct and is included as 6 units, from A to D we must pass through intermediate points and the symbol X is given to this link in the matrix. We must now try and see if we can improve on the data given in Matrix 1.

Exhibit 6.3 Matrix 1

	A	B	C	D	E	F
A	0	6	7	X	X	1
B	6	0	X	X	6	2
C	7	X	0	8	X	X
D	X	X	8	0	2	7
E	X	6	X	2	0	4
F	1	2	X	7	4	0

To try this, we start by saying that if there are any better routes between each of the points than those in Matrix 1 then they must pass through one of more of the other points on the matrix. To test this we simply try all the possible routes from each and every point in the network. Thus we take the first line of the matrix which gives us the data for the routes from point A to the other locations in the matrix. A—A will always be 0 so there is not much room for improvement there. What about the next route A—B? From the original matrix the direct route (there are only direct routes in Matrix 1) is 6. Can this be improved? If it can, then the new route must pass through one or more of the other locations in the network so we try them all as shown in Exhibit 6.4 This means that we add all

Exhibit 6.4 A to B improvement

```
AA + AB = 0 + 6 = 6          i.e. move from A to A and from A to B
AB + BB = 6 + 0 = 6          i.e. move from A to B and from B to B
AC + CB = 7 + X = 7 + X i.e. move from A to C and from C to B
AD + DB = X + X = X + X i.e. move from A to D and from D to B
AE + EB = X + 6 = X + 6 i.e. move from A to E and from E to B
AF + FB = 1 + 2 = 3          i.e. move from A to F and from F to B
```

the possible ways in which we might move in the network from A to B. The information for this move is contained in the original matrix. Again we deal only with direct data. Whenever an X appears in the original matrix the same appears in the improvement calculation, such as AE + EB. We can see from Matrix 1 that the link EB is 6 but the link AE is unknown therefore it is carried through as such. We regard any link whose total contains an X to be of greater magnitude than any one which does not. When the improvement calculation is completed we select the lowest link value for inclusion in the second matrix. We then move on to the next link A to C; again all the possible ways which might include improvement are evaluated (see Exhibit 6.5).

Exhibit 6.5 A to C improvement

```
AA + AC = 0 + 7 = 7          i.e. move from A to A and from A to C
AB + BC = 6 + X = 6 + X i.e  move from A to B and from B to C
AC + CC = 7 + 0 = 7          i.e. move from A to C and from C to C
AD + DC = X + 8 = X + 8 i.e. move from A to D and from D to C
AE + EC = X + X = X + X i.e. move from A to E and from E to C
AF + FC = 1 + X = 1 + X i.e. move from A to F and from F to C
```

Again we select that link which gives us the best improvements for this particular route. It is very important to remember that this is a method which relies on doing the same thing over and over until we arrive at the best answers. The only way to check is to use the data given at the end of the exercise to complete

Exhibit 6.6

```
AA + AD = 0 + X = X       i.e. move from A to A and from A to D
AB + BD = 6 + X = 6 + X   i.e. move from A to B and from B to D
AC + CD = 7 + 8 = 15      i.e. move from A to C and from C to D
AD + DD = X + 0 = X       i.e. move from A to D and from D to D
AE + ED = X + 2 = X + 2   i.e. move from A to E and from E to D
AF + FD = 1 + 7 = 8       i.e. move from A to F and from F to D
```

another matrix. If this is the same, then you have the correct matrix. One more example takes the link A–D (see Exhibit 6.6).

The three examples given above should be sufficient to show the method of proceeding.

After each evaluation we select the lowest link value and place it in our next matrix. In this way we see that the lowest value for A to B is 3, and from the link evaluation we know that to reach this improvement we must move to B by way of F. The best route at this stage is from A to F and from F to B. Likewise we see the next route for the movement A to C as 7 and the link with this value is AA to AC, that is the direct route. In the final example, the best link for the A to D route is 8 moving through F.

The entire route matrix is drawn up in this fashion. If in the course of the iteration any best links have alternative routes the best method of dealing with this will depend on the original purpose of the study. It is always safe, however, to make a note of those routes having alternatives. This would allow the manager greater flexibility in planning in the future.

Assume that the procedure is carried out and we get Matrix 2 (see Exhibit 6.7). Now we return to a point mentioned above. On the simple network which we have drawn for this example, it is obvious by inspection that the route B to C is not best accomplished by the figure and directions given in Matrix 2, i.e. from B to C passing through A. But we mentioned that we must resist the temptation to jump ahead. Inspection might work on a network like this, but not with 15 or so nodes. We must see if this is the best matrix and we do this by exactly the same method as before, except at this stage we do not refer back to the original matrix for our data but use that evaluated for Matrix 2. Thus for the route B to C, for example, we obtain the figures shown in Exhibit 6.8. It will be noticed this time that the lowest link is not as before but is 10 passing through F and through A. This is shorter than before by 3 units.

Exhibit 6.7 Matrix 2

	A	B	C	D	E	F
A	0	3F	7	8F	5F	1
B	3	0	13A	8E	6	2
C	7	13A	0	8	10D	8A
D	8	8E	8	0	2	6E
E	5F	6	10D	2	0	4
F	1	2	8A	6E	4	0

This is built up because the first link from our evaluation equation is B to F and the next link is F to C; but we have already calculated another, that the best route at this stage between F and C is A going through the node A. Therefore the best route now becomes 10FA. We have once more repeated at this stage. This is really how the method works. At each successive calculation of the best link, the best value from the previous matrix is used and as already mentioned the best result will be obtained when there are two calculations the same.

We carry out the usual procedure for the evaluation of a network and we arrive at Matrix 3 (see Exhibit 6.9). In fact, this is our final matrix. Although this simple problem has come out quickly it will be obvious that in a real work situation the greater number of nodes will make the calculations more laborious.

It will be obvious, however, that it is only necessary to calculate half of any network. Moreover, initial inspection might help in the smaller problems by eliminating some direct route possibility. As already mentioned, however, this practice can be dangerous, especially with the larger problems. In the final matrix it will be noticed that two of the links are in bold type. These are the links with alternative routes.

When the problem is small enough, it is worth keeping a note of these alternative routes since they can often help to improve loading utilisations. The journey from B to D gives an illustration of this. In the final matrix the route is given as 8 units going through E but there is also an alternative route of the same magnitude moving through F and E.

If in the future it becomes important to have drops at both F and E on the way to D, then of course the alternative route can be chosen without increasing the journey times/distances. Or there might exist congestion on the direct route but not so on the alternative; or there might be variances in the distances of these two routes but the network survey we first drew up might have been measuring

Exhibit 6.8

```
BA + AC = 3F + 7   = 10FA  i.e.  B to A and A to C
BB + BC = 0 + 13A  = 13A   i.e.  B to B and B to C
BC + CC = 13A + 0  = 13A   i.e.  B to C and C to C
BD + DC = 8E + 8   = 16E   i.e.  B to D and D to C
BE + EC = 6 + 10D  = 16D   i.e.  B to E and E to C
BF + FC = 2 + 8A   = 10FA  i.e.  B to F and F to C
```

Exhibit 6.9 Matrix 3

	A	B	C	D	E	F
A	0	3F	7	7FE	5F	1
B	3F	0	10FA	8E	6	2
C	7	10AF	0	8	10D	8A
D	7EF	8E	8	0	2	6E
E	5F	6	10D	2	0	4
F	1	2	8A	6E	4	0

times. If this was the case then the longer route might be chosen because the matrix calculations showed it to have equal times and since wages can account for over 65 per cent of vehicle costs, then this might prove a saving. In other words the interpretation of the results is as important as the calculation.

There are objections raised to this type of calculation: the first is usually the length of the calculation. I do not think this is a very valid proposition since the calculations are so simple that a fairly complex problem can be dealt with in a relatively short time. The next objection is usually complexity, i.e. for a medium to large size firm the number of nodes to be included is so large that people become confused in the calculation. This is certainly valid, to a point. The best way of dealing with this problem is to divide the problem into a number of parts and allocate these accordingly. We could, for example, do it in two stages. Stage one would be the calculation of the routes between the major distribution depots for the firm (as in the example). This will usually reduce the number of points to manageable proportions. The second stage is the calculation of the best routes from the major depots to local drops. Or even greater subdivisions could be made.

There is always the problem of deciding whether to try to minimise time or distance. This will depend on the particular situation of the individual company, but if cost investigations were to be made then I believe that most firms would find that the greatest single item of costs for the average vehicle's daily running burden is wages. Therefore the best way to increase effectiveness is to increase the utilisation of vehicles, i.e. the best data for inclusion in the original survey and in the original network is times. There are exceptions to this rule, naturally, but each firm should find out for itself; certainly not enough do. The most basic objection is perhaps the quality of the information being used in the first place. This has already been dealt with and it is really an area for the application of industrial relations rather than mathematics.

Flexibility is also important. It is often pointed out that the conditions recorded in the original surveys will not last forever; this is true. If, however, the results of the survey are worthwhile then it is likely that if conditions deteriorate drastically this will be shown on the performance figures of the fleet. Therefore another survey will also probably pay for itself. It is a question of management deciding when the increasing costs become great enough. The other answer to this argument is that conditions are likely to get worse with or without a survey. At least if one is carried out some profits will be reaped instead of continually escalating losses. In other words we come back to our primary assumption:

> *We do not change theory to practice. We use theory to set a possible target in terms of profit and efficiency. Then we change practice to get as close to this possibility as we can, knowing that it will never be fully achieved.*

This is a question of interpretation. It may very well be that the best routes are impossible to use but we have at least introduced positive targets at which to aim. All mathematical methods in transport must be looked at in this way, otherwise disappointment is guaranteed.

It is true to say that there will arise many situations, especially in the smaller firm, where the methods discussed above will be found useful. They do however have certain limitations. The most obvious and probably the most important is that they lack a capacity variable, i.e. there is no facility in the methods to allow for the size of vehicle employed, for the demand at any node, or for the length of the working day. To improve on the more simple methods, techniques must be used that can in some way handle these extra considerations. Many are available and we will examine a few, especially those suitable to manual methods of computation. The ultimate aim is to allow our route planner to arrive at a solution which has a good answer to the basic difficulty of how many vehicles, what routes and what size of reserves.

The savings method

This approach to the problem is one of the most simple to apply, but at the same time can adequately handle the conditions noted above. As is the usual case we collect our basic data. This consists of the distances between our depot and the customers, and between the customers themselves. We will select a route giving us the best times or distances between our customers and the depot on the basis of constructing routes with the constraints of capacity of vehicle and customer demand. To see the rational of the method, consider Exhibit 6.10. In this basic

Exhibit 6.10 Savings method

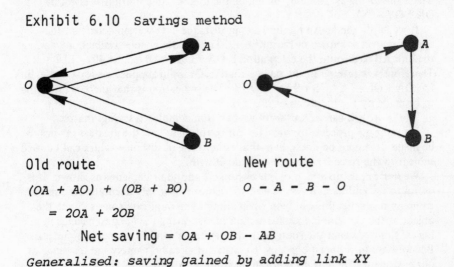

Old route

(OA + AO) + (OB + BO)

= 2OA + 2OB

New route

O − A − B − O

Net saving = *OA + OB − AB*

Generalised: saving gained by adding link XY is OX plus OY minus XY

situation we can see that we have two customers A and B served by our depot at O. At this stage of the problem let the capacity of the vehicles involved be such that it requires one lorry each to deliver to A and B. Let us also assume that our route plan is such that a vehicle leaves the depot, completes the drop and returns to base. Under this plan the total movement would be O−A−O plus O−B−O. Put another way this is 2OA + 2OB.

There might be a saving available if we include in our plan the link A−B. The effect of this can easily be seen. The new journey would still have to include the links O−A and O−B, but now they would be covered only once, so the amount O−A and O−B is deducted from our total journey, and since we have a new link, A−B is added. This can be put in a more usable form by saying that the net saving equals OA + OB − AB. In fact this can be shown to have a general application

Exhibit 6.11 Distance data

Depot	O	A									
A	78	X	B								
B	40	114	X	C							
C	104	150	118	X	D						
D	110	72	124	206	X	E					
E	130	132	126	232	70	X	F				
F	106	160	70	184	140	100	X	G			
G	120	100	156	164	172	226	204	X	H		
H	72	158	100	54	158	194	168	66	X	I	
I	92	170	68	98	192	186	106	180	116	X	J
J	128	60	154	210	50	120	184	152	158	220	X

where the saving available by including the link XY in a journey is given by OX + OY − XY.

If we apply the above method to our distance data we can construct the savings matrix as shown in Exhibit 6.12. To find the savings available by adding the link AB to a route the calculation is OA + OB − AB = 78 + 40 − 114 = 4. Therefore 4 is entered in the savings matrix. Or again suppose we look at the link IA: OA + OI − IA = 78 + 92 − 170 = 0. The indication is that there is no saving to be made by the inclusion of this link.

The process is carried out until we have the completed savings matrix.

We can now proceed to calculate our routes based on the greatest savings to be made. It should be noted here that either time or distance values can be used subject to the considerations already dealt with.

We must draw up a map of our customers and their demands as shown. It is useful to try and keep the spatial relationships reasonably accurate as in more complex problems this can help when eliminating duplicate routes. Since the object of the exercise is to construct a route showing the greatest savings it is logical that we select the route with the greatest saving to commence our plan. But we have introduced one simple constraint already, namely the demands of our customers. There is no point in planning a route with all the best savings if at

Exhibit 6.12 Savings data

	A									
A	X	B								
B	4	X	C							
C	32	26	X	D						
D	116	26	8	X	E					
E	76	44	2	170	X	F				
F	24	76	26	76	136	X	G			
G	98	4	100	58	24	22	X	H		
H	52	12	132	24	8	10	126	X	I	
I	0	64	98	10	36	92	36	48	X	J
J	146	14	22	188	138	50	96	42	0	X

the end of it we find that we have exceeded vehicle capacity. So we will assume that we have a standardised fleet of lorries, each with a capacity of 16 tons. From this it will be apparent that we can only add links up to the point where a vehicle is fully loaded.

If we examine the matrix we can see that the link DJ has the greatest saving with 188 (see Exhibit 6.12). Therefore the route starts as O–D–J–O; the demand at these two points is 8 and 4, well within our 16-ton limit so the route is feasible. The next best with 170 is ED. Our route then becomes O–E–D–J–O. The sum of the demand on this route is 14, still within our upper limit. The next greatest saving is JA with an improvement of 146. When this is added to our route it becomes O–E–D–J–A–O. The total demand to be met now becomes 16 tons. Therefore we have completed a route for one vehicle. This is noted and the satisfied customers eliminated from future consideration.

By applying the same methods we can arrive at the routes and number of vehicles required as shown in Exhibit 6.13.

The effective solution of this problem has resulted in us knowing the minimum number of road vehicles required within the constraints of customer demand and lorry capacity. It will be noted that there is a very strict limitation involved, namely that all vehicles are of the same capacity. Furthermore we have ignored the likelihood of certain lorries not being available because of operating problems. These further limitations can be dealt with by inspecting past records.

Exhibit 6.13 Customer demand (in brackets), locations and routes

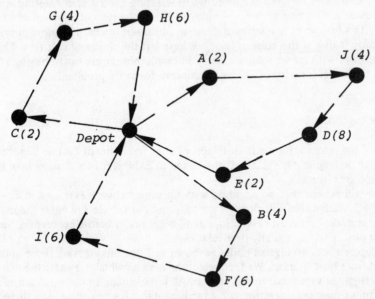

The number of vehicles off the road and the frequency of these occurrences can be used in conjunction with standard deviation to allow us to obtain a good estimate of the number of reserve lorries required to maintain a predecided

service level. A fuller discussion of standard deviation and its implications is to be found in the section dealing with inventory control. Suffice it at this point to say that it is a measure of dispersion which when applied to a normal distribution allows the calculation of a given coverage of occurrences.

As will be shown later, 1.28 times the standard deviation added to the arithmetic mean will cover 90 per cent of happenings within the normal distribution. If we look at the service record the usefulness of the standard deviation can be illustrated. Assume that we are a nationwide concern and that from our calculations by the savings method we require 1000 vehicles as a minimum fleet. From our past records we find that up to 13 vehicles have been off the road at any one time; the frequencies of other failures are as noted. The standard calculation is completed and will give a standard deviation of 2.75. The average number of vehicles off the road is 7. If we decide that the level of service cover we require is 90 per cent then the number of reserve lorries we must have is 2.75 × 1.28 or 3.5, i.e. 4. Therefore we must have a reserve pool of 11 vehicles. If 80 per cent coverage were sufficient then the pool would need to consist of 2.75 × 0.84 or 3 vehicles extra, giving us a total of 10 vehicles.

The essential element is naturally profit. The above approach does not include this. If, however, the section dealing with inventory control under conditions of uncertainty is looked at it will be obvious how service levels and profitability can be combined.

In the discussions above the basic problem was always taken to be the finding of the shortest or best routes within a network. This is not the situation in every case in the real world. Very often we may just require a good route through the network. We may be given the objective of selecting a route plan entering at a given node and leaving wherever we please. This is the type of problem most often met with when we have a series of drops in a chain of towns. The most obvious difficulty is that at this stage at least, we have left the choice of exit free. This can be dealt with (as we shall see later), but with most larger towns having a 'ring road' facility, it is no longer of crucial concern for every problem.

Tree method

One of the most useful methods to apply to the requirement outlined above is the tree technique. One glance at the layout in Exhibit 6.14 will show how the method gets its name.

We will assume that we are faced with the same network as is used in Exhibit 6.2, except that this time we are told that our vehicle will enter the network at node A. It must make drops at all other nodes before proceeding but it is not crucial to leave at any particular exit.

Step one is to arrange all nodes as shown with the links leaving those nodes listed from least to most. We then select the node at which we enter the matrix and assign the value zero to this station. All links leading to this node are eliminated from future consideration and a further table reflecting these alterations drawn up.

We now have our entry point around which to plan our route. We are trying to find the shortest way through our network, we have a starting point and a distance moved of 0. We proceed by examining our table selecting the shortest link to be added and, since this will bring us to the next node, we delete all other

Exhibit 6.14   Tree method

A=	B	C	D	E	F
AF=1	BF=2	CA=7	DE=2	ED=2	FA=1
AB=6	BE=6	CD=8	DF=7	EF=4	FB=2
AC=7	BA=6		DC=8	EB=6	FE=4
					FD=7

Exhibit 6.15   Tree method

A=0	B	C	D	E̲	F	A
AF=1	BF=2	~~CA=7~~	DE=2	ED=2	~~FA=1~~	
AB=6	BE=6	CD=8	DF=7	EF=4	FB=2	
AC=7	~~BA=6~~		DC=8	EB=6	FE=4	
					FD=7	

(handwritten:) 0 + 2 + 6
AF + FB + BE +

Exhibit 6.16   Tree method

A=0	B	C	D	E	F	A-F
~~AF=1~~	~~BF=2~~	~~CA=7~~	DE=2	ED=2	~~FA=1~~	
AB=6	BE=6	CD=8	~~DF=7~~	~~EF=4~~	FB=2	
AC=7	~~BA=6~~		DC=8	EB=6	FE=4	
					FD=7	

Exhibit 6.17   Tree method

A=0	B=3	C	D	E	F	A-F-B
~~AF=1~~	~~BF=2~~	~~CA=7~~	DE=2	ED=2	~~FA=1~~	
~~AB=6~~	BE=6	CD=8	~~DF=7~~	~~EF=4~~	~~FB=2~~	
AC=7	~~BA=6~~		DC=8	~~EB=6~~	FE=4	
					FD=7	

Exhibit 6.18   Tree method

A=0	B=3	C	D	E=9	F=1	A-F-B-E
~~AF=1~~	~~BF=2~~	~~CA=7~~	~~DE=2~~	ED=2	~~FA=1~~	
~~AB=6~~	~~BE=6~~	CD=8	~~DF=7~~	~~BF=4~~	~~FB=2~~	
AC=7	~~BA=6~~		DC=8	~~EB=6~~	~~FE=4~~	
					FD=7	

links into the chosen node. As we move forward we note the distance moved with each successive step, and at the same time write the letter designation at the side of our calculation so that by the end we have the best route through our matrix ready for use.

In this case it can be seen to be worked out as follows. In Exhibit 6.15 we have all our nodes and the links leading from them arranged as mentioned above. We know that the entry point is A, therefore we assign a zero value to A. Delete all links into A and construct the table shown in Exhibit 6.15. The next link to be added to our route must be AF with a distance of 1 unit; therefore all links into F are removed and another table constructed as shown in Exhibit 6.16. From F

Exhibit 6.19 Tree method

A=0	B=3	C	D=11	E=9	F=1	A-F-B-E-D
~~AF=1~~	~~BF=2~~	~~CA=7~~	~~DE=2~~	ED=2	~~FA=1~~	
~~AD=6~~	~~BE=6~~	~~CD=8~~	~~DF=7~~	~~EF=4~~	~~FB=2~~	
AC=7	~~BA=6~~		DC=8	~~EB=6~~	~~FE=4~~	
					~~FD=7~~	

Exhibit 6.20 Final calculation of tree method plus format for one-move table: route = A-F-B-E-D-C

A=0	B=3	C=19	D=11	E=9	F=1
~~AF=1~~	~~BF=2~~	~~CA=7~~	~~DE=2~~	~~ED=2~~	~~FA=1~~
~~AD=6~~	~~BE=6~~	~~CD=8~~	~~DF=7~~	~~EF=4~~	~~FB=2~~
~~AC=7~~	~~BA=6~~		~~DC=8~~	~~EB=6~~	~~FE=4~~
					~~FD=7~~

the next most attractive link is FB and the total distance of 3 is included as shown. The process is carried through as described. The final result is that the best route through the network becomes as follows: A-F-B-E-D-C with a total time or distance of 19.

It will be realised that in the example above many tables have been used, but with practice most examples can be carried out on the one table as shown in Exhibit 6.20.

When our objective is to find the shortest route through a network given the entry point and the exit node, then the technique is just as simple. The matrix approach can certainly be of use, especially if the operation is one dealing with unknown demands over a fixed territory (some form of maintenance or quick service contract, for example). A matrix with shortest time or cost routes between all known locations could be drawn up, and as each point was dealt with, central control could relay the next location together with fastest route.

There are, however, likely to be just as many occasions when the straight-through route is requested. This is especially so when we are moving goods over long routes dropping material at only one point in a town before moving on. In these conditions we will know the entry point and the destination.

Looking back at the simple matrix example already used let us assume that we know that we must enter at node C and leave at B. We wish to find the shortest route to satisfy this task. The technique is basically the same as the one illustrated above. We fan out from our origin or point of entry, each step being made after we have identified the shortest link between where we are and the next step towards the exit.

All nodes are listed. Below each all links leading out of the node are noted in ascending order, the only exception being that we are not interested in links into the origin or links out of the destination. The first step is to identify the original node. From this we determine the next closest link. This is done by looking at the lists below the node. These are circled or marked in some way. The distance from the origin to the node in question is placed above that nodes list. The procedure is repeated until the destination is reached (see Exhibit 6.21). As C is the point of origin, the nearest node is A. Circle link CA and place 7 above A's list and delete all other links into A. We are no longer interested in these as we have now reached node A.

Our original nodes are now C and A. The nearest node to C is now D, the link distance being 0 + 8 = 8. The nearest to A is F, the distance, 7 + 1 = 8. We have a tie. Circle both, and delete all links leading into them (see Exhibit 6.22).

Exhibit 6.21

	7				
C	A	D	E	F	B
(CA=7)	AF=1	DE=2	ED=2	FA=1	
CD=8	AB=6		EF=4	FB=2	
			EB=6	FE=4	
				FD=7	

Exhibit 6.22

	7	8		8	
C	A	D	E	F	B
(CA=7)	(AF=1)	DE=2	ED=2	FA=1	
(CD=8)	AB=6		EF=4	FB=2	
			EB=6	FE=4	
				FD=7	

Again we see which is the closest node to our original ones — A, D and F. C is removed from our considerations because there are no longer any links left to form possible routes. We find that B is closest to A with a value of 7 + 6 = 13; E is nearest D, 8 + 2 = 10, and F is closest to B again with a value of 8 + 2 = 10. Since it will be remmebered that B is our destination then the link we would choose is FB. The final table is shown in Exhibit 6.23.

Exhibit 6.23

7	8		8	10
C	A	D	E	F	B
CA=7	AF=1	DE=2	ED=2	FA=1	
CD=8	AB=6		EF=4	FB=2	
			EB=6	FE=4	
				FD=7	

For the sake of explanation we have laid out each step on a different list. In practice of course, almost all problems of this nature can be solved in one list. All that is required is to take a note of each node as it is added to the list. The shortest route in this case is CAFB.

There is a further situation which frequently arises — where we have a range of different performances for the same route. This may come about through vehicle size, the ability of the individual driver or whatever. This problem is shown in the table in Exhibit 6.24. Here we have a range of vehicles with varying times for the routes. We have to allocate a route to each vehicle so that the best overall performance can be achieved.

Zero allocation technique

This task is carried out by the application of the zero allocation method. As is the case with all techniques discussed here a good answer can be obtained by applying a simple discipline.

We look first at the rows (see Exhibit 6.24-6.26), locate the best time and subtract this from all other values in the row itself. This will indicate the best allocations for all the rows. The same procedure is carried out for the columns. To check if an optimum allocation (as indicated by the zeros) has been achieved, we apply a simple rule. All zeros in rows and columns are covered by the least number of vertical and horizontal straight lines required. Where this number equals the sum of the rows or columns then an optimum solution has been reached.

As can be seen from Exhibit 6.27 our first scheme is, in fact, an optimal one.

Exhibit 6.24 Zero allocation: basic data

Routes covered

Van salesmen		1	2	3	4	5	6
	A	8	4	16	8	10	8
	B	12	16	14	10	14	10
	C	6	12	6	10	10	3
	D	6	12	4	6	14	16
	E	14	12	6	16	8	6
	F	14	8	10	8	10	6

Exhibit 6.25 Zero allocation: row application

	1	2	3	4	5	6
A	4	0	12	4	6	4
B	2	6	4	0	4	0
C	0	6	0	4	4	0
D	2	8	0	2	10	12
E	8	6	0	10	2	0
F	8	2	4	2	4	0

Exhibit 6.26 Zero allocation: column application

	1	2	3	4	5	6
A	4	0	12	4	4	4
B	2	6	4	0	2	0
C	0	6	0	4	2	0
D	2	8	0	2	8	12
E	8	6	0	10	0	0
F	8	2	2	2	1	0

Exhibit 6.27 Zero allocation optimum test: minimum
number of horizontal and vertical straight lines
required to cover zeros = set number

	1	2	3	4	5	6
A	4	0	12	4	4	4
B	2	6	4	0	2	0
C	0	6	0	4	2	0
D	2	8	0	2	8	12
E	8	6	0	10	0	0
F	8	2	2	2	1	0

If this had not been the case, however, the following steps would have been taken. A search is made for the lowest element in the matrix not covered by a line. This is then subtracted from all uncovered values and added to squares covered by a line in both row and column, i.e. at all intersection points of lines. This can be seen in Exhibit 6.31 where the lowest number of lines required to cover all zones is 3. The number of lines and rows is not compatible with this being an optimal solution, therefore the step already mentioned is carried out. The result of this move can be seen in Exhibit 6.32, and this is also an optimal solution. It should be noticed that it is a basic feature of this type of assignment problem that the number of rows and columns will always be the same. They are really only a

Exhibit 6.28 Zero allocation: final allocation.

1 Select K's (columns) with only one allocation
  circle.
2 Cross out all zeros in same row as allocation
  appears.
3 Select R's (rows) with only one allocation
  circle.
4 Cross out all zeros in the same column as
  allocation appears.

In this case:

RCK1☐ Cross out = RCK3:RCK6   A will serve route 2
RAK2☐ Cross out = none   B will serve route 4
RBK4☐ Cross out = RBK6   C will serve route 1
REK5☐ Cross out = REK3:REK6   D will serve route 3
RDK3☐ Cross out = none   E will serve route 5
RFK6☐ Cross out = none   F will serve route 6

	1	2	3	4	5	6
A	4	[0]	12	4	4	4
B	2	6	4	[0]	2	⌧
C	[0]	6	⌧	4	2	⌧
D	2	8	[0]	2	8	12
E	8	6	⌧	10	[0]	⌧
F	8	2	2	2	1	[0]

Exhibit 6.29 Zero allocation: procedure when first application is non-optimum. Basic data

	1	2	3	4	5
A	160	130	175	190	200
B	135	120	130	160	175
C	140	110	155	170	185
D	50	50	80	80	110
E	55	35	70	8	105

Exhibit 6.30 Row application

	1	2	3	4	5
A	30	0	45	60	70
B	15	0	10	40	55
C	30	0	45	60	75
D	0	0	30	30	60
E	20	0	35	45	70

special application of our usual transportation methods. Unlike the usual problems we have to solve it is not a question of a minimisation of unit costs of movement, but the minimisation of opportunity costs. We are faced with a number of tasks each being capable of performance by an equal number of vehicles (machines or people), the actual cost of one doing the job is the cost of another not doing it. These conditions make the method one of very specialist application, but there is little doubt that having say six units to cover six routes is not a method that will never be met with. This simple technique discussed above will allow us to solve it reasonably quickly and at an acceptable level of accuracy.

It should be noticed that although we have applied this method only to vehicle allocation it is suitable for any similar situations, say order pickers within a ware-

Exhibit 6.31 Row and column application plus test   85
for optimum: minimum number of horizontal and
vertical lines = 3. Therefore non-optimum. Smallest
non-covered value = 15

	1	2	3	4	5
A	30	0	35	30	15
B	~~15~~	0	0	~~10~~	~~0~~
C	30	0	35	30	20
D	~~0~~	0	20	~~0~~	~~5~~
E	20	0	25	15	15

Exhibit 6.32 After applying rule: minimum number
of vertical and horizontal lines now equals set
number (5). Therefore optimum

	1	2	3	4	5
A	15	✗	20	15	[0]
B	15	15	[0]	10	✗
C	15	[0]	20	15	5
D	[0]	15	20	✗	5
E	5	✗	10	[0]	✗

K1RD ☐ Cross out RDK4
K3RB ☐ Cross out RBK5
K4RE ☐ Cross out REK2:REK5
K5RA ☐ Cross out RAK2
K2RC ☐ Cross out none

house or deciding which salesman will operate on which route. These applications
will be looked at in the warehouse section.

To return to the example in hand, we have now solved the matrix. Thus we
know the lowest cost routes between all the routes and every van salesman
and we can then schedule our delivery patterns accordingly.

The next stage in our investigation is to look at the local situation for each of the main depots. At a later stage in the section on warehousing a method for deciding the optimum area to be served by a warehouse is given. We will assume that this has been done and our problem is to decide upon a route for vehicles calling at customers within the area. Suppose that Exhibit 6.33 gives the layout of our customer locations. (Variations between direct data and figures going through a link will be caused by traffic conditions varying with direction and so

Exhibit 6.33

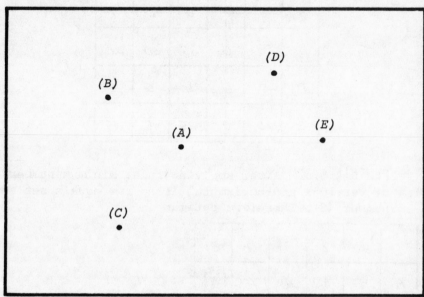

on. BA is 3 units and AD is 2 units but B to D is 6. This could be caused by the fact that a journey from B to A is not the same as BD even though the route is, because time may be consumed on BD passing through A.) The first piece of information which we require is, of course, the best route between each of these points. This is achieved by the method already described and the matrix shown in Exhibit 6.34 obtained. If, of course, there had been links involving indirect

Exhibit 6.34

	A	B	C	D	E
A	0	3	4	2	3
B	3	0	5	6	5
C	4	5	0	7	4
D	2	6	7	0	3
E	3	5	4	3	0

first part of the project. What we must now do is to select a route beginning at
our major depot, in this case A, and passing through all the other points and back
to the depot. This is completed in much the same way as before, the method being
first developed by Krag and Thompson.

First we choose a route, any route, then we find the shortest way to complete
that route. We take this and continuously add all the other points to be visited,
finding the shortest route at each stage. When all the points to be visited have
been included and the shortest route found then we have arrived at our answer.
First the simplest route, A to B and back to A: thus A—B—A from our matrix; we
can substitute the values for this as 3 + 3 giving us 6. This is our basic route and
we build up from here. The next point to be visited is, say, C. We evaluate all the
possibilities: A—c—b—A or A—b—c—A. If we evaluate these possibilities we get 12
units for the first two. Therefore the best route to follow would be either
A—c—b—A or A—b—c—A. The final choice will depend on whether there are any
special characteristics on the ground that must be taken into account; let us
choose A—c—b—A. The next point to be passed through is, say, d. We can then proceed as before the routes being as follows: A—d—c—b—A or A—c—d—b—A or
A—c—b—d—A. All of these must be evaluated. When this is completed it will be
found that the route A—d—A—c—b—A is the best at 16 units which leaves us the
final point to be included as shown in Exhibit 6.35. Therefore, we have arrived at
the best route whereby a vehicle leaving its main depot A and visiting customers

Exhibit 6.35

$$A-e-d-c-b-A = 3 + 3 + 7 + 5 + 3 = 21$$

$$A-d-e-c-b-A = 2 + 3 + 4 + 5 + 3 = 17$$

$$A-d-c-e-b-A = 2 + 7 + 4 + 5 + 3 = 21$$

$$A-d-c-b-e-A = 2 + 7 + 5 + 5 + 3 = 22$$

b, c, d and e using all the shortest routes would involve us in the theoretical
minimum cost. This route is, of course, starting from A moving to D, then to E,
through C and B, finally returning to A. This would, of course, represent only one
vehicle's route, but the others would be dealt with in a similar fashion.

As before this method must only be used as a theoretical target. There are a
great many variables which will affect this theoretical answer. The real key to the
successful application of this method, as before, is flexibility. These methods are
aids to management not a substitute for it, and there will always have to be a
compromise between the benefits to be had from a particular method and the
costs of introducing and controlling it.

One general point will now be made about both the methods used above. It
will be obvious that the figures used in the original networks and matrix can be
nothing more than averages gleaned from the data sheets of our original traffic
surveys. To introduce a note of realism into our methods we must make a true
assessment of the likelihood of these averages being realised. When we translate
the averages from the original record sheets to the diagrams we must make a
weighting which will give us some measurement of the risk of the times not being

realised. The easiest way to do this is to use the standard deviation. A full explanation of this is given in the section on inventory control. For our purposes we decide what level we want our network data to operate at and weight the average accordingly. Thus if we wanted to say that the data we included in the networks was correct 80 per cent of the time then we would take our average figure plus 0.84 times the standard deviation. If we wanted greater reliability say 90 per cent of the time, then it would be the average plus 1.28 times the standard deviation, and so on.

There is a danger which must be looked at here, however; care must be taken not to put too great an emphasis on reliability and accuracy. As the reliability we want increases, then of course the less likely a route link is going to be chosen as the best route. Care must be taken to ensure that we do not find ourselves in the position where we have routes of great reliability but higher cost. For example, a particular link may be susceptible to variable traffic conditions but may also at certain times offer a considerable time saving. If we try and include a realistic figure to reflect the variation, i.e. our average plus a high standard deviation weighting, we might make the route so undesirable that all general routes miss that link, yet it can often be very beneficial. The judgement here will depend on the skill of the particular manager in deciding what risk he is willing to take. This decision will be made when the weighting factor is decided upon when the original networks are drawn up.

This concludes the discussion of these methods. As mentioned in the introduction, these are not the only methods or even the most accurate. They are, however, ones that can be applied by anyone and they will give results. I see no point in looking at methods which are theoretically very accurate but are next to impossible for the average transport manager to apply. It is far better to use techniques which will give a good answer than ones which are too costly or complicated to justify themselves. As always the cost of the investigation should not be greater than the results nor should the results require an elaborate and expensive control system.

LINEAR PROGRAMMING

There remains however one more useful method to apply in these situations. We have been looking at problems where the target was simple and low in number. This often happens, but more likely we will find that we have not one depot in an area but two or three or more. In these conditions the methods described above are not the end of our routing problem, only the first stage. Suppose there are three sub-depots within an area and five different customers. Naturally, as always, this is a simple problem, but the method is the same for greater numbers.

To attack this set of circumstances we must use linear programming. This is not difficult and is essentially the same as the methods discussed above. We decide on a solution to the problem and then continually improve upon this until we can go no further. There are many methods of completing the actual computations. The one described here is one of the oldest and also one of the slowest, so it is best to explain why its use is preferred.

Too many of the shorter methods require calculations for the short cuts which are done 'in the head' and not fully written out. This is fine when we are dealing with the textbook type of problem, for no difficulties arise. When there are, say, 4 supply points and 25 delivery points the problem becomes extended and a great deal of simple arithmetic must be done. It is all too easy to make a mistake under these conditions.

In the method described here all the calculations are written out; more laborious yes, but extremely easy to check. There is one further reason: this method, like all linear programming methods, can be taught to assistant staff. I think this is one of the easiest to teach and to learn. These are, of course, purely personal opinions, disagreed with by many. There is really very little to choose between all the methods available except for what has already been said. They will all produce the same end result anyway.

The very first step is to collect the relevant data. Since our aim is to minimise costs then we must discover the cost of movement between the depots and the customers. Since we have already mentioned that the most likely element here is time, this is what we must first find out and then weight it appropriately to give us the cost of movement per unit moved. It must be mentioned here that there are two approaches to this question of costs to be included. The first, the most simple, and hence likely to be the least accurate, is to concentrate simply on transport costs as mentioned above. This would involve us in calculating all the best routes between the various locations as described previously. We would then simply convert these times into costs by allocating the proportionate times with their share of the total costs for a period. Suppose that a particular route takes 4 hr for an 8-hr day, then the proportion is half. If the total costs for the day are £10, then this route will receive £5 and if the average number of units dropped there is 5, the cost per unit on this route is £1.

This is a very simple approach which will give results and when the method described is applied then economies will be made. But this is the elementary approach. While we have stated time after time that this volume is intended above all as an introduction, we can nonetheless not allow this to rule out completely the more sophisticated problems, even if they are only mentioned in passing. Linear programming is a case in point. While it is true to say that the approach outlined above will give results it is not the total approach and this is after all what we are trying to encourage.

The cost of movement of the goods between the depots and the customers is not quite as straightforward as above. Later, in the section on warehousing, mention is made in passing of the Stewart Bowman formulation in the location decision. The first step in this is to arrive at the total cost of the operation of the warehouse per pound sterling of merchandise moved through it. This includes the costs associated with delivery but goes much wider.

For us to arrive at the optimum solution in our delivery problem we should really allocate costs on this basis, but this is beyond the scope of an introductory volume on the subject. As always we draw up our information in a matrix, and the result will only be as good as the information fed in (see Exhibit 6.36).

Now let us explain the layout of this first matrix. On the extreme left hand side we have the depots or supply points S1, S2 and S3. At the extreme right hand side we have their normal capacities S1 with 14 units, S2 with 21 units and S3 with 8 units, giving us a total supply of 43 units.

The columns are our demand points or customers (D1, D2, D3, D4, D5), the very bottom row their expected demands: D1 with 10 units, D2 with 12 units, D3 with 6 units, D4 with 7 units and D5 with 8 units. Again total demand is 43 units.

In the body of the matrix are the unit costs of moving these products from the supply points to the demand points. Thus to move a unit of product from S1 to D1 would cost 10 monetary units, from S1 to D4, 12 monetary units, from S3 to D4, 7 monetary units, and so on. Because the monetary units are costs, they are given a negative sign. This is the basic matrix from which all others are to be constructed.

Before moving into this, some elementary rules. The first of these is that the problem to be solved must be symmetrical, i.e. demand and supply must be equal. In our example this has been artifically assured. In the real work situation this is seldom the case. To deal with this problem dummy rows or columns are inserted to ensure balanced rim conditions. Thus if we find that demand exceeds expected supply then we add a dummy warehouse to balance the conditions up. This procedure is, of course, merely a convenience; we cannot satisfy all our customers whom we can accommodate.

Likewise if we find that supply exceeds demand we simply add a dummy customer. The end result is that we will be left with excess unshipped products, but we will have once more ensured that the real customers have been serviced at the lowest costs. It will be obvious that we must pay attention to the costs we allocate to these dummy rows or columns. Since we want to ensure that all the real customers are serviced and all the real capacities used as much as possible, then we allocate an arbitrarily chosen high cost of shipment of products from dummy warehouses or to dummy customers. Since these are theoretical costs anyway they are usually set equal to one another. The dummies in a matrix are then treated as normal.

When we have so arranged our problem that there is balance, we then proceed to the first allocation or solution. This can be done by inspection in the simple problems, but for the larger ones some formal rule is useful. To keep some degree of uniformity we will use one of the formal rules. This is one of the most common and is known as the North West Corner Rule, because we start our allocation at the north west corner. When an allocation is made it is boxed and called a stone square. Those squares without a stone in them are referred to as water squares.

The north west corner rule is that, starting at the north west corner square of the matrix, examine supply and demand. If supply is greater than demand, then allocate full demand and move *horizontally to the next square.* If supply is equal to demand, then set demand equal to supply and move *diagonally to the next square.* If demand is greater than supply, set demand equal to supply and move *vertically to the next square.*

Matrix 2 (Exhibit 6.37) shows this allocation. Starting at S1D1, demand is for 10 units, supply is 14 units, therefore we set this square equal to total demand and move horizontally to S1D2. At this point we have already used up 10 units of our supply leaving us 4 units. The demand at D2 is for 12 units, therefore demand exceeds supply, so we set S1D2 equal to supply (4 units) and proceed vertically to S2D2. We have already supplied D2 with 4 units from S1. Thus the demand remaining is for 8 units (12 − 4). Supply at S2D2 is 21 units therefore satisfy demand and move horizontally to S2D3. Demand here is for 6 units, supply is 13 units (21 − 8), therefore satisfy demand and move horizontally to the next square S2D4. Demand here is for 7 units, supply is 7 units (13 − 6), therefore satisfy demand and move diagonally to the next square S3D5. Demand here is for 8 units and supply is 8 units, so satisfy demand.

Exhibit 6.36   Matrix 1

	D1	D2	D3	D4	D5	
S1	-10	- 7	-10	-12	- 8	14
S2	- 9	-12	-14	- 2	- 7	21
S3	-14	- 9	- 6	- 7	-12	8
	10	12	6	7	8	43/43

Exhibit 6.37   Matrix 2

	D1	D2	D3	D4	D5	
S1	(10)	(4)	1	15	6	14
S2	6	(8)	(6)	(7)	(0)	21
S3	- 6	- 8	-13	0	(8)	8
	10	12	6	7	8	43/43

The reason for circling the allocations will become apparent as we progress. Examine our initial allocation: all demands have been satisfied and all capacities used. S1 supplies D1 with its entire demand, D2 with 4 units thus using its entire capacity of 14 units. S2 completes D2 demand by supplying 8 units, completely satisfies D3 with 6 units likewise with D4 and 7 units, thus using up its entire supply of 21 units. S3 completely satisfies D5 with its capacity of 8 units.

It must be remembered, however, that this is simply an initial solution. There may be occasions when it turns out to be the best solution, if not then we must improve on it.

Before we start this, however, one check must be made. Some problems degenerate, i.e. become insoluble, by linear programming methods. This will occur when the number of stone squares is less than the number of rows plus the number of columns minus one, i.e. when R + C −1 is less than the number of stone squares. Check this after the initial allocation. In our example there are 3 rows and 5 columns, therefore we have 7. The number of stone squares is 6; therefore our problem is degenerate. To make the number of stone squares equal to R + C − 1 we add a stone square of zero value. This is added in the best place to solve the problem. When degeneracy occurs during initial allocation there is usually a stair pattern to be seen. Add the zero stone square where it completes the stair pattern. Thus we add a zero stone allocation at S2D5 completing the stair pattern. This stone is hereafter regarded like any other stone allocation.

What we now do is evaluate the opportunity cost of not using the water squares in our initial allocation; and so long as there is a negative value there we have not reached the best solution. To do this select any water square, i.e. one not having a stone allocation: let us select, say, S1D3. To evaluate a water square we must trace a critical path for the square. This is done by moving along the row which the water square is in until we come to a stone square in the same row which is also in the same column as another stone square. A path is then traced out using only right-angled turns and stone squares until the original square is reached. Once the path has been traced out it is evaluated. This is achieved by referring back to the original matrix. The costs of movement can be obtained, and these are summed algebraically to arrive at the cost of not using that particular square.

Thus for S1D3, the nearest stone square in the same row also in a stone column is S1D2. Thus move to S2D2, move to S2D3 and then back to the home square. This is the path to be evaluated.

$$S1D2-S2D2-S2D3-S1D3 = +(-7) - (-12) + (-14) - (-10) = 1$$

The values in the brackets are the costs from the original matrix. They are summed algebraically, the result being 1. The value for water square S1D3.

S1D4 . . . . . . S1D2-S2D2-S2D4-S1D4 . . . + (−7)−(−12) + (−2)−(−12) = 15
S1D5 . . . . . . S1D2-S2D2-S2D5-S1D5 . . . + (−7)−·(−12) + (−7)−(−8) = 6
S2D1 . . . . . . S2D2-S1D2-S1D1-S2D1 . . . + (−12)−(−7) + (−10)−(−9) = 6
S3D1 . . . . . . S3D5-S2D5-S2D2-S1D2-S3D1 . . . + (−12)−(−7) + (−12)
                                        −(−7) + (−10)−(−14)−6 = −6
S3D2 . . . . . . S3D5-S2D5-S2D2-S3D2 . . . + (−12)−(−7) + (−12)−(−9) = −8
S3D3 . . . . . . S3D5-S2D5-S2D3-S3D3 . . . + (−12)−(−7) + (−14)−(−6) = −13
S3D4 . . . . . . S3D5-S2D5-S2D4-S3D4 . . . + (−12)−(−7) + (−2)−(−7) = 0

All these values are placed in their respective squares in the matrix as shown in Matrix 2. Since there are negative values in the water squares we have not yet reached an optimum solution. We must then proceed to another improvement. We first of all select the greatest negative water square, in this case S3D3 with a value of −13 and mark it with a rectangle for the purpose of identification, as in the illustration. We then retrace the path which we used to evaluate this square S3D5−S2D5−S2D3−S3D3 and note the values of any stone allocation in the path. These are taken in the same order as they appear in the path and prefixed as before with alternating plus and minus signs: + (8) − (0) + (6).

A new matrix is laid out as in Matrix 3 (see Exhibit 6.38). All the stone evaluations are left in the same locations as before, only without any values in them. There is one exception to this, the smallest positive value stone allocation in the path we have just retraced. In this case the value is + (6); this is placed with its old value in the square which contained the greatest negative value, in this case S3D3 with −13. This can be seen in the illustration. We now move on to Matrix 4 (see Exhibit 6.39) and reallocate values for our stone locations. Usually we would not use a separate matrix for the move of (6) to S3D3; it is done here for illustration only.

In Matrix 4 we again give values so that all supply is used and all demand satisfied. Starting at S1D1 demand is 10 units, supply 14. We can thus satisfy this demand so we place the value 10 in the stone. We move to S2D2: demand here is 12 units, we only have 4 left so as before we allocate 4 units and move to S2D2. Demand is for 8 units, (12−4) supply 21 units so we fill 8 in the stone and move to our next stone location which is at S2D4. Demand is 7 units, we have 13 left so demand can be fully satisfied and we move to the next stone location. The supply here at S3 is 8 units, but we have already allocated 6 of these to S3D3, so we have only 2 left. These are given so that D5 has its demand catered for, 6 units from S2 and 2 from S3 making the total 8.

If we examine the matrix we have again satisfied all demands and used all supplies. We must now see if this is the best solution. This is done as before by evaluating all the water squares in this next matrix. Select any water square, move to the stone square in the same row which is also in the same column as another stone value and using right-angled turns trace a path back to the original water square. Then we find the algebraic sum of the cost values of those stone squares we used in the path. To give a few further examples:

S1D3...S1D2-S2D2-S2D5-S3D5-S3D3-S1D3... + $(-7)-(-12)+(7)-(-12)+(6)-(-10) = 14$
S3D1...S3D5-S2D5-S2D2-S1D2-S1D1-S3D1... + $(-12)-(-7)+(-12)-(-7)+(-10)-(-14)$
$$= -6$$

All the water squares are evaluated in this manner and the results placed in the matrix as shown. Again we select the water square with the greatest negative value, which in this case is S3D2 with -8. Retrace the path and select the stone square prefixed by a positive sign which has the lowest value in the path. In this case it is the stone (2) at S3D5.

We then move on to our next matrix. In Matrix 5 (see Exhibit 6.40) we place all the stone squares appearing in Matrix 4 in the same position only with no values in them. We have only one exception to this; this is (2) which is placed with its value in the location of the water square having the greatest negative value in Matrix 4. This is, of course, S3D2.

We then allocate as before. S1D1 gets fully satisfied with 10 units. Our next stone is at S2D2. We have only 4 units left in supply so this is all we can allocate. This is done and we move to the next stone at S2D2. The total demand at D2 is

Exhibit 6.38 Matrix 3

	D1	D2	D3	D4	D5	
S1	( )	( )				14
S2		( )		( )	( )	21
S3			(6)		( )	8
	10	12	6	7	8	43/43

Exhibit 6.39 Matrix 4

	D1	D2	D3	D4	D5	
S1	(10)	(4)	14	15	6	14
S2	- 6	(8)	13	(7)	(6)	21
S3	- 6	- 8	(6)	0	(2)	8
	10	12	6	7	8	43/43

12 units. We have already allocated 4 from S1 and 2 from S3 therefore to complete demand requirements we allocate 6 units and move on. The entire stone allocation is made and we have the picture as before. We must see if this is the best pattern of servicing which is done by evaluating the water squares.

As can be seen from the illustration, Matrix 5 is not the best allocation as we still have a negative value at S2D1. Again the path is traced and again the stone value preceded by a plus sign having the lowest allocation in the path is chosen, in this case being S2D2. A new matrix is constructed and (6) placed in S1D1 with the other stones as before. The new allocation is made as shown in Matrix 6, (see Exhibit 6.41), the water squares evaluated and as shown they are all found to be positive. Therefore this is the best pattern of servicing. There may be other patterns giving the same costs, but not a lower cost. The total cost of this pattern would be 288 monetary units.

It is worth mentioning yet again that this is the theoretical best and should be used as a target figure, not as an inflexible prophecy. There may very well be policy reasons which would prevent this pattern being put into operation.

There is, of course, the question of speed and application to be considered, and whilst it is true to say that the method discussed above will produce good results, especially when applied to the small, classroom type of problem, it is cumbersome. This aspect of the North West Corner Method led to the pursuit of more manageable techniques. Over the years a great many of these have been developed and here we will examine only two.

THE VOGEL APPROXIMATION METHOD

The first of these, The Vogel Approximation Method (VAM), was developed by W. R. Vogel of the Rock Island Arsenal. The method is simple to learn — and to apply — and can be easily taught to clerical personnel as no maths other than arithmetic are involved. The technique was originally developed as a time saver, an initial solution, and as such does not guarantee an optimum answer. There is no reason however, why the initial solution arrived at by VAM cannot be processed in the normal way to develop an optimum allocation. The real attraction of VAM is that it is a great time saver. This arises through the near optimality which the initial application will produce. To illustrate the superiority of VAM we will initially at least apply it to the problem looked at above.

Steps in the use of VAM

In the application of VAM the original information is set out in a manner very similar to the North West Corner Method except, as can be seen from Matrix 1 (Exhibit 6.42), an additional column and row are drawn. These are known as the difference row and column.

The difference value is calculated for each row and column. This is the absolute difference between the most desirable value (lowest cost), and the second best value. Enter this difference value in the respective row or column. This value represents the 'improvement' value for the row or column, or to look at it another way the desirability of allocating to a row or column will be indicated by the difference value. A high difference value indicates that there is a large

Exhibit 6.40   Matrix 5

	D1	D2	D3	D4	D5	
S1	(10)	(4)	6	15	6	14
S2	- 6	(6)	5	(7)	(8)	21
S3	2	(2)	(6)	8	8	8
	10	12	6	7	8	43/43

Exhibit 6.41   Matrix 6

	D1	D2	D3	D4	D5	
S1	(4)	(10)	6	9	0	14
S2	(6)	6	11	(7)	(8)	21
S3	2	(2)	(6)	2	2	8
	10	12	6	7	8	43/43

discrepancy in a particular row or column; the greatest difference will indicate where the greatest proportional improvement between all allocation possibilities is.

The next step is to select the row *or* column with the greatest difference value and allocate the greatest amount possible to the lowest cost allocation, ensuring that the allocation is within the constraints of available supply and demand. If demand has been fully satisfied, or supply completely consumed, cross out all remaining squares in the row or column and insert F in the difference square for that row or column. If either demand or supply are not fully completed then make sure that the allocations made are deducted from original figures.

Repeat all the steps until demand and supply are fully utilised. When repeating the process it is important to ignore all crossed out squares.

As can be seen the method is simple in practice, the only real problem encountered is remembering which stage you are at if interrupted, so it is important to complete one cycle before leaving the computation.

It must be remembered, however, that this is an initial allocation which we end up with, not a final one. To check the VAM solution, we must apply an artificial set of values known as shadow costs. This method is another application of the check applied to the North West Corner Method. We set $R1 = 0$. The other check values are set relative to it by equating each cost, where there has been an allocation made, to the sum of its row and column check values. If we select a square where an allocation has been made, say R1K1, we proceed as follows: For a square with an allocation it has been decided the row and column check values or shadow costs will equal the cost of unit movement for that square and that $R1 = 0$. If we examine the square R1K1 we can see that the cost of unit movement is 10. Since we have said that $R + K =$ cost then $R + K$ must equal 10. But we have also said that the shadow cost of R1 = 0; therefore if R + K = 10 and R = 0, K must equal 10. Therefore the shadow cost for R1 we know is 0 and the calculated shadow cost for K1 is 10. We can use this information to calculate the shadow costs for all other rows and columns by using stone squares. Thus R1 + K2 = 7, therefore K2 must equal 7. Likewise R3 + K2 = 9 therefore R3 must equal 2. This is because we said R + K values must equal cost at stone squares This method is repeated until R and K values are obtained for all rows and columns. If during the calculation a gap in the spacing of stone squares is en-countered such that no link up can be made, then another 0 value is allocated to the row and the calculation is continued as above. It should be remembered that shadow costs can be positive or negative.

When all the shadow costs have been calculated, the test for optimality is applied. Select the first square with no allocation from the first application of VAM; this first water square must be positive, i.e. the row plus column value must not be greater than the unit cost of movement. If this is the case, then a negative quotient applies to this square and improvement through reallocation is possible. If C − (R + K) is positive, then move to next square. If all squares prove to be positive then we have an optimum solution; if not then proceed as below.

Select the water square with the greatest negative value. As on page 92, trace the shortest path using only stone allocations and making right-angled turns back to your selected square. List alternating plus and minus signs at each square selected for the path. Select the smallest positive-path stone. Subtract this from all positive-path stones *including itself. Add* the smallest positive-path stone to all negative allocations and *the original water square.* Re-check shadow cost values. If still a negative then repeat process until all water squares show a positive value when the shadow cost check is applied.

To illustrate the method we will apply VAM to the simple problem looked at

Exhibit 6.42 VAM layout

		D1	D2	D3	D4	D5	
		10	12	6	7	8	Diff.
S1	14	10	7	10	12	8	
S2	21	9	12	14	2	7	
S3	8	14	9	6	7	12	
Diff.							

under the North West Corner Method. Our basic cost data is laid out as before. We construct Exhibit 6.43 and apply the difference method. For ease of calculation amounts available at supply points have been moved from the right- to left-hand corners and demands from bottom of the columns to the top. The unit cost of movements are placed in the top left-hand corner of each matrix square.

In the first column the lowest cost is 9 units and the next lowest 10. Therefore the difference value for this column is 1; this is entered as shown. K2's lowest cost is 7; the next lowest is 9. Therefore the difference value is 2. Applying the same method to the other columns gives difference values of 4, 5 and 1.

The same procedure is carried out on rows R1. The lowest value is 7, the next lowest 8. Therefore the difference value is 1. For R3 it is 5 and for R3 1.

The next step is to examine the difference columns to locate the greatest difference value. In the case of this particular problem there is a tie, since both R2 and K4 have a value of 5. When ties occur special rules apply as to which row or column is selected. If the tie in difference values occurs only between columns, select the second best value in each tied column and calculate the difference between this value and the best value in the *row* that it appears in. This is known as the KT value (column tie). Allocate this to the column having the greatest KT value.

In the case of a tie between rows or in rows and columns then allocate to the saddle point. The saddle point is the square that has not only the best value for its row but also the best for the column in which it appears. Where more than one saddle point exists then allocate to the one associated with the greatest difference value for both the row and the column. Where there are several independent saddle points, allocate to any.

In our case then it can be seen that we are faced with a tie between a row and a column so we search for a saddle point. R2K4 with a value of 2 is both the best

Exhibit 6.43

		D1	D2	D3	D4 F	D5	
		10	12	6	7 = 0	8	Diff.
S1	14	10	7	10	12	8	1
S2	21 = 14	9	12	14	2 [7]	7	5
S3	8	14	9	6	7	12	1
	Diff.	1	2	4	5 F	1	

in R2 and the best in K4 so this is our saddle point. If we look at the top of column 4 we find that the demand to be satisfied is 7 units; to the left of row 3 we see that the supply available is 21 units. The allocation then is 7 units from warehouse 3 to customer 4. We enter this allocation in the lower right-hand corner of our square. *It is important that the demand and supply situation is altered to take account of this.* Therefore since we have completely satisfied this customer we reduce the demand to zero, draw a line through the column and place F at top and bottom. We subtract 7 units from the available supply, reducing this to 14 units. We have now completed one cycle of application. In practice, we would continue another cycle on the same matrix but to make it more easy to follow we will construct Exhibit 6.44 showing us ready to start another cycle. We start as before by calculating the difference values.

It can be seen that K1 remains the same at 1, K2 at 2, K3 at 4; K4 we are no longer interested in, since that demand has been satisfied, and K5 also remains the same at 1. R1 is unchanged at 1, but since we have removed K4 from our calculations then R3 must have a changed difference value. The best value is now 7 and the next 9 so the difference is now 2. R3 changes from 1 to 3.

We now proceed as before. Examine the matrix for the greatest difference value. This can be seen to be column K3; 4. We therefore examine K3 for the lowest unit cost square. This is, of course, R3K3, at 6 units. Therefore, by the above-mentioned rules, we must allocate to the lowest cost and this involves an allocation of 6 units to this square. This satisfies demand; therefore K3 is drawn through and F inserted to indicate completed demand. To take account of the satisfaction of this demand point we must subtract 6 units from the supply point, leaving us with 2 units of supply at warehouse 3.

We have now only to recalculate the difference values to complete another cycle. As can be seen from Exhibit 6.44, the values are: K1 remains as before at 1, K2 remains at 2, K3 we have removed from our calculations as we have K4 and K5 nonetheless remains at 1.

Let us now examine the values of the rows. R1 remains as 1; R2 also stays as 2, and R3 now has a difference value of 3. Therefore the next allocation must occur in R3, since this has the greatest difference value. We then look for the best square allocation. In this case it is R3K2 with a unit cost of movement of 9. We therefore allocate the maximum available — 2 units. This reduces the demand at this point to 10 units and the supply available to 0. The supply point at R3 has therefore been allocated as many customers as can be served, so R3 is then crossed out and F placed on that row.

To complete the cycle we must now calculate any new difference values as required. As mentioned before this would usually be carried out on the same matrix, but for the sake of clarity this will be shown (at this stage at least) on a new matrix, Exhibit 6.45. Again we follow the usual procedure; K1 remains the same, but K2 now becomes 5, K3 and K4 are satisfied and K5 stays as 1. R1 is unchanged, as is R2; and, of course R3 is removed from our calculation. The greatest opportunity for cost improvement is presented in K2. Therefore we start another cycle. The most attractive square location in that column is at a unit cost of 7. We therefore must allocate to that location. As we have already decided to deliver 2 units to this customer from warehouse 3, then the maximum we can now assign is 10. If we examine the source of supply at the left-hand side we see that this is 14 more than enough. Therefore 10 units are assigned to be delivered to customer 2 from warehouse 1. *We must alter supply and demand to accommo-*

Exhibit 6.44

		D1	D2	D3 $\overset{F}{6}=0$	D4 $\overset{F}{7}=0$	D5	
		10	12			8	Diff.
S1	14	10	7	10	12	8	1
S2	2̸1=14	9	12	14	2	7	$\not{5}$ 2
					⌐7		
S3	8̸=2	14	9	6	7	12	⌐3
				⌐6			
Diff.		1	2	4 F	5 F	1	

Exhibit 6.45

		D1	D2 $\not{12}=10$	D3 $\overset{F}{\not{6}}=0$	D4 $\overset{F}{\not{7}}=0$	D5	
		10				8	Diff.
S1	14	10	7	10	12	8	1
S2	2̸1=14	9	12	14	2	7	$\not{5}$ 2
					⌐7		
S3	8̸=2̸=0 14	14	9	6	7	12	⌐3
	F		⌐2	⌐6			F
Diff.		1	2̸ 5	4 F	5 F	1	

date these deliveries. To complete the cycle we recalculate difference values. This new state of affairs is shown in Exhibit 6.46. K1 is still 1; K2, K3 and K4 are finished; K5 remains as 1. R1 becomes 2; R2 still is 2; R3 is finished. We therefore repeat the cycle. We now have a tie between two rows, namely R1 and R2. The rule mentioned above must be followed. Since the tie is row and row we look for a saddle point. If the matrix (Exhibit 6.46) is examined carefully it will be seen that R2K5 is the only saddle point; therefore it is to this square that the next allocation must be made. Since the quantity demanded is 8 units and 14 units are available to make the maximum delivery, namely 8, we must remember to alter the columns and rows accordingly. This brings the column to F and the row to 6. To complete the cycle we must now recalculate difference column values: K1 = 1; K2 = F; K3 = F; K4 = F; K5 = F (see Exhibit 6.48). If we now examine the rows: R1 = 10; R2 = 9; R3 = F, the greatest difference is obviously 10. Therefore we allocate to the lowest cost square in that row, namely at R1K1; supply available 4; demand 10. The demand at K1 is therefore reduced to 6 units and the supply available at warehouse 1 is reduced to zero, so that row is allocated an F. We then complete a further cycle: K1 now becomes 9; K2-K5 are F; R1 = F as does R3; there is therefore only one allocation possible, i.e. 6 units at R1K1.

After this final allocation all supply requirements and demands are met. We have therefore arrived at an initial solution. There are naturally certain things we must observe about this initial solution. The most important of these is that we have, for the sake of illustration, used more than one matrix. In practice, as can be seen in the final matrix (Exhibit 6.49) it all can be done very quickly on the one matrix; only practice is required.

There is, nonetheless, a further and more important consideration. Is what we have arrived at an optimum solution? Since we have already solved the same

Exhibit 6.46

		D1	D2	D3	D4	D5	
		10	F ~~12~~=~~10~~=0	F ~~6~~=0	F ~~7~~=0	8	Diff.
S1	~~14~~=4	10	7 [10]	10	12	8	~~1~~2
S2	~~21~~=14	9	12	14	2 [7]	7	~~5~~ 2
S3	~~8=7=0~~ F	~~14~~	~~9~~ [2]	~~6~~ [6]	~~7~~	~~12~~	~~1 3~~ F
Diff.		1	~~2~~5 F	4 F	5 F	1	

Exhibit 6.47

	D1	D2	D3	D4	D5	Diff.
	10	12=10=0 F	6=0 F	7=0 F	8=0 F	Diff.
S1 14=4	10	7 [10]	10	12	8	1̸ 2
S2 21=14=6	9	12	14	2 [7]	7 [8]	5̸ 2
S3 8=7=0 F	14	9 [2]	6 [6]	7	12	1̸3 F
Diff.	1	1̸5 F	4 F	5 F	1̸ F	

Exhibit 6.48

	D1	D2	D3	D4	D5	Diff.
	10	12=10=0 F	6=0 F	7=0 F	8=0 F	Diff.
S1 14=11=0 F	10	7 [4]	10 [10]	12	8	1̸ 2 F
S2 21=14=6	9	12	14	2 [7]	7 [8]	5̸ 2
S3 8=7=0 F	14	9 [2]	6 [6]	7	12	1̸3 F
Diff.	1	1̸5 F	4 F	5 F	1̸ F	

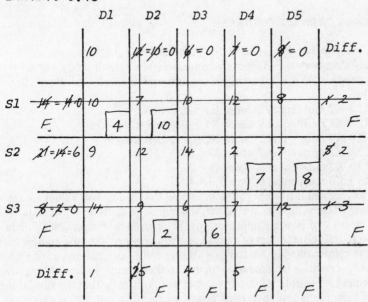

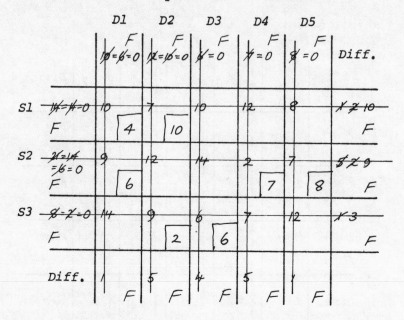

problem, albeit by a more laborious method, we already know that we have achieved the same allocation straight away. But suppose we did not know this. We would have to apply the shadow cost test as already described.

Test for an optimum solution

Given the technique that we have used, the best test for an optimum solution is, as already discussed, the shadow cost approach (see Exhibit 6.50). Let $R1 = 0$. Therefore, since $R1 + K2$ must equal the unit cost of movement, $K1 = 10$. Similarly,

   $R1 + K2$ must equal 7. Since $R1 = 0$, then $K2 = 7$.
   $R2 + K1$ must equal 9. Since $K1 = 10$, then $R2 = -1$.
   $R2 + K4$ must equal 2. Since $R2 = -1$, then $K4 = 3$.
   $R2 + K5$ must equal 7, then $K5 = 8$.
   $R3 + K2$ must equal 9, then $R3 = 2$.
   $R3 + K3$ must equal 6, then $K3 = 4$.

In this way we can introduce to the matrix all the shadow cost values for rows and columns. Once this has been done, it is simple to apply the final tests.

The measure of possible improvement (PI) is given by the general formula $PI = C - R - K$, i.e. the cost of a particular square minus the row shadow cost minus the column shadow cost. Where this is positive or equal to zero no improvement is possible by allocating further to that square. Where it is negative improvement is possible. This, put another way, is namely that the sum of the row and column shadow costs must not be greater than the cost of unit movement at a square: $C - R + K$ must be positive.

If we examine row one we can see that, when the above test is applied, square

Exhibit 6.50 All cycles and shadow costs; all water squares positive

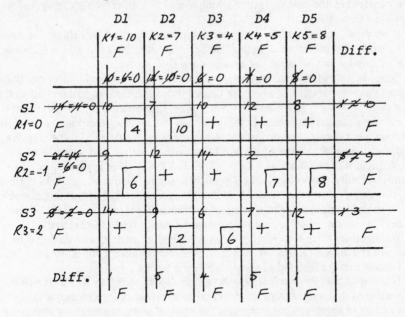

	D1	D2	D3	D4	D5	Diff.
	$K1=10$ F	$K2=7$ F	$K3=4$ F	$K4=5$ F	$K5=8$ F	
	10-6=0	12-10=0	6=0	7=0	8=0	
S1 — 11-11=0 — R1=0 F	10	7	10	12	8	7≠10 F
		4	10	+	+	+	
S2 — 21-14 =6=0 — R2=-1 F	9	12	14	2	7	8≠9 F
		6	+	+	7	8	
S3 — 8-2=0 — R3=2 F	14	9	6	7	12	7≠3 F
		+	2	6	+	+	
Diff.		1 F	5 F	4 F	5 F	1 F

Exhibit 6.51 Showing negative value: path traced with alternating positive and negative signs circled. Previous calculations to reach this point ignored

	D1	D2	D3	D4	D5	Diff.
	$K1=10$	$K2=7$	$K3=4$	$K4=-3$	$K5=2$	
	10	12	6	7	8	
S1 14 R1=0	10	7	10	12	8	
	⊕ 10	⊖ 4	+	+	+	
S2 21 R2=5	9	12	14	2	7	
	⊖ -6	⊕ 6	+	7	8	
S3 8 R3=2	14	9	6	7	12	
Diff.						

R1K3 is found to be less than the cost of movement, so no improvement is possible. We then move to R1K4 and find that this is also as before. R1K5 is not greater than the cost so again nothing would be gained by allocating further supply to that square.

If we proceed through all non-stone squares then we find that this is the case every time. This indicates, of course, an optimum solution (alhtough we already knew this since the problem has already been dealt with).

Suppose we had not had an optimum solution, then we would apply the procedure discussed above. To illustrate this let us assume that we had arrived at the allocation shown in Matrix 5 of the North West Corner Method. The first step is to calculate our shadow costs. It will be found that with a little practice this can be done mentally, at least on such an elementary matrix (see Exhibit 6.51). We find that the shadow costs of R1 and R3 remain as before, as does those of K1, K2 and K3. R2 becomes 5 and K4 = −3 while K5 = 2. If we apply our improvement possibility test we find that it is positive for all squares except R2K1. Here the row and shadow costs total 15 whilst the cost associated with the square are 9. We therefore have a negative value of 6. Notice this is identical to that found under the more involved technique used in the North West Corner method.

We therefore trace the closed path as described on page 92 and find that in this case it is R2K2–R1K2–R1K1. It will be found useful if the alternating plus and minus sign are inserted as the path is being traced.

It is found that the smallest positive stone allocation is 6 in R1K2. It will be remembered that we subtract this from all positive allocations *including itself* and add to all negative allocations *and the original home square being evaluated*. The result can be seen in the improved matrix illustration (see Exhibit 6.52). We have subtracted 6 from R2K2 thus reducing this to zero, and from R1K1, this resulting in the allocation becoming 4. Six has been added to R1K2 resulting in 10 and to R2K1 making an allocation here of 6.

Strictly speaking we should then calculate the shadow costs for this new matrix to see if we have reached an optimum solution. In this case we do not

Exhibit 6.52 Result of stepping-stone procedure

		D1	D2	D3	D4	D5
		$K1=10$	$K2=7$	$K3=4$	$K4=5$	$K5=8$
		10	12	6	7	8
S1	14	10	7	10	12	8
$R1=0$		4	10	+	+	+
S2	21	9	12	14	2	7
$R2=-1$		6	+	+	7	8
S3	8	14	9	6	7	12
$R3=2$		+	2	6	+	+

need to do this because we can see that this is in fact the usual allocation which we know is optimum.

We have gone through this problem step by step, and the reader may well be asking himself where the great time saving is. In practice we would not continually redraw matrices for the VAM method. All our calculations would be on one matrix as is shown in the VAM composite matrix illustration (see Exhibit 6.49). A little practice is all that is required for a significant time saving to be realised.

There are further adaptations which we must now examine. We have assumed this far that no special constraints have been introduced and that rim conditions always balance, i.e. supply and demand are always equal. This would be nice, but practical problems are seldom of this nature. If demand exceeds capacity, a dummy warehouse is introduced, i.e. we insert a fictitious warehouse with an imaginary supply of products. We assign a 0 value to the costs associated with this warehouse. We then solve as in the text above, treating the dummy warehouse the same as any other. If capacity exceeds demand we simply insert a dummy customer.

To illustrate these points assume that demand at customer 1 is not 10 but 15. We now have demand exceeding supply by 5 units. As can be seen in the matrix (Exhibit 6.53) we simply introduce a warehouse with 5 units available. We then proceed as usual to calculate our difference values. The greatest difference is in K1 so we allocate the maximum possible to the lowest cost, i.e. 5 units from the dummy warehouse. It must be remembered that the real situation is that demand exceeds supply, therefore somebody must be left unsatisfied; in this case it is customer number 1.

Exhibit 6.53 Layout if D1 is increased to 15, i.e. demand exceeds supply. D1 will have a shotfall of 5 units

		D1	D2	D3	D4	D5	Diff.
		~~15~~ 10	12	6	7	8	
S1	14	10	7	10	12	8	1
S2	21	9	12	14	2	7	5
S3	8	14	9	6	7	12	1
Dummy	~~5~~ 0	0	0	0	0	0	0
F		5					F
Diff.		9	7	6	2	7	

Exhibit 6.54 Layout if S3 supply was 18, i.e. supply exceeds demand. Dummy customer absorbs extra units. S1 left with 10 units

		D1	D2	D3	D4	D5	Dummy F	Diff.
		10	12	6	7	8	~~10~~ = 0	
S1	~~14~~ = 4	10	7	10	12	8	0	7
							10	
S2	21	9	12	14	2	7	0	2
S3	18	14	9	6	7	12	0	6
Diff.		1	2	4	5	1		F

If supply is greater than demand, then again some warehouse is going to be left with excess merchandise. To decide which one we use a dummy customer as shown in Exhibit 6.54. Assume that the supply available at warehouse 3 is 18 units instead of 8. This time our imaginary customer has a demand of 10 units as shown. We proceed as usual to calculate difference values. The greatest now is in row 1 and the maximum is allocated; again the dummy is removed from further calculations.

There may be marketing constraints to be introduced. It is not impossible for general management to decide that a particular warehouse for outside considerations must not supply a specified customer. If this situation arises then it is dealt with by allocating a very undesirable cost to the square combination involved. This cost will be, for example, X, where this is greater than any other cost on the matrix. On the other hand it may be required that a particular customer or customers always be supplied. It will be obvious that this instruction will only become effective under conditions where demand exceeds supply. If this is the case, however, a very undesirable cost is allocated to the square at the intersection of the customer and the dummy warehouse. This ensures that the cell will be driven out of the solution; or to be more accurate, into the normal solution.

We might also find that the particular pattern which we arrive at in our final solution is not desirable. This might arise because of management structures. We could find that we cut across regional boundaries and so on. To accommodate this we check to see if there is more than one optimum solution. We examine the values calculated when evaluating the water squares by means of our shadow cost matrix. It can be seen that they are all positive, greater than zero with the exception of R1K5 this square has an improvement possibility of 0. If this is pondered for a few moments the implications are obvious, namely that there is another optimum allocation possible. If there had been more than one zero value then an infinite number of alternative patterns would be available. We then take R1K5 and retrace the path that would be required to subject it to a reallocation. This would be R1K1–R2K1–R2K5–R1K1. When alternating plus and minus signs are inserted, the smallest stone allocation is R1K1 at 4. This value is subtracted from itself, added to R2K1, subtracted from R2K5 and added to R1K5. The result of this on the cost structure of the solution can be easily determined. We have moved an allocation of 4 units from a square with a cost of 10 units. Therefore we have deducted a cost of 40 units. We then add these 4 units to a square with a cost of 9 units, thus increasing our costs by 36 units, leaving our total improvement at −4 units. We then remove 4 units at a cost of 7 units, i.e. 28 units, and add them to a cell which involved a movement cost of 8 units, thus increasing our total cost by 32 units. It is obvious that the net result of all this is a zero movement in the total costs involved for this pattern of deliveries. This is confirmation of what we would expect, since after all we did move into a cell with a 0 improvement possibility, i.e. −40 + 36 − 28 + 32 = 0.

There is, of course, no guarantee that the new optimum pattern will conform with, say, the regional sales structure either. If this is the case, then we would recommend that all other possible patterns are evaluated. Since in this particular example there was only one other optimum solution all other choices will be more expensive. A table is drawn up showing all the water square values in descending order of magnitude. The procedure outlined above is then employed starting with that water square with the lowest value.

It is an easy matter to calculate the cost of these alternative patterns and general management will be able to see whether the present sales structure, or

Exhibit 6.55 Most to least method: layout of basic data

		D1	D2	D3	D4	D5
		10	12	6	7	8
S1	14	10	7	10	12	8
S2	21	9	12	14	2	7
S3	8	14	9	6	7	12

whatever the original reason for the exercise, is worth the extra costs involved A further point must be added here concerning the VAM method. Degeneracy can be recognised during the course of a solution when one allocation simultaneously satisfies a row and a column. This is dealt with by inserting a zero stone in any available cell in either the row or the column.

There is little doubt that VAM is one of the most useful of the 'transportation problem' methods and it can be used in most such situations. There are however conditions under which its use becomes very difficult or even impossible. This is especially true of seasonal inventory or outside capacity problems. These situations, in which the distribution manager is faced with a choice of, say, overtime working at peak demand periods or storage of inventory produced during slack periods, are suited to solution by the above methods, but because of the nature of VAM other approaches are best used. Indeed, under some problem constraints, VAM cannot be used at all.

To accommodate these situations we can either use the North West Corner method or a slight modification of this, where instead of evaluating the squares we apply the shadow cost method. There is another useful approach. The initial allocation is made purely on the most-to-least basis. An examination of the matrix is made, the location of the lowest cost cells noted and as great as possible allocation consistent with supply and demand is carried out.

As can be seen in the most-to-least matrix (Exhibit 6.55), the basic information is laid out in a form very similar to that used for VAM, except that there is no need for difference rows or columns. As is obvious, the lowest cost square is R2K4 with a value of 2. The demand for this customer is 7 units and the supply available 21. Therefore he is fully supplied from this depot. We must remember to note any allocations made so a line is drawn through the customer (as in VAM) and the corresponding amount deducted from supply. The next lowest is at R3K3; as 6 units are required and 8 are available, the allocation is made. There is then a tie in the lowest cost cells, both R1K2 and R2K5 having values of 7 units. In these circumstances it is always best to allocate to the greatest demand, in this case R1K2, where 12 units are demanded and supply is 14. We then satisfy R2K5 with 8 units. This procedure is carried on until all supply points are depleted and all demands satisfied. The result can be seen in Exhibit 6.56.

We then apply the shadow cost test to see if this is an optimum solution. As can be seen in the matrix, it is not. The greatest negative square is R3K2 with a value of −2. We therefore trace the evaluation path: R3K1−R1K1−R1K2−R3K2. The smallest stone allocation with a positive sin is R3K1, with a value of 2. We add this to R1K1, subtract it from R1K2 and add it to R3K2. As can be seen in Exhibit 6.57 this gives us the familiar solution to our little problem. We should, of course, now apply a further shadow cost grid to check that this is indeed an optimum solution but we already know it is. It is worth noting that although this method is shorter than the North West Corner approach, it still required one reiteration, whereas VAM gave us a better answer. In more complex problems it is much more likely (indeed, usual) to have reiterations with VAM.

It should be remembered, of course, that the variations and constraints discussed in connection with VAM apply to other techniques as well.

We have assumed in the methods discussed above that our aim has been to reduce costs, but it must be emphasised that the techniques can be as easily applied to profit-maximisation problems by looking at profit possibilities rather than unit costs. The only difference would be that rather than looking for the

Exhibit 6.56 Most to least method: initial allocation, shadow cost calculation and stepping stone path

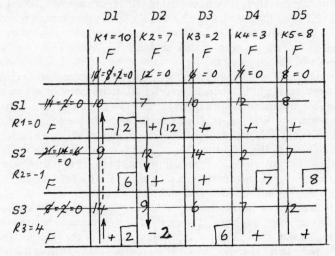

Exhibit 6.57 Most to least method: result of re-allocation of $+\boxed{2}$ shadow costs now positive

		D1	D2	D3	D4	D5
		$K1=10$	$K2=7$	$K3=4$	$K4=3$	$K5=8$
		10	12	6	7	8
S1	14	10	7	10	12	8
$R1=0$		$\boxed{4}$	$\boxed{10}$	$+$	$+$	$+$
S2	21	9	12	14	2	7
$R2=-1$		$\boxed{6}$	$+$	$+$	$\boxed{7}$	$\boxed{8}$
S3	8	14	9	6	7	12
$R3=2$		$+$	$\boxed{2}$	$\boxed{6}$	$+$	$+$

lowest cost as our best cell, we would search for the highest profit and then subtract from this the next best, or next highest, profit possibility.

So far in our discussion we have assumed a basic condition — that all movements in our scenario are direct without the possibility of trans-shipment or subsequent handling at different locations. In the real world this is usually an oversimplification of the situation. Some form of redirection is normally available. We are assuming that where this double handling is considered then the overall cost of movement is lower. This can and does come about in a variety of ways. For example, there may be depots in our system where handling costs are significantly lower than at others. This could offset higher transport costs to this location. There might be other firms who can provide lower throughput costs in specific locations simply because they are local employers. There may be local operations who are prepared to offer attractive rates in the hope of future business. Or there might just simply be occasions where local management operating on a smaller scale just might be prepared to offer attractive rates. In any or all of these situations and others, such price differentials must not be ignored — they should be included in our basic matrix. If we can do this and we are faced with a choice of costs, then not only can we decide which warehouse will serve each customer, but also (subject to the conditions below) which routes should be utilised. This assumes that we have already calculated the most attractive routes between all our sources of supply and our destinations anyway. This final method is a selection from the uncombined most desirable routes.

The technical term usually employed to describe the situation outlined above is the 'trans-shipment problem'. The method of solution is to reshape the basic data in such a way as to allow the application of any of the transportation algorithm techniques already discussed. We regard vehicle trips as the unit question rather than truck journeys. In this way we allocate customers, not to warehouses but to vehicle trips between the supply points, the customers and the trans-shipment depots, ensuring not only lowest costs but at the same time giving final route decisions.

Let us look at our base data already used and suppose that, in addition to the three warehouses already present we also have three possible trans-shipment points. As can be seen from Exhibit 6.58 a variety of routes are now available between some customers and certain warehouses. These are in addition to the direct ones. Notice that it is quite likely that not all customers will be capable of being serviced from our trans-shipment points. For these we leave a cost larger than any other on the matrix. This we will call M. This, remember, only signifies an impossible route.

The information which must be included in the matrix must include all points desired in the final solution. We must therefore include all warehouses, all customers, and, of course, all trans-shipment depots. In the case under examination this becomes 3 warehouses, 5 customers and 3 trans-shipment points. All of these are regarded as possible sources and destinations giving a total of 3 warehouses + 5 customers + 3 destinations, or 11 sources and destinations to be considered.

Since we are now regarding all trips as included in our data then the total number of trips must be regarded as having the same final number of destinations as locations, i.e. no vehicle can leave an origin without arriving at a destination, be this customer, supply point or trans-shipment depot. In other words, all locations and demands must ultimately balance.

Since the particular pattern of supply and demand is not known in advance, a slack or space capacity is introduced at each supply point and demand location to accommodate any imbalance which might be produced as a result of allocation. In theory this would be the notional number of units shipped and demanded by any location from and to itself. Thus the real number would be the actual number of vehicle loads, in this case $14 + 21 + 8 = 43$, minus any excess loads moved.

Exhibit 6.58 Transhipment basic data: here customers cannot supply themselves or anybody else. If sub-warehouses were included instead of customers, relevant data would be entered

		Supply points			Junctions		Demand points					Diff.
		1	2	3	1	2	1	2	3	4	5	
Supplies	1	–	16	2	3	16	10	7	10	12	8	14
	2	16	–	12	13	15	9	12	14	2	7	21
	3	2	17	–	16	3	14	9	6	7	12	8
	4	3	13	16	–	17	2	14	18	8	10	
Junc.	1	16	15	3	17	–	15	3	5	15	17	
	2	2	2	2	2	2	1	2	2	2	2	
Demands	1	2	2	2	2	2	2	2	2	2	2	
	2	2	2	2	2	2	2	2	2	2	2	
	3	2	2	2	2	2	2	2	2	2	2	
	4	2	2	2	2	2	2	2	2	2	2	
	5	2	2	2	2	2	2	2	2	2	2	
Diff.							10	12	9	7	8	

Exhibit 6.59 Transhipment layout for solution: as in VAM

		Supply points			Junctions		Demand points					Diff.
		1	2	3	1	2	1	2	3	4	5	
		14	21	8	43	43	10	12	6	7	8	
S_1	1	—	15	2	3	16	10	7	10	12	8	√
S_2	2	15	—	12	13	15	9	12	14	2	7	
S_3	3	2	17	—	16	3	14	9	6	7	12	
J_1	1	3	13	16	—	17	2	14	18	8	10	
J_2	2	16	15	3	17	—	15	3	5	15	17	
D_1	1	√	√	√	√	√	√	√	√	√	√	√
D_2	2	√	√	√	√	√	√	√	√	√	√	√
D_3	3	√	√	√	√	√	√	√	√	√	√	√
D_4	4	√	√	√	√	√	√	√	√	√	√	√
D_5	5	√	√	√	√	√	√	√	√	√	√	√
Diff.												

Since these are notional amounts anyway, then let their unit cost of movement 113
equal zero. Notice what we have done. We have simply acknowledged the fact
that all points in our system must come into our final calculation, but at the
same time we know that some of them are handling units which they themselves
are not producing or indeed demanding; they are throughput points only. Therefore, any movement into them must be counterbalanced by a movement out.
This must be capable of being handled by the points in question; therefore theoretical capacities and costs must be given them. In other words a safe upper limit to
capacity is added. Since it is most unlikely that it would ever be worth returning
a vehicle to the same trans-shipment point more than once, then the safe upper
limit to allow for all movements must be the total number of units in the problem
which in this case is 43. It is important to notice that the total number of routes
available, as in Exhibit 6.58, is 5 + 3 + 3 = 11. As is shown in Exhibit 6.59, the
problem is solved in the usual manner.

7 The railways

BACKGROUND PROBLEMS

'This country does not know what to do with its railways and at the same time does not know how to do without them.' This may seem a contradictory statement to make, but as we shall see it is very likely a true one in some ways, although not completely so. Over the last ten years there has been an overall growth in the movement of goods of about 26 per cent. In terms of tonne-kilometers, rail's share of this movement has remained fairly steady around the 20 per cent level; the share moving by road is about 77 per cent. The government forecast that up to 1985 rail's share is expected to grow modestly.

It is fair to say then that not only has the financial performance of the railways been poor (with only about three years in surplus since 1950), but they would seem to be in a stagnant position as far as their share of the expanding freight market is concerned. Perhaps the most widely raised issue concerning rail's financial performance and problems is that it is a tapering cost industry, i.e. in the long run the unit costs decrease as output increases. The opposite is also true: as output decreases the unit costs increase. The railways are not, of course, the only tapering cost industry, but in the transport sector they would seem to be the most extreme case, especially as far as their main competitor, road, is concerned. This comes about through the relationship between fixed and variable costs on the rail network. For the railways a larger than usual share of its total costs are fixed. A moment's thought will confirm this; think of the track, the signalling network, maintenance costs, and so on. If spare capacity exists, if it is possible to take more traffic on the tracks, then average costs will decrease as the volume increases. The marginal costs will be below average costs, thus as output increases cost per unit will come down. Remember we have very high fixed costs so the marginal cost, i.e. the cost of producing one extra unit (assuming spare capacity) must be below average costs, because average costs will include all costs for all units. To illustrate the point, suppose that our fixed costs are, say, £10. We know that the marginal cost per mile of output is, say, 6p.

Suppose then that a shipment was moved by rail because we have spare capacity. The average cost per mile assuming in the first case a 50-mile trip would be the fixed cost (£10) plus the cost per mile, 6p X 50 = £13, divided by the distance covered, i.e. 26p per mile. For a 100-mile trip the average cost per mile would come down to 16p and for a 500-mile to 8p per mile. We have assumed here that cost functions are straight lines. This is not the case in practice but the point is illustrated. It can also be seen that as output declines the average costs will increase and since the railway's share of the freight market has declined from around 38 per cent in 1955 to the 20 per cent already mentioned, it is argued that a vicious downward spiral has been induced. As the volume of traffic decreases, the remaining traffic is faced with increasing average costs. Because of this prices have to be raised. This in its turn frightens more traffic away, thus giving another boost to the spiral.

It is obvious that there are two basic methods of solving rail's problem. Either they must in some way alter their cost burden in such a manner as to escape from the spiral, or they must attract additional traffic sufficient, in conjunction with their cost relationships, to allow a sound cost-versus-revenue base. It would of course be even more desirable if both methods of attack could be achieved at the same time.

There are, naturally, difficulties. Reduction of costs as far as the railways are concerned is a nice easy phrase to me but is fraught, in practice, with difficulties, not least owing to their inherent nature and the fact that they are nationalised. The second concept suffers from the very advantages that the railways have as being very suitable for large-bulk, long-distance movement. The sad fact of the matter is that most freight movements are not large bulk, long distance. Most of those that are already go by rail anyway.

Reduction of costs for the railways is a complex concept — as it is for any industry where the direct material costs involved in the product are low. For example, if we think in terms of variations in capacity of individual services then we are likely to find very few savings of any significance that can be made. If, for example, we reduce the capacity of a particular train then the costs escaped are very small indeed — probably only the costs of the paperwork involved in dealing with the loads foregone. Indeed, only the cost of the paper is likely to be saved as the wages of the staff involved will not be cut.

It has already been pointed out that many of rail's costs are fixed. To provide a service, a track must be laid. This is true whether one train per day uses it or its technical maximum. We are faced not only with these difficulties of fixed and indivisable costs, but also with time considerations. If an early morning train is removed from the schedule, the costs avoided might be small because the network and all its facilities might still be required for train movements later in the day. If on the other hand the last three late-night services were cut — assuming no other trains until morning — then there might be large savings possible.

Costs incurred jointly and in common also produce problems. If a service from A to B is on a track of such a nature that the train must return to B then the costs of the A to B to A service are said to be produced jointly — a situation often met in rural districts. If we then ask what costs can be avoided by cutting the trip from B to A the answer is very few, except some paper at the B terminus.

Common costs are slightly different in concept. Such costs must be incurred if a particular output is to be produced although no individual service must of necessity result in the provision of any other one. In the case of the journey from

A to B common costs would exist for traffics originating at A or B or for goods which only use this stretch of line as a feeder service to reach the much wider national network. There are many stretches of track used by both passenger and freight services. Thus in these situations we are very much in the position that dropping one service might produce only small savings in costs.

As was mentioned at the start of this discussion one aim of a policy to help the railways might be to try and reduce the great proportion of total costs represented by fixed costs. From what has just been said it is fairly obvious that with the entire network faced with a stagnant or nearly stagnant growth future, then wide-ranging small cuts on some services in different regions will not help in any positive sense. To reduce the burden of the fixed costs then reasonably large changes must be made in some parts of the system.

Various authorities [for example, Joy and Foster in the *Proceedings of the Institute of Civil Engineers* (February 1968)] have suggested that drastic reductions in the track costs incurred by British Rail could be achieved by the widespread use of single-track lines with much-simplified signalling systems. An important reduction in the contribution these make to the fixed costs element would be obtained in this way.

There are, however, problems in achieving this desired reduction in fixed costs, especially where we have over-capacity. The reduction can only be achieved at a price. The removal, for example, of long stretches of track would involve considerable dis-investment costs. A balance must be struck between the cost of ceasing certain activities and the cost of the continuance. Then there is the problem of quality of service. The railways must be careful to ensure that attempts to reduce fixed costs do not reduce the level of service offered to their remaining customers. Otherwise these may leave the railways and go elsewhere. This would only add to the difficulties in the manner already discussed.

In an article entitled 'Pricing and investment in railway freight services' [*Journal of Transport Economics and Policy* (September 1971)] , Joy carries the capacity argument to its logical conclusion by advocating that the demand side should be considered to be largely outside the control of the railways. The railways should then decide the total revenue available from particular services, i.e. likely prices and traffic flows, and then adjust their costs, or capacities accordingly. There will obviously be cases where revenues will not cover costs. In these circumstances, the services in question should be regarded as social necessities and subsidised by the government or quite simply withdrawn.

The major problem to be remembered here is that such hard and fast rules might very well have an adverse affect on the general quality of service that the railways can offer overall.

LABOUR COSTS

It is often argued that labour costs are a major indivisible cost that the railways have to bear and some evidence of the difficulty can be seen in the statement in the 1967 Railways Policy White Paper to the effect that Beeching's policies 'could be described as effecting a reduction in total annual railway working expenses of about £115 million between 1962 and 1966, but of this £95 million was absorbed by wage and other price increases'. In the 1977 Transport Policy White Paper the government says: 'But the future of rail freight depends far more on the Board and the rail unions than any set of measures that the Government may take'.

The 1976 Consultative Document on Transport Policy makes the point that more than two-thirds of the cost of operating the railways is accounted for by wages and salaries. There might be a case for regarding these as fixed costs in the short run and therefore an area where substantial reductions might help the overall financial position of the railways. This is especially so when the productivity per employee of the home network is compared with some foreign systems. Taking the passenger-kilometer and tonne-kilometer of paying freight per employee and the UK as a base of 100, we find the German figure 110, the Netherlands 177, the French 179 and the Japanese 277. Much the same picture by the way results if we look at the use of assets per tonne-kilometer of paying freight traffic per tonne of capacity of waggon stock. Here the figures for the same countries in the same order are 107, 244, 178 and 442.

There is little doubt that great things were achieved in the sixties. Between 1963 and 1970 manpower fell from 476,545 to 253,395, a drop of some 223,150 men; in the six years 1970 to 1976 the labour force fell from 253,395 to 230,972 or a drop of 22,423. As the Government says in the Consultative Document: 'The unions indeed have a crucial role and their co-operation is essential in the long-term interests of the industry. British Rail have therefore invited them to discuss a large number of specific proposals for improving productivity over their whole range of operation and administration, including train crews, station and depot staff, track and signalling employees and, of course, office workers.'

The unions and some management are of the opinion that such drastic reductions as we have mentioned are not the way to help the railways. What is needed it is said is a new investment programme to encourage more traffic onto the railways. This is a difficult area to discuss because we are always faced with the situation that we do not really know what the result of an investment programme would be until it is carried out. There are, however, some steps we can take. We can, for example, examine past experience and look at the likely available market the railways might capture. This available market it will be remembered has already been mentioned in the context of the two basic methods of attacking the railway's difficulties.

POSSIBLE MARKET CAPTURES

Let us look first at freight movement. There is a feeling encountered frequently that there are vast amounts of freight traffic just waiting to go by rail, but for some reason or other (preferably a government conspiracy) it just does not materialise. As far as the facts can be ascertained, they would seem to support the other argument that this pool just does not exist.

It will be recalled that the railways are ideally suited to long-distance bulk haulage. The facts more or less bear this out. The average resource costs for rail is given in the Consultative Document as 1.2p/tonne-km compared to that of road of 8.5p/tonne-kilometer. But it must be borne in mind that the nature of the average trip on road is very different from that on rail. The average length of haul on the railways is approximately 135 km and for road about 55 km. It is estimated elsewhere that bulk goods carried over 75 miles by road account for only about 5 per cent of road ton-mileage. In other words there just is not a vast pool of freight of the most suitable kind available to redirect onto the railways. They already have the major share of such traffic. They have, for example, about 75 per cent of bulk coal movements. It has been estimated that if all goods traffic of hauls of more than 100 miles were to be moved from the roads to the railways, road traffic would drop by about 2-4 per cent. Even if there were to be an increase in the rail movement of freight by 50 per cent this would reduce road traffic by under 8 per cent. As a final point, about 66 per cent of the tonnage carried by road over the period 1964-74 was on hauls of 25 miles or less. On the railways such hauls accounted for less than 33 per cent of movements. Such short hauls are, of course, exactly the kind of traffic the railways are not suitable to handle, and bear in mind that road carries 85 per cent of total tonnage (as opposed to ton-miles) moved.

The same position can be seen in the passenger market. In terms of passenger-kilometers the market for rail has remained more or less stable over the past ten years, although the number of journeys have fallen dramatically. The increasing length of average trips has made up the difference.

There are a great many reasons behind these facts but in all probability the most important centre around the attractiveness of the private motor car. There has been a significant growth in car ownership and a favourable movement of the indices of car purchase and operation in comparison with other modes. There is also the perceived cost problem that we have already mentioned in another context, the point being that for most motorists the costs of a particular journey are regarded as the direct costs. This is especially true for fairly short journeys repeated frequently. Very few drivers calculate their labour cost and the cost of tyres, oil and depreciation on every journey.

Whilst it is true to say that the railways have greatly improved the quality of their service on many trips, it is just as true to point out that the extensive motorway network now in existence has improved the relative quality of car travel for many people. Motoring has increased its share of total expenditure on passenger transport by users from 77 per cent in 1974.

There is one area where likely growth is probably still available. This is the Inter-City service. Fares in this area increased in January 1975 by 12½ per cent, in May 1975 by 16½ per cent, in September 1975 by 15 per cent and in March 1976 by 12 per cent, yet there continued to be an increase in revenue, although there was a slight drop in volume. The answer to this is probably the fact that upwards of 35 per cent of Inter-City passengers are businessmen with a more inelastic demand. Moreover most other regular users are from higher income groups — again less likely to be tolled off easily.

Even from this brief survey it is fairly obvious that there is no great pool either of freight or passenger traffic that is available to be easily directed onto the railways. At best, freight and passenger transport demand will slowly increase over the next decade but new massive investment schemes would on the evidence just saddle the railways with even greater fixed costs to help them further down the decreasing traffic/increasing average costs spiral.

SUBSIDIES AND COSTS

Just before we examine the past history of such attempts it is as well to bear the following facts in mind. According to the Consultative Document, subsidies to the railways in 1976-77 were to account for about 69 per cent of the total funds available for subsidy to inland transport. British rail investment will amount to about 20 per cent of total public investment in inland transport and all this on a method of transport *that carries about 18 per cent of freight movement and 8 per cent of passenger movement.* To quote: 'This is a lot of money. We must therefore ask first whether we are getting proper value for it in transport terms. . . . We must ask these questions in the light of previous conclusions that indiscriminate subsidies are seldom justified. . . .'

A quick look at past experience might be of value now. One argument that is usually raised concerning the railways is that they were starved of capital in the period from just before the Second World War to the early fifties, Redfern [*Journal of the Royal Statistical Society*, Series A, Volume 118 (1952)] estimates that for the period 1937-53 a disinvestment of about £440 million at 1948 prices took place. There was some attempt during 1953-60 to rectify this but the position was never fully recovered. When monies did become available under the 1955 Modernisation Plan little evidence was presented that all that had been lacking was money. So ineffective were the results that rather than new fresh revenue being reaped in viable amounts to cover expenditure, all investment expenditure prior to 1955 still on the books and half of the 1955-62 expenditure had to be written off. Very soon then after full nationalisation, some evidence was available that forces were at work in the transport needs of the country that indicated that large investment schemes for the railways would not necessarily solve their problems.

Another argument often heard is that the valuation of the assets taken over by nationalisation in 1948 was an overestimate of their true value. This may or may not be true, but the fact remains that if all charges associated with these burdens are excluded from the accounts then by 1962 on working account a deficit of some £200 million had accumulated. In 1962 a £705 million capital debt incurred before 1956 was suspended interest free. Half the investment of the £612 million modernisation plan was written off. In 1968 the suspended £705 million and an additional £557 million were written off. Given these figures, it is fair to say that whilst the original capital debt of the railways may have given some problems in the early years, subsequent performance left no doubt that it was not the sole difficulty.

The first attempt to solve the rail's problems in a systematic way was the 1955 Modernisation Plan. This was to be implemented over the fifteen years up to 1970. The plan was ambitious; estimated costs were around £1200 million. The basic aim was to attract custom through the modernisation of rolling stock, signalling equipment, stations, track, freight waggons and the replacement of steam by diesel and electric locomotives. It rapidly became obvious that the plan was not succeeding for the following reasons. First, there was a dangerous lack of basic management information. The Ministry of Transport and railway officials, for example, before a Select Committee of the House of Commons could not agree on the criteria to be applied on the appraisal of a major electrification scheme. Surely such a conflict on so basic a matter indicates a weakness either on technique or agreed objectives or both. Either way such a situation does not engender confidence on the uses to which the railways management were putting such large sums of money. The same trend can be seen on operational information. It was not until Dr Beeching was called on the scene that a large-scale survey was carried out to collect basic data. Nobody knew which services or areas were contributing what revenue. Nobody knew which service routes or indeed stations were covering their costs and which were not. It is tempting to say, and probably not be too wrong, that as far as operational performance was concerned nobody seemed to know very much. It would appear that there was a belief that the introduction of diesel units and generally improved operating methods would cut the losses on most services. The net result of this was that there was little if any selective investment. Areas with potential for high profit were not pinpointed and did not receive the more than average investment they could justify. Those areas where disinvestment might have been more desirable were likewise not known in sufficient detail.

Then there was the fact that no planning seemed to have taken place in the isolated railway world. Little attention seemed to have been paid to the upsurge in incomes that was taking place, the movement towards higher car ownership and a premium being put on personal independent mobility. There was much talk at the time of the 'Drift to the South', but apparently little interpretation of the future results in industrial and house concentrations — and hence different patterns of transport. There was, in other words, no realisation that rail traffic was likely to remain fairly constant over the fifteen years of the plan. There was, therefore, investment in facilities to cope with the expected increases in traffic, which when they arrived were almost non-existant in terms of their need for much greater facilities. The end result was that the fixed charges of the railways were increased — without attracting the extra traffic that would be required to use the new capacity to bring down average costs. The result was predictable. The fifteen-year plan was cut short and in 1962 Dr Beeching was called in by the government. And at the same time the financial structure of the railways was altered as already indicated.

BEECHING

The Beeching Plan failed, due in part to the government's attitude to certain of its recommendations and also to some internal weaknesses. It was, nevertheless, probably the first reasonable attempt to gather the really necessary basic information about the railways that had been lacking for so long.

If management is to improve the operations of an organisation — nationalised or not — then it must be able to correct past errors and plan appropriate action for the future. Neither of these actions can be carried out if there is no basic knowledge of the locations or costs and revenues.

The Beeching Report certainly threw up some interesting facts in this area. Of the total available route mileage, 33 per cent carries 1 per cent of passenger mileage; 33 per cent of the route mileage carries 1 per cent of the freight ton-mileage. One half of the entire rail system did not generate enough revenue to cover even track and signalling costs. The other half covered these by a factor of six. Of the passenger stations 50 per cent generated only 2 per cent of revenues and half the freight stations accounted for only 3 per cent of receipts. In neither of these cases was the revenue enough to cover the station costs alone. The report contains example after example in a similar vein.

The action required was obvious. At the root of the problem was our old friend of fixed costs. Since it seemed that many of these could be removed it is no wonder that the phrase 'Beeching's Axe' came into popular usage. The axe was to fall on passenger services and passenger stations, lines were to be closed and some have maintenance reduced from passenger standard to freight. Some passenger rolling stock was to be removed and the number of freight waggons reduced. Workshop staffs were to be reduced and new costing methods introduced. Working expenses were to be reduced in the coal traffic and the conversion to diesel and electric traction was to be continued. General traffic was to be re-organised and an investment programme instituted to develop liner trains. Inherent in the plan was a forecast that some £10-15 million revenue would be added by traffic attracted to the railways from other transport modes.

All in all the plan seemed reasonable and when it is remembered that the railways also received very favourable financial treatment, a positive forecast for the plan's future seemed justified. With the benefit of hindsight (a wonderful tool for solving other people's problems) we know that the plan failed. Can any reasons be put forward? Many.

In the first place social consideration ensured that the government (either colour) was not prepared to tolerate the level of passenger closures that the report recommended. The original Beeching target of a rail network of about 8000 miles was revised upwards in 1967 to 11,000 miles where it has remained. According to the most recent government publications, it is likely to remain for some time. Probably more important, however, the plan was hopelessly over-optimistic in its forecasts relating to the volume of traffic that Freightliners would attract to the railways. It was forecast that by 1973 this service would make about £18 million profit. In fact even after much higher inflation rates than were thought of in the plan about £1 million was made in 1973, although the service had changed somewhat.

The reorganisation of the sundries traffic which was a feature of the plan did not take place at anything like the rate or so successfully as was envisaged. Indeed from 1961 to 1967 the deficit increased from £13 million on a turnover of £38 million to one of £18 million on a reduced turnover of £22 million. The same position existed in the waggon load traffic. A basic tenet of the plan had been a move towards larger unit loads (preferably company trains) away from waggon load traffic. Yet in 1969 about 75 per cent of the revenue from general freight was coming from waggon-sized loads and, not surprisingly, failed to cover its direct costs.

A very high proportion of the bulk movement on the railways is in the form of coal and coke. It was forecast that growth would take place here, but because of the general low level of activity (in growth terms) of the coal and steel industries there was a shortfall here as well.

There was a very bad failure in basic industrial relations in the plan's attitude to the unions. Many of Beeching's suggestions, especially those on the freight side, required increases in labour productivity, both in the positive sense and in the wastage sense, i.e. more output from fewer men. This is fine in theory, but it is unrealistic to expect the unions to accept this without some form of higher wages for the men still employed on the railways. No allowance would seem to have been made in the plan's forecast improvements in revenue for this factor. We have already seen that from Beeching's expected savings of £115 million, about £95 million was absorbed in wage increases and other price rises.

The objective set for Beeching was to make the railways pay their way. From the figures available it would appear that there was underestimation of the revenue that would have to be generated to achieve this. In the first place an operating deficit of £87 million remained from 1961. This had to be paid for. To be met this would amount to about £30 million and the depreciation required to maintain the network would add, approximately, another £50 million. Therefore something in the order of £167 million was required in the first instance, followed by a surplus of at least £80 million a year just to stand still. Nobody at their most euphoric could have expected a performance of that order. Certainly, when the government's reaction to the plan and the failures to implement certain of its proposals are taken into account, there is little wonder that it failed. We have already examined the 1968 Transport Act with reference to its road provisions but it must be remembered that a central part of the Act was related to the railways and, indeed, the Act was in many ways a reaction to Beeching's failure to solve the problems of the rail network.

THE 1968 TRANSPORT ACT

The basis of the 1968 Act's attitude to the railways was a desire to see the railways paying their way on a normal commercial footing. This new reconstruction was to put the railways on their feet and from then on any new projects must be financed from within. There was the feeling that the management of the railways had become too dependent on the Treasury and that new investment was seen as a right rather than something which had to be earned by improved levels of service, better productivity and more efficient management decision-taking. To achieve this better 'morale environment', The National Freight Corporation was to take over the responsibility of the sundries traffic. Subsidies were to be paid for socially necessary services, grants were to be made for surplus track capacities, and the capital structure was reorganised in such a way as to move the system into surplus in 1969.

Instead of block subsidies to cover deficits the idea was that specific subsidies would be paid, thus allowing (it was hoped) greater financial control. The services requiring long-term subsidy would be identified and a conscious decision made as to whether they justified, on social grounds, a continued payment, or whether they should be cut. Very specific conditions were laid down to allow justification of a subsidy – if competitors' prices fell below marginal social costs, for example. The idea here was obviously to cover the situation where users of other modes were bearing only marginal private costs and not marginal social costs. In this case it was felt that a subsidy to the railways would in certain circumstances be more effective than making the consumer bear full marginal social costs. If the railways were to be the only or least cost transport available in an area then, if its withdrawal would cause hardship, subsidies could be justified on social grounds. If factor prices (especially railway wage bills) exceeded true opportunity costs, then the price to the railways in private costs would exceed the social costs of providing services. In other words, if the actual costs to the railways of, say, labour exceeded what the labour could obtain elsewhere, then the service would be justified on social grounds. Think of services not paying their way. The government did not implement the cuts suggested in the Beeching Plan. Therefore, of those large number of routes and services where revenue was not covering costs, the service continued to run for social reasons.

Spare capacity grants were justified for social reasons also. There are times of the year when demand for rail travel increases dramatically. Capacity must be held if this is to be carried. This excess capacity, however, only earns revenue when in use. If this feature is to be continued to be provided then it is only reasonable that the railways received some form of subsidy to cover its costs when not itself earning.

The problems of the railways were not solved by the 1968 Act, however, and further legislation was forthcoming. The main problems were difficulties with cost increases, lack of price-fixing freedom and a failure to increase its share of the available markets. The cost problem would seem to have revolved around the burden of wages. Although progress was made in this field, most authorities feel it has been insufficient especially when it would appear that British Rail appear to be recruiting at a rate that exceeds the reduction in numbers. Fears have been expressed that redundancy payments are such that little net financial benefit accrues to the railways anyway. There might be a case for greater government participation in this particular field.

It has been suggested that the railways did not tale full advantage of the freedom conferred on them by the 1962 Act in respect of pricing decisions. Prior to the 1962 Act the Transport Tribunal had powers to fix maximum prices. This is a little unfair since many proposed increases were postponed or reduced between 1971-74 as a part of government price policies. The failure to extend further into markets has already been mentioned. The upshot was that in the 1974 Railways Act a return was made to blanket subsidies, the government tacitly admitting that the objectives and general framework of the 1968 Act were just not workable. A further capital write-off of about £190 million was made and provision was included for a fund of about £5 million per annum to encourage private industry to invest more in rail facilities such as private sidings for the use of company trains.

THE PRESENT SITUATION

To date, in spite of several different 'plans' and the writing off of over £3000 million pounds, the railways seem no further forward and, indeed, are unlikely to be if the old schemes of more investment to bring more traffic are adhered to. In the Consultative Document, the basic facts of life were set forth and the subsequent White Paper showed no desire to soften them: 'Difficult choices will have to be made between a number of options such as concentration on essential renewals to track and signalling, a selective approach to product improvement, limiting further electrification, a less comfortable and slower service, and slower introduction of the High Speed Train (HST) and Advanced Passenger Train (APT).' It has been decided to stabilise investment at present levels and these are lower than those forecast in 1972. The intention is to devote a larger share of the available funds to the 'key sector of freight and parcels'. Total investment of about £260 million is available. A prime target is set of eliminating freight losses of some £70 million which were incurred in 1975, and the government will not extend any freight subsidy after 1977. There will be, however, an extension of the time period over which grants will be available for private sidings: 'No worthwhile scheme will be rejected on the grounds that funds are not available'.

The main hope that the government holds out for the future is that the implementation of EEC regulations will improve the competitive position of the railways against road. Further, the ability of the railways to carry bulk commodities long distances efficiently will 'enable them to carry more freight and to earn substantial profits for investment to replace assets and to develop other parts of the industry'. If this last quote stirs up memories of other such prophecies which were not fulfilled, one can but agree, especially when you remember that the governments' own forecast is for a modest growth in the future.

NATIONALISATION – ITS PROBLEMS

We have spent some time looking at the problems facing the railways and it will be noticed that a great many of them are tied either directly or indirectly to the fact that they are nationalised. Nationalisation is a very emotive and interesting topic but not really central to our theme here. If we were to be asked one basic difficulty brought about by nationalisation perhaps the word 'objectives' might spring to mind (among it must be admitted a host of others). For those firms who operate to the simple commercial rule of profitability (I think some still exist), many of the kind of decisions we have been discussing resolve themselves into: Objective – can this be made to pay? If yes, how and can we afford it? If it cannot be made to pay, must we keep it? If so, why is it worth it? If not, use the resources elsewhere. This can be a very complex and tortuous process, but at least the ultimate objective is usually quite clear. Not so in a nationalised industry such as the railways. Beeching was asked to make them pay; his remedy was not accepted. The 1968 Act put them on a normal commercial basis: 1974 changed that, and now again in 1977 the government is pointing out that subsidies will be cut for freight and held for passengers. It is very difficult to draw up long-term plans when the objectives of the entire organisation can be altered or can have its emphases changed with bewildering regularity.

THE RAILWAYS AND THE DISTRIBUTION MANAGER

We have perhaps overspent our time on these background difficulties of the railway network, but it is essential for good planning to be aware at least in outline of the record and likely future of the mode to be employed.

What use therefore should the transport and distribution manager see the railways being put to in his organisation? That, of course, depends very much on what his organisation's products and markets are like. For whilst it is true that the railways have many problems it is also true that they have many specialised advantages. At the outset we must recall that 65 per cent of rail tonne-kilometers are accounted for by three product categories: coal and coal products; iron and steel products with their raw materials; and petroleum. Therefore, by and large, if we are engaged in the movement of these products in bulk over long distances then there would have to be very special circumstances indeed if rail were not the first choice. But there are other products moved by rail and other rail facilities than bulk waggons. The most important of these from our point of view is Freightliner. At the present time this service still comes under the control of the National Freight Corporation, although there is the remote possibility of it being returned to British Rail.

The problem that rail faced in the past was one common to any form of movement that required the assembly of many small units into a large economic load, i.e. time consumption at origin to consolidate the load and time consumption at the destination to allow for breaking down the large load and the distribution of the individual consignments. The most obvious way to overcome these difficulties is to move consignments of greater bulk, and, if possible, introduce mechanical handling to speed up loading and unloading. This can be achieved by using standard containers. More will be said of these later, but for the present the simple description of large metal boxes with standard dimensions and handling fitments will suffice. The normal sizes met with in this country are 8 ft by 8 ft 6 in by multiples of 10 ft. Once we have the boxes as the answer to the load size and handling problem we still have to move them from place to place. This is accomplished by Freightliner trains. These are special trains carrying (ideally) only containers on specifically designed rolling stock. The basic attraction is that they operate on a timetable service, i.e. just like any other train service. Departure times, destination and arrival times are known in advance. Indeed, so determined were British Rail to achieve reliability on this service that only Inter-City trains have a higher route priority than Freightliners.

To accommodate the handling facilities a network of depots was gradually set up in the industrial centres of the country and no major centre of commercial activity is now far from a Freightliner depot. These depots are simple in layout, consisting of railway frames for the assembly of trains. This is accomplished usually by straddle carriers which straddle the road vehicle which brought the container to the depot and in one cycle lift the box off the lorry and onto the running flat. Not only can this be achieved rapidly, but the possibility of damage caused by heavy shunting is removed. Once the time set for departure is reached the total loaded consignment leaves. This arrangement was intended to, and in fact does, overcome a worry that plagued users of general freight facilities, namely unpredictability. Under the general system waggons were laid in frames and as each small consignment arrived the nearest station to its destination was looked up, and it was placed in a waggon going to the next break-bulk assembly point. As each waggon was filled up it was sealed, the relevant documents attached and shunters would ensure that it was eventually taken out and placed in a train moving to the next shunting station; a time-wasting process indeed! It is obvious though that this method was just not suited to effective programming. Indeed, internal surveys by BR have shown that upwards of 60 per cent of movements by this mode did not arrive in the estimated time given. With Freightliner, however, we have a forecastable, reliable and safe method of transit for containers. The uses to which these can be put are legion and vary from individual firm to firm. We could for example look upon the service as an extension of a production line with components moving at specified times in bulk from diverse manufacturing points to a central assembly point. It might be looked at as a mobile warehouse facility with suitably scheduled container loads leaving, say, Glasgow and travelling to perhaps London overnight, being picked up by company vehicles in the morning and the products delivered to local customers from the container. The container is then returned to BR, or consigned back to Glasgow with goods from the London end to carry out the same service there. If it is not possible to schedule in this way, then, with the minimum of facilities, an outdoor 'warehouse' can be created simply by storing containers for short times in the open.

One interesting operation which I came across was an individual supplying a small range of products to a large number of small users in the London area. To cut costs to the minimum, a container load of material was picked up in the morning, taken to a central point and used as a temporary warehouse. Customers were informed previously of time and location and simply came along, collected their orders and left. An extreme example, perhaps, but the thinking behind it could have wider applications.

So the usefulness of the system could go on, but let there be no mistake about it, the basic and ideal role for Freightliner is the movement of large amounts of material over long distances.

Why then are the railways not snowed under with customers for the service? In the first place remember our old statistic namely that 66 per cent of road hauls are 25 miles or less, and since road carries most goods moved it is fair to say that there just is not a large market available. However there are still an awful lot of tons moving on these longer trips — so why not by Freightliner.

Perhaps a major reason is attitude. There are many businessmen who for reasons no more soundly based than political myopia are very reluctant to trust their goods to a nationalised industry. Certainly BR are not blameless but perhaps they have been cast as too much the villain, at least with this service. It is up to BR to get up, get out and sell the service and in all honesty this should not be that difficult to do.

There are problems, however, that this approach would not solve. There is a good *prima facie* case that extensive regular use of containerised services offer returns to scale. A smaller manufacturer with small customers may just not have the flow of goods to regularly use containerised methods. BR will provide collection and delivery services, but there is the difficulty here that the final scheduling and face-to-face contact with customers are lost to employees who have no direct interest in the final customer — in practice anyway.

Therefore, for the large firms moving sufficiently large volumes the Freightliner service is certainly ideal in many ways; for the small operator much more thought is required.

When we remember that the overall concentration ratio of British Industry is low, i.e. that the typical firm is small, then of course BR have a problem. This is reinforced by the fact that many of the large firms are also road fleet operators and for many reasons prefer their own transport anyway.

The firm or company train is a useful method of movement by rail. The idea is of itself simple and like most such ideas effective. Instead of moving one or two containers why not a complete train of one firm's products? Consolidation problems are reduced to a minimum and distribution difficulties in many cases removed altogether. There must be certain simple conditions present though before such a scheme would prove worthwhile. In the first place there must be a sufficient supply *and* demand for the product in question to ensure regular large movements. Railway sidings must also be available at points of departure and destination. Whilst many firms are close to railways not all have private sidings. It is as well here to bear in mind what the government say in the 1977 White Paper: 'Funds are available to encourage industry to build such sidings and that no good project would be turned down on the basis that no funds were available.'

Many specialist waggons and handling facilities are provided by the railways, but the key must remain large bulk, with markets separated by long distances, 100 miles and over being ideal, unless, like coal, the bulk is really large.

8 Sea transport

The antiquity and importance of seaborne trade is too well known to need any restatement here, but over the past few years there have been momentous developments in management thinking and practice in this field. The chief problems likely to be encountered with sea transport are those of consolidating various small loads into a larger load that is economically viable to transport and breaking down this load into its separate consignments at the ports of destination. This can involve a great deal of handling at the ports of loading and unloading. This situation is represented diagramatically in Exhibit 8.1.

From the factory to final customer the same difficulty is constantly met; namely that the individual load may be small either because of the size of the order or because of the mechanics of the transport involved. The absolute fact of size means that no advantage can be taken of technical economies of scale, as far as handling methods go. At the same time, again because of the varying sizes encountered along the way, multiple handling further adds to the costs involved.

Starting from the factory the path followed is like this. The product in question will be held in a warehouse on or near the factory premises. This will have been designed around a standard module, i.e. the layout, operation and economics of the warehouse will rely on a unit of particular dimensions always being moved in the warehouse (normally a pallet). Here we have the first handling cost, namely the assembly of the product coming off the line into standard modules for the use in warehouse.

When an order for the product is received it will normally have to be once again handled with the object of changing its size. This may take the form of breaking down for orders of less than pallet size; more usually it may involve consolidation up to units of greater size. The breaking down movement tends to be more expensive since these small orders will most likely have to undergo a subsequent consolidation process when groupage becomes feasible for a particular destination.

For our purposes it really does not matter which particular path is followed. The real point to bear in mind is that once more costs and time have been added

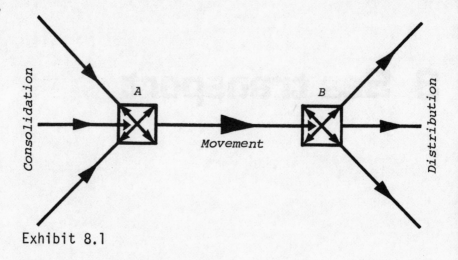

Exhibit 8.1

through the changing of the size of the module which the firm is moving its product in. Once the orders have been finally assembled they then must be moved to the port of exit. This will normally involve the firm once again in costs and time through changing the size of the moving unit. This time it takes the form of loading the vehicle in question with the completed orders. This will normally be done in the largest vehicle that circumstances will allow. Once this consignment reaches the port of exit further handling and perhaps changes in size will again have to be added to the already proportionally large costs of these movements. These will take the form of again unloading the vehicle in question, i.e. reversal of the last consolidation process. The goods will once more be placed at a storage point of some description and this possibly might involve the repetition of the various consolidation moves already mentioned as taking place before the consignment left the factory in the first place. Then the vessel will have to be loaded which in its turn may involve the shipment repeating yet again the whole process of consolidation.

The problem is not solved when the merchandise is eventually aboard ship, for the materials will have to go through a very similar procedure at the port of destination. The basic lesson is plain. The movements outlined above are expensive not only in the direct sense of the actual costs involved with the physical handling, but also in the indirect sense of extending the total time required to move goods from origin to the customer.

COSTS INVOLVED IN MOVEMENTS

If we look at the various cost centres mentioned above it will be seen that they break down (broadly speaking) into two distinct categories, i.e. those of distinct interest to the shipping operator and those of direct interest to the manufacturer using the shipper's services. Both of these areas are of importance to the final customer because they will be reflected in the price which he must pay for the products being moved.

We can say that it is in the best interests of all concerned to try to develop a method whereby the costs discussed can be reduced. This fact has been obvious for some time and the answer to the problem (in many a person's opinion) is the use of containers. The problem resolves itself into finding some way to remove, or at least drastically reduce, the number of consolidations and break-bulks that shipments incur. This will reduce both the direct and indirect costs involved.

CONTAINERS

The standard definition of the container is something which many people would like to see agreed upon, but until there is general agreement on the standardisation of the containers themselves there must be some room for argument. Most of the problems in this field are of academic interest since for all practical purposes the definition laid down in 1956 by the UNO Economic Commission and later developed by the International Standards Organisation is generally recognised as the most practicable. This states that a container is:

1   An article of transport equipment.
2   Of a permanent character and accordingly strong enough to be suitable for repeated use.
3   Specifically designed to facilitate the carriage of goods by one or more modes of transport without intermediate reloading.
4   Fitted with devices permitting its ready handling, particularly its transfer from one mode of transport to another.
5   So designed as to be easily filled and emptied.
6   Having an internal volume of 1 cubic metre or more (35.3 ft^3).
7   The term freight container includes neither vehicles nor conventional packing.

The picture that emerges from this is perhaps best described by the good but unfashionable 'large metal box with lifting devices' definition and indeed this is what a freight container basically is. The idea is not new but the scope and extent of the modern concept is large and new enough to warrant the term 'container revolution'.

The basic idea is simple enough. The major problem facing the shipping lines was the cost in terms of both money and time of the loading and unloading of vessels. The best method of tackling the increasing costs of operation was to reduce this burden.

The root of the difficulty lay in two areas, the size of the average unit load moving through the ports and the lack of mechanisation. The answer would lie with a method that would allow an increase in the size of unit load and at the same time introduce qualities suitable for mechanical handling.

The container is the obvious answer. After some original problems it would seem to have settled down on the 8 ft by 8½ ft section in 10-ft modules, the most common at sea in British lines being the 20-ft type. At the same time the use of standardised handling fixtures has allowed the introduction of mechanical handling.

THE ADVANTAGES OF CONTAINERISATION

The consolidation of shipments in containers is not limited to seaborne traffic, but we are of course dealing with this aspect in this section. It will be remembered from above that we can divide the total costs of a movement of material into those costs directly of interest to the operator and those of greatest importance to the use of the operator's services. The container affects all of these costs and in theory at least is of benefit to both the shipper and the operator and also (again in theory anyway) to the final customer. The costs are affected by allowing a much larger consignment to be moved at a time.

Thus the container is packed at the factory and from then until the final destination is reached there will be no further consolidations or breaking of bulk required. When movement takes place, the entire container load is moved. This will obviously reduce the costs and time additions dealt with above, and it should also reduce the total time required to move the shipment from point of origin to destination.

Let us first examine how this can benefit the operator. Like any other business, the shipping operators must make profits and to do this they must constantly attempt to reduce costs and increase efficiency. To achieve these aims it is first necessary to have available basic information as to how the total costs of your operation are composed.

One of the most interesting of these investigations was the *SS Warrior* study as mentioned in *Transportation and Economic Policy* by Lansing. This study went into the costs involved in the transport of general cargoes between New York and Germany. The total costs were given under seven headings, the percentages being given in Exhibit 8.2. The really important figures from the point of view of the container are, of course, the receipt, handling and loading and unloading percentages. These together add to some 37 per cent of the total costs involved. It can be seen that the costs attributable to handling are in fact about three times greater than the cost of the sea voyage.

Other figures quoted in *Containerisation: A Modern Transport System* by Van Den Burg highlight the above statistics. These second figures are concerned with percentage composition of operating costs for some 22 ships. They break down as shown in Exhibit 8.3. Here A refers to total accounts examined, B to typical cargo vessels on a long voyage and C on short voyages.

From these two sets of figures many important conclusions have had their original impetus, but it is obvious that the handling operations present a fertile area within which the shipping companies could make economies. With such a significant proportion of the total costs going on the handling operations, the use of containers was seen as a quick way for the operators to reduce their costs, increase their efficiency and at the same time not only increase profits but also benefit the customer through faster services.

The National Ports Council commissioned a report by consultants Arthur D. Little and McKinsey (quoted in Van Den Burg's *Containerization*) which confirmed the general conclusions made from the type of data looked at above. These reports pointed out that the containerisation of cargo on the North Atlantic routes produced 'significantly lower' port-to-port costs than the conventional cargo methods. This was true even when the shipper was responsible for the cost of packing and of unpacking 75 per cent of the containers carried. This is an important point.

One of the problems with containers is who is going to pack and unpack them. There is no real problem here when dealing with really large firms, since they will frequently be able to utilise the full capacity of standard-size containers.

The difficulty arises with the smaller firm when full container capacity is too large and groupage of some sort must take place. When this is the case the operator might find himself responsible for the loading and unloading operations. The fear of unacceptable costs in this eventuality were somewhat smoothed out by the 75 per cent figure quoted above.

It was also stated in these reports that the cost advantages enjoyed by container vessels could be 'diminished, eliminated or even reversed by longer routes, lower cost ports and with diminished load factors'. This would seem to reduce the advantages of container services for many routes, but it must be borne in mind that the North Atlantic route together with short sea routes (cross-Channel and North Sea) are extremely important for this country.

The shipping operators were then in the position of knowing that the composition of their total costs was such as to make it obvious that they could make economies on handling; containerisation seemed to achieve just this. It is not surprising that the idea caught on.

There were and are other savings to be considered. The smaller the portion of total round trip time that is spent in port, the happier the operator is; in port the vessel is not making money but is incurring costs. The use of containers can

Exhibit 8.2

USA	
Domestic movement	37%
Receipt and handling	6%
Loading	18%
Voyage	12%
GERMANY	
Discharge	8%
Receipt and handling	5%
Delivery	14%
	100%

Exhibit 8.3 (Figures are percentages)

	A	B	C
Crew	30	30	19
Fuel	12	9	5
Repairs	6	6	4
Insurance	8	6	5
Port expenses	10	6	5
Cargo handling	25	37	55
Other costs	9	6	7
	100	100	100

drastically reduce the turnround time of the vessel, reducing the time spent in port and increasing the utilisation of the investment.

With the use of containers the output per man-week can be raised from around 20-25 freight tons to around 500-600 freight tons. This is assuming that the unions cooperate and allow full use of mechanisation. These increases in productivity will also allow a reduction in the total number of vessels required to service routes which used to operate on the old general cargo methods.

Let us review what we have said so far with regard to the shipping operator. He gets cost savings from containers by reductions in those costs which make up important parts of the total operating costs of a vessel. These, for the purposes on hand, are basically handling costs. These are reduced by the container acting as a consolidated unit allowing greater quantities to be moved each time. There are also benefits to be gained from increased productivity in port, allowing the proportion of time which a ship spends in port to be reduced (sometimes by as much as 50 per cent). This allows the operator to give as good a service (probably better) with a reduced number of vessels.

Bearing these advantages in mind let us now look at the advantages which the operator's customer can achieve by his usual shipping service going over to containers.

In this context we are once again thrown back on to dealing in general terms. Every firm will view the advent of containers in a different light. Exactly how they are greeted will depend on the markets served by the firm, their location and density, the absolute volume of material moving to the markets and the nature of the products in question.

We can, however, examine certain general considerations. Let us be honest about this subject; by far the greatest advantages and savings which containers generate are of no real interest to many of the customers of the shipping lines. The most important economies undoubtedly accrue to the operators themselves. This is not to say that there are no benefits, but recently there has been a great deal of publicity which gives the impression that the shipping lines are doing their customers a favour by using containers. As far as a great many firms are concerned this is just not going to happen, at least not in the form they would like to see it.

These remarks do not apply to the larger companies who can take full advantage of the containerisation of their product, but to the medium to small firm. Why is this? When a firm sends its product by container the procedure is as follows. The container arrives at the factory, it is filled, sealed, loaded onto its vehicle and despatched to the collecting point. Documentation is relatively easy and packaging may offer some savings. Nothing could be simpler, in theory anyway.

This is fine, always assuming that the firm in question has sufficient products going to specific destinations to fully load the container. If this is not so the shipment must be moved to a consolidation point (as for general cargo), made up to container loads and experience the same procedure at the destination. When this is the case the customer is in a peculiar position. He is not likely to find the shipping rates any lower, because of consolidation and distribution difficulties. The overall time in transit is not likely to be significantly less, yet he is expected to believe that containers are a great benefit to him. All he sees, rightly or wrongly, is that he is receiving pretty much the same service at practically the same price. But because of the benefits of handling containers, the operator is reducing his costs, yet is not passing them back down the line in the shape of lower rates.

It can, of course, be pointed out that although rates are not going down, increases are being held. But even so, many customers feel that containerisation is of benefit only to the shipping lines. They often find that they must install extra facilities for the handling of containers. This cost might apply to the large manufacturer as well as to the smaller. He might, for example, find that while he does not have full container loads going to every destination very frequently he can consolidate several days' orders for a variety of customers fairly often. In this situation a very careful examination of the real benefits and costs of using the service must be made, including the costs of any extra expenditure on, say, handling equipment space and time.

In the smaller manufacturer's case it can often be found that apparent cost savings are in fact hidden sources of cost transfer. This might take the shape of, say, economies on pack but increased handling costs. Care must be exercised to ensure that the total cost situation is appraised. This also applies in those cases where reduction in rates is in fact offered. The largest reductions are, of course, for full containers, and against these savings the additional costs incurred in other areas of the transit process must be examined.

These points, as already mentioned, are of greatest importance for the smaller manufacturer, but this is not to say that only the large manufacturer will find it economic to use the container services. The general lesson is that disadvantages may exist and great care should be exercised by the individual firm before it decides to commit itself to a particular mode of transport. No form of transport is ideal for all markets and products.

The larger firms will most likely find that containerisation in fact offers very similar benefits to those discussed for air transport in the following chapter; indeed the basic economies are almost identical from the customer's point of view if not from the operator's. The faster transit times for full container loads (assuming the unions will allow) will result in less capital tied up in the pipeline, smaller inventories, warehouse savings, packaging and so on. Simplified documentation and the easier tracing of individual consignments should also bring benefits.

To conclude this section, can we say that the greatest benefits likely to arise out of containerisation will fall to the operators of the services involved in the changeover. The larger customers of the operator will be most likely next in line, at least from the point of view of internal economies, followed by some of the smaller customers.

The two groups of customers will, however, benefit either because of a reduction of freight rates, or at least through the opportunity being there for the operator to absorb inflation to a greater extent than would be possible if he relied on the traditional methods of cargo handling.

POTENTIAL CATCHMENT

In the above discussion it was seen that the container concept can have a great many advantages for the customer as well as the operator of the service in question. The next point for consideration is the likely catchment area available for this method of transport.

There have been many studies carried out to determine to what extent the trade of this country (and others) could be containerised. This is not the place to enter into a detailed discussion of these various reports since each firm must decide not only on the physical suitability of its product but also on the costs involved. But almost all of these reports have estimated that upwards of 75 per cent of exports and upwards of 35 per cent of imports could be containerised. The major problem has been that very little cost data has been made available and this, of course, may be crucial. Simply to say that 75 or 80 or 85 per cent of all cargo is capable of being shipped in containers does not mean very much. This situation might be extremely suitable to the operators, but does it mean that the firms who are responsible for these exports will find it financially attractive? This is again something only the individual firm knows.

The problem of the attitude of the unions is another facet which must loom in the minds of the customers as much as the operators. At the time of writing there has not yet been an overall agreement concerning the compensation of labour made redundant or moved to areas of lower wages. Such agreements will certainly be made, but if there is a full swing to the container concept then more trouble must be expected.

If such a swing takes place then we must expect a drastic reduction in the number of vessels which will be required to keep the services going. This will be coupled with further manpower reduction due to mechanisation and in this way there will be contraction on two fronts. On top of this it would not be at all surprising if over-capacity were to appear due to too many firms jumping on the bandwaggon and causing even further problems.

These difficulties should pass in time; certainly they do not and will not deter operators from going over to containers. But they must give some cause for thought to the customer. There is no point in going over to another form of transport whose benefits are tied in some degree to time savings door-to-door if these economies cannot be achieved. One always remembers the tale of the stevedors in a major East Coast US port insisting that all containers be unpacked at the port before being allowed to move on.

In this context the dispute over container traffic which took place in Liverpool (Spring 1972) is a case in point. By insisting that all containers were to be loaded by registered dock labour, the union concerned was in reality hitting at one of the basic advantages claimed for the container: speed and ease in developing a full economic load. If the manufacturer is to be refused the loading and unloading of his container, he might find that he has no alternative but to send the unit to the docks for loading; the likely delays this would involve again would strike at a major container advantage, namely speed.

In the long run, however, given the economic state of our major ports, containerisation in a well utilised form must come — though it is not the answer in every case, as the following will show.

PRE-PALLETISATION

Pre-palletisation is held by many to offer very similar results to containers without the large capital investment involved. On the other hand the people who favour containers point out that the results on which the above statement is based have come about by less than accurate comparisons.

As is their way, the dispute will continue. One important point is to be remembered, however, that the key lies in turnaround times and labour productivity. In a manning dispute at Tilbury there is little doubt that the container berth in question was selected for dispute because it was close to a pre-palletisation berth. Productivity was high in the pre-palletised berth, turnaround times were short and this fact was reflected in the higher wages paid in this berth.

The fact that the operators in question could make pre-palletisation function effectively indicates one thing, that the method offers at the very least an alternative to full containers on some routes. In the description that follows nothing more than this is assumed.

As usual before any individual decision can be made, the relevant costs of the two systems must be rigorously analysed. Extreme judgements on the general economics of either system should be avoided; one will suit a specific firm/product/market though it may not suit a similar one.

It will be remembered from our earlier discussion on the container that one of the basic opportunities for economies arose because of the consolidation of merchandise that the container allowed. There was a reduction in the handling costs and also in time consumed by breaking bulk and consolidation operations. Pre-palletisation also achieves this, but at a lower load factor. The pallet is met throughout industry and needs no description here. The palletisation methods adopted as complementary to containers use the basic pallet as the module to move through the system.

The product is loaded at the factory on either the firm's own pallet or one from the shipping line. These are then loaded onto vehicles by means of lift trucks. They are then transported to the docks in the usual manner. At the quayside they are loaded onto specially designed ships. This is achieved through side ports with lift trucks operating within the vessel. Thus the entire operation from factory to storage on board is based on one module. The same applies at the point of destination. Fred Olsen lines are an ideal example of this type of operation and Exhibit 8.4 shows the sequence.

Exhibit 8.4 Fred Olsen Lines' distribution system

It will be noted that the major differences between palletisation and the use of containers are, firstly, that the basic module is smaller, requires no great investment on the part of the operator or customer and once assembled the pallet gives a more reasonable through module for the smaller manufacturer, 2.5 tons compared to the container. Secondly, the basic equipment required by the customer for handling is most likely already in operation within his factory for other reasons and in any case is not too expensive. Thirdly, the operator does not require extensive dockside facilities such as are needed for containers. The most important advantage from the customer's point of view is that he can get a fast door-to-door service with a module likely to be commonly used by his customers.

The main disadvantages are that, firstly, there is a wide range of goods not suitable to palletisation because of the difficulty which may be experienced in protecting the product from the elements. Nor can there be easy humidity/ temperature control, except in cases where the entire hold is brought into action, which may not be convenient. The operator reaps the same advantages as were discussed under containerisation, although whether to a greater or lesser extent only the firms concerned know.

There is little doubt that for certain products pre-palletisation is the best form of movement. This is especially the case (to state the obvious) where fully developed container services are not available. There is hardly a port in the world where lift trucks are not in service.

The smaller operator not willing to get involved in containerisation will most likely find palletisation very attractive. In 1967 something like 70 per cent of lorries passing into the Port of London had loads of less than 3.5 tons. There is obviously a great deal to be done by palletisation yet.

PALLETS VERSUS CONTAINERS

The economics regarding the relative benefits to be obtained by the operating of either a container or palletised service will be argued about for a long time to come. Reliable figures are difficult to come by, and even the best data is open to bias in interpretation.

This is, however, a relatively simple problem for the insider; the criterion is the profitability of the firm concerned. And at least with a goal to work toward the problem becomes manageable. It is not so easy for the customer to reach the decision since, at least, there will be a section of his product range which could move either by container or by pallet. These products will as usual have to be examined within the overall context of the firm's policies. This might, for example, involve some of them being moved by container when it might easily be more economical to use pallets. This might be due to, say, the firm being prepared to sacrifice economies over a small section of its product range because the practical costs involved in setting up two systems of control might easily outweigh the savings for some products if they went pre-palletised. The reverse situation may also be found.

The pallet is ideally suited for those products which are, first of all, not extremely sensitive to weather damage. This problem is often exaggerated by the extreme enthusiasts of containers. The only times when products shipped on pallets are subject to weather damage are when the vehicle is being loaded for movement to the docks and intermediate storage points, if in fact these are not under cover. These are small dangers and can be protected against fairly cheaply.

It should not be too expensive to have some sort of weather protection at storage points at the firm's loading point. If the operation is a large one and space at a premium, then some sort of weatherproof cover over the individual pallet might be used. Movement to the docks will normally be provided with shelter by means of the usual vehicle protections. Intermediate storage at the docks can be tackled in the same way as at the factory. Some form of industrial polythene-type cover would be both cheap and practical. This is not to say that there is no weather protection problem but the relative costs must be examined first.

If the product can either be adequately protected or does not need cover, then the next quality suited to palletisation is that the form should be regular and relatively small. This allows easy storage on pallets and also enables maximum handling economies to be made. Cartons, cement bags, fertiliser, fruit boxes, small components and so on are the type of merchandise in mind here.

A major problem often raised when pallets are discussed is standardisation. There is little doubt that a very wide range of pallet sizes is in use. This makes for difficulty in the cooperative movement of goods on pallets from firm to firm. No one questions this, but when this is raised as an objection to pre-palletisation as a shipping method more examination is required. The answer to the problem is for customers to agree to standardise on the shipping line used. Since the palletised vessel depends to a very great extent on standardisation of pallet size the problem is solved, e.g. Fred Olsen Lines' 2.5-ton pallet.

The same problem also exists to some extent with containers of different sized cross-section; again the simple answer has been to standardise on operators, this being very often the same as on module sizes.

ROLL-ON/ROLL-OFF FERRIES

The innovations discussed above refer in the main to changes that have taken place in the handling of cargo. There have been other developments, of course, just as important in their fields. One of the greatest growth areas of these new approaches has been the roll-on/roll-off ferry.

The basic idea of this ferry is that vehicles are driven on to the vessel at the port of exit, shipped across the channel in question and driven straight out at the other side. First on being first off, no complicated manoeuvering is required, the ship being designed so as to provide a straight- through drive.

As the above suggests, these vessels are aimed at the short sea journey. They provide a sea bridge for goods vehicles, getting them across the water in the fastest time with the least trouble. There are a great many connections leaving the United Kingdom to most of the more usual Continental jumping-off points. These services provide many advantages for goods vehicles moving to the Continent and must not be ignored.

CONCLUSIONS

To conclude this section on sea transport, let us not forget the basic aim which we are trying to achieve, irrespective of the particular choice we eventually make between the various methods available. The target is to reduce the costs of movement of the firm's product to the customer within the broad service policies of the company. There is sometimes a danger in regarding as the ultimate criterion only the reduction of cost. This we must not do. We look not simply for the lowest cost method, but for the method having the lowest costs consistent with the distribution policies of the organisation within which we operate.

As far as the two improvements we have looked at above go, it is fair to say that the maximum economies will be reaped from each only when there is a total approach within the firm to transport and distribution. So long as both continue to be regarded as related but separate fields then the full potential of any system will not be realised. This may be the reason why, in spite of the potential catchment area for containerised traffic on the North Atlantic route, such a small percentage is moving in containers.

9 Air freight

When dealing with air freight the total approach must always be used if any reasonable conclusions at all are to be reached. The straight comparison of transport rates between the different transport modes is no longer acceptable when deciding the choice of method. The reason for this is simply that we have already seen that the transport decision can have a great effect on other sectors of the distribution function, and because of this these effects must also be examined before a final choice is made. Since the total approach is the only really acceptable one, then another conclusion must follow. There is no point in trying to think that air freight can be introduced into a firm on a regular basis without any effort, other than costing the problem, being made on the part of the firm. Under the right conditions the introduction of air freight into the company can result in substantial savings in that firm's total costs of distribution, but such an introduction requires new attitudes and new methods; too often a firm tries air freight only to change its mind within a short period.

In a very large number of cases the reasons for the disappointment really have nothing to do with the transportation method at all, but stem from the fact that the firm expected to be able to reap the advantages of the new mode while at the same time retaining the old familiar operating routes. This is just not possible. The full benefits will be obtained only when new procedures and attitudes are introduced at the same time and adhered to.

There is a tendency in the UK to look upon the air freight alternative as a fire-brigade service, one that is only brought into use when something goes wrong elsewhere along the line between production and final customer. As said before, the full advantages of air freight cannot be reaped when this is the only attitude, although in this situation air has a positive role to play as will be seen when we examine two-tiered ordering systems.

Broadly speaking the available economies from air freight can be broken down into two categories. The first of these depends almost entirely on the nature of the product and its market so we will call these the marketing benefits. The second type also depends on the product but in a different way and is moreover more deeply influenced by the actual mechanics of the mode. These we will call technical economies.

There are quite a number of products whose market penetration relies on speed in reaching the market. These can be either food products or merchandise that is subject to a varied short selling season such as fashion. In either of these cases the value of air freight is high because its speed will allow an extension of profitability through either increasing the scope of the market or extending the period over which a fashion-type can be in the shops.

In the case of perishable products the implications are obvious: by the use of air freight, markets which would normally be out of the question can be serviced with a high degree of reliability.

Fashion goods are more complicated. The first advantage is simply being able to have a shorter lead time between repeat orders. It is extremely difficult to be fully accurate about just exactly which particular model of a range is going to be the greatest success, and miscalculations can and do happen. The effect of these mistakes is felt more heavily in the fashion trade because of the rather long manu-facturing pipeline in comparison to selling time. The final designs to be pushed later in the year must be decided upon very early in the year, orders must be placed for materials and the actual manufacturing process must take place. If even a small miscalculation occurs and the public swing in favour of a model which was not at the top of the list, a great deal of revenue can be lost through non-sales which happen because there is just not sufficient stock. The lack of stock will, of course, occur even if air freight is used. After all, the mistake was made in the past, but substantial time can be made up for repeat orders by cutting the travelling time down to a minimum through the use of air freight. Not only will the manufacturing time be reduced but selling time will be extended.

Similar considerations apply to other categories such as after-sales service. By using air freight, service can be improved. Often the increase in service will be at a lower cost or a higher service level can be provided at the same cost as when surface transport was employed.

One of the most common sources of costs when new machinery is introduced is down-time caused by inexperienced operators using the machinery incorrectly and causing damage. Every manufacturer realises this possibility may occur and tries to reduce the time lost to the minimum by having a comprehensive after-sales service. This is expensive because it will involve investment in spare parts in all his major markets. If the market he serves is worldwide then the investment can be substantial. Even when spares-holding points are set up in all the major markets, too much time can often elapse between a spare being required and the part actually arriving at the point where it is required. If selected stock-holding points are linked by air the cost and speed can often both be improved. Costs might well be reduced by concentrating demand.

Individual patterns may not be easily discernible for the man on the spot. He is too close to stand back and see the overall movements. At a central holding point this is often not so and future forecasts become more accurate. It is a known fact that as the inventory holding increases the proportion required for safety stock does not increase at the same rate. In other words by locating inventory in fewer and larger holding points the total investment in inventory required for a given service level will decrease. The savings here can be large.

Once the decision has been taken to install a new piece of equipment then the longer it takes to arrive and be put to work the more expensive it becomes. Suppose that a particular piece of machinery was going to increase the productivity of a particular plant by, say, 1000 units per day. If the equipment could arrive at its destination ten days faster by air than it would have arrived by surface then the firm in question could gain an additional production of 10,000 units.

Finally, on the marketing side, there is the question of flexibility. Most companies are always looking for new outlets and markets for their products. Their search inevitably means the servicing of their new markets and this, in turn, implies a commitment to these new markets in the form of after-sales services, distribution depots and so on. Every firm hopes that the new markets will be profitable but if traditional methods are used for distribution then a certain amount of avoidable risk must be taken.

Modern competition being what it is, most organisations find that they have virtually to set up an entire selling operation before they can really accurately confirm their first impressions of the available opportunities in new sales areas. If they are confirmed, well and good; but a mistake can be extremely expensive, not only in terms of hard cash but in damage to the image of the firm.

The costs and risks involved in this type of operation can sometimes be reduced by using air freight. Instead of committing the firm to capital expenditure in distribution depots or agents, throughout the market, the number required can be reduced. Salesmen on the spot can complete orders from samples knowing that they are backed by the ability of air freight to ship out in such a short time that he can often give local industry a shock when it comes to service times. He can carry out test marketing without the firm committing itself to an expensive investment in a logistics system.

Air freight has substantial marketing benefits to offer the manufacturer who is prepared to change his methods to suit the new conditions required by new distribution techniques.

TECHNICAL ADVANTAGES OF AIR FREIGHT

But the broad general advantages outlined above are not the only economies available through the use of air freight. Even when these are recognised and full advantage is being taken of them there are more direct hard financial economies that can be achieved. These are, as we have mentioned, basically built on the speed advantages that air has over the other transport modes. They rely on the fact that time costs money.

One point must be cleared up here and this concerns the already mentioned difference in long-haul and short-haul routes. Technical financial economies depend on the fact that the total elapsed time between an order for material being placed and it being received into the customer's stores can be shorter by air than by surface transport. While transit times, i.e. time actually spent in moving, are important they are only part of the total time cycle which we are interested in. On short-haul routes such as those in Western Europe the transit times advantage which air freight has can be quickly lost through ground delays and poor company organisation. There is no advantage in an aircraft having a transit time of, say, 2 hr between London and Milan if the freight is going to stay on the ground for another day before it is cleared and collected. When these types of delay occur then the time advantage that air has over surface methods becomes so small as to be of theoretical interest only. It is quite possible to show that even a 2-day difference can have significant effects on stock levels, but the margin is often too fine for practical use.

On the other hand if the firm in question realises the importance of time and is organised in such a way as to eliminate possible delays at the airport and in the collection of material, then short-haul air freight can have a bright future on some routes. I recall a trip taken to Northern Italy by TIR road vehicle leaving Dover on the midnight ferry on the Monday and delivering a 30-ton load of material to the customer in Bologna at 11.00 a.m. on the Thursday. An aircraft could make the same trip with a much shorter transit time but from factory to customer with 30 tons of product the difference would probably be small.

Even in the unlikely event of the total journey being cut by two days this is a very small period for practical lead time economics to come into play. The moral is simple; the technical advantages of air freight must be examined very carefully on short-haul routes before a final decision is made. Moreover trial runs under normal operating conditions should be made before the final commitment.

On long-haul routes, say transatlantic, the situation is entirely different. It would be hard to imagine conditions where substantial economies in time were not available through the use of air freight. This is, of course, assuming that congested airports are avoided. One well known manufacturer of electronic equipment has estimated that by using air freight between the eastern seaboard of the United States and Europe it can save about 30 days in the total time of movement from point to point. It was found that the total elapsed time by surface was approximately 40 days, and that by air 9 days. The times involved covered such classes as movement from plant of origin to airport or sea-port, transport across the Atlantic, clearance by customs at port or airport of destination and finally the movement inland to final customer. When we reach time savings of this magnitude then substantial economies are available.

It is one of the well known problems of any army that as its supply lines increase in length its effectiveness begins to suffer. The same applies to a business. When a firm has a long logistical tail it is wasting money. Capital tied up in goods in the pipeline is of no use to the firm. It is important to think of this pipeline as consisting of physical products. If the pipeline concept is treated in too theoretical terms then it can sometimes be difficult to put across to non-distribution management. It must be regarded as having physical properties, as a definite line of the firm's products which exists. In this way the idea of extra costs being incurred by the firm if the pipeline is too long is easily assimilated. The money tied up in the merchandise in the pipeline has an opportunity cost; the longer material is in the pipeline then the greater will this category of cost be.

Opportunity cost simply means that money has a great many uses. However, since the supply is limited we must make a decision between the competing uses to which our money can be put. Once we have made this decision and carried it out we can say that the real cost of the operation to which the capital was channelled is the alternative which was foregone. In business this usually means the other project which we could have put the money into and received at least an equal return to that we are getting from the project we pushed through. We can then say that if we have money tied up somewhere the cost of that money is the return we know we could achieve elsewhere. This return is usually stated as a return per £100 invested.

If we now return to our pipeline problem, the relevance of opportunity cost can be seen. If we have a longer pipeline inventory tie-up than is required, then the material in this pipeline is costing the firm money. Moreover this is not just represented by the value of the products in transit, but also by their opportunity cost.

If there were not a cost here then all material in the UK would still be sent by barge since, after all, this is the cheapest form of transport. Remember to think of the pipeline as a physical entity whose existence is required to provide the firm's customers with the products they want to buy. But the shorter this line is the cheaper it is.

To determine the costs involved then we must have available certain basic information: the annual value of the material we ship plus our opportunity cost of capital. This is taken usually as the cost of capital to the firm, since it is assumed that this is the absolute minimum return which a project would have to provide if it was to prove at all feasible for the firm to invest in it.

By multiplying these two together we can arrive at the total cost of the annual pipeline to the firm, i.e. we can arrive at the total sum which the firm is paying out for its pipeline each year. It will be remembered, however, that what we are really interested in just now is the effect on the pipeline that air freight as opposed to surface would have. To calculate this then, of course, we simply take the values we have above and multiply them by the annual time saving possible by air.

Thus, pipeline savings available through switching to air equal annual value of shipments by surface times the proportionate time saving available by air times the cost of capital for the firm. For example, if we ship £3,000,000 by surface and upon investigation we realise that about 30 days would be the advantage we could expect on the average shipment time by changing to air and that the opportunity cost of capital in our firm was 10 per cent, then the annual savings from the pipeline would equal:

$$£3,000,000 \times (30/365) \times 10\% = £24,100$$

This amount is best looked upon as a cost which no longer has to be borne by the firm. The cost of the pipeline has been reduced by this amount.

There are other ways of looking at the advantages of reductions in the pipeline. If, for example, the firm we were discussing above was not supplying an outside customer, but was moving components between one plant in the USA and another in the UK then we could say that the components not only represented capital tied up in them, as already described, but that they also had an additional value because the journey was in fact really only part of a very long production process. By cutting the time of material involved in this step in the production line benefits will also occur.

INVENTORY SAVINGS

The pipeline concept above is not the only saving available through the time reductions possible by air. Some firms disagree with the thinking behind the pipeline concept on the basis that it does not matter how long it takes for their products to arrive at their destination. Payment will only be received in accordance with the accounting practices of their customer. True this will reduce to some extent the effectiveness of the pipeline savings but it cannot wipe them out. They do not depend on the money for the products being available more quickly but on fewer products being in the line between the firm's plant and its tardy customer. The savings arise not from the customer's side of the pipeline but from the manufacturer's. Besides, payment practices are likely to be the same for air and surface.

Exhibit 9.1 shows the basic function of inventory. It will be noticed that a residue of inventory is left at each time a new order is received. This is safety stock to allow the maximum expected demand to be satisfied on those occasions when it arises.

When demand is known and lead time is certain there is no need for safety stock. Usage and replacement cycles are all the same, following the path of the unbroken line. A maximum level is decided upon, A, which will maintain service levels over a certain lead time. Inventory will be depleted until there is zero stock left at time BE. At this point the replenishment shipment arrives bringing levels back up to A and so the cycle continues. If demand fluctuates as represented by the broken line then inventory would be 0 at time F and a stock-out occurs over the period EF. To prevent this an estimate is made of the fluctuations expected and the amount consumed over the period FE; this becomes the safety stock C. Exactly how comprehensive this buffer will be depends on the costs and benefits involved.

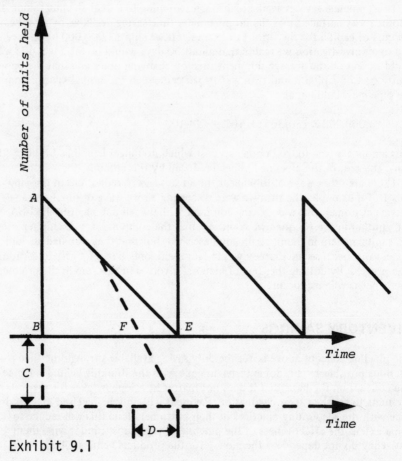

Exhibit 9.1

If only average demand were carried in the form of stock then there would be occasions when inventory ran out before the next shipment arrived. These fluctuations in demand and their effect on safety stock provide another area where operating economies are available from air freight.

One of the basic factors affecting the size of safety stock carried is the length of time that will elapse between placing an order and receiving it. If this lead time is reduced then so also will be the amount of reserve inventory held. This is illustrated in Exhibit 9.2. As in Exhibit 9.1, we have a fluctuation in demand, except that now the basic situation is changed since we have a shortened lead time as shown by the broken line. The continuous line represents the situation before a change in lead time. As before, demand increases so that inventory would be 0 at F_1 instead of time E_1 thus causing a stock out. As before, the estimated time F_1E_1 is converted into consumption and this is added to the base line at B to allow this variation in demand to be accommodated. It will be seen that by reducing the replenishment lead time we have also reduced the required safety stock for a similar fluctuation.

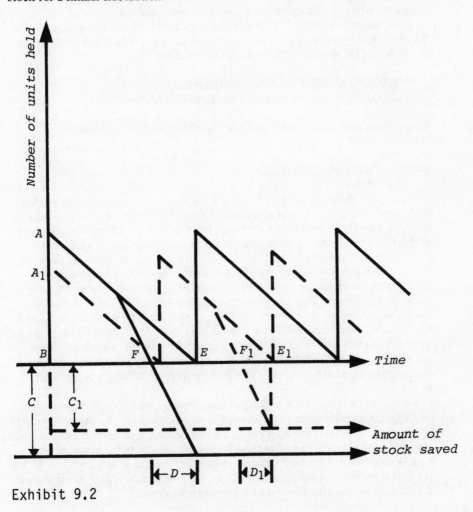

Exhibit 9.2

To calculate the money savings available here, then again we must know the amounts involved. This will usually be possible to gather from the warehouses concerned. This will then be multiplied by the cost of capital to the firm in question.

There are two approaches to this figure. The simple one holds that, as before, the plain cost of capital to the company should be used. The second school, however, points out that inventory has other costs besides those that would be represented by the opportunity cost of capital. These are carrying costs which are dealt with in greater depth in the part on inventory, but suffice it for now to say that they average about 20 per cent over wide ranges of industry. The second school points out that the use of the relevant carrying cost would give a more realistic picture of the inventory savings made through safety stock reductions. Since they include some categories of warehousing costs and since these are dealt with in our next section then the best practice would seem to be to include only those costs in the carrying costs which are not connected with warehouse operations. If this segregation is performed there would seem to be no objections to using the revised inventory carrying costs in this calculation.

Thus the savings made would equal the reduction in safety stock times the costs (or cost of capital). If we found that we could reduce our safety stock commitment by, say, £200,000 then we would save:

£200,000 × 10% = £20,000 (cost of capital)
£200,000 × 15% = £30,000 (revised carrying cost)

Under either method it can be seen that significant savings are possible.

WAREHOUSING SAVINGS

In the section above we have seen that the use of air could result in a reduction in the levels of inventory held in particular markets. Since inventory is usually held in a warehouse then it follows from above that we would expect to benefit in this cost area as well. To calculate the potential savings here we must first arrive at some weighting factor that would relate the cost of operating the warehouses to the amount of inventory held in them. This is done by dividing the total annual warehousing costs by the total value of the inventory in the warehouse or warehouses. This will produce a factor relating the cost of the warehouses and the value of the inventory in them per unit. The value of the reduction in safety stock translated into warehousing terms is obtained by the product of this factor and the reduction in safety stock. Assume that we have reduced our safety stock by £200,000 and we find that our weighting factor is 0.06; then the savings here would be £200,000 × 0.06 or some £12,000, an acceptable saving.

Care must be taken when looking at these warehousing savings. What we have calculated is a saving related to operating costs but there may be others. Obviously there will be extra space available in the individual warehouses. If our reductions are great or the system extensive then the volume of warehouse space involved may be significant. Two methods are available for looking at this problem. We can say that since warehouses are indivisible we are now underutilising our space and this is reducing the effectiveness of the entire operation.

Or we can say we now have the chance to bring in more revenue by leasing the space made vacant by the inventory reductions. On the other hand it might be said that, due to a lack of flexibility in the organisation, these savings will be ignored because the firm does not want to lease space in its warehouses to other firms and it feels that underutilisation of space will counterbalance any likely savings anyway.

Both of these approaches can be turned by pointing to the dynamics of the business. It is likely that the firm will be experiencing an increasing demand. Because of this it is reasonable to expect that in the future the warehousing requirements in the market would also increase, and some or all of this increase can be accommodated in the surplus space made available by the use of air freight reducing safety stock requirements. Thus it can be said that the extra space made available does not really create the problems of alternative use and underutilisation mentioned. Indeed it provides desirable flexibility for the future expansion of the company's operations.

OTHER SAVINGS

There are other savings claimed for the air freight alternative, the most important being insurance and packaging. As far as insurance is concerned the field is too wide to deal with briefly. Some airlines show significant improvements over others, but in general it is fairly safe to say that there is a movement towards a lowering in differentials — where they exist at all — between the various transport modes. The destination and the route, even the airline, can and do affect the premium that will be required. The best that can be said here is that some savings are possible but that the situation can vary a great deal. The only really effective way to approach the problem is to price the route and commodity individually.

Packaging is another of the often publicised advantages of air freight. The argument usually takes a form similar to the following: because of the high level of handling and the very low risk of in-flight damage the cost of protective packaging can be drastically reduced by sending your shipment by the named airline. This is reasonably true; there is indeed less likelihood of in-transit damage to cargo in an aircraft as opposed to say a ship, but handling hazards do occur.

There are two broad areas that must be guarded against in air freight packaging as in any other variety of packaging. These are, of course, the danger of overpack and the danger of under-pack, i.e. care must be exercised to ensure that neither too much protection or too little is used. The amount of material involved in these decisions will be affected by the nature of the product, the destination and the handling method likely to be employed. There is no point in using the minimum possible packaging at the UK end of the operation where handling will be relatively safe, if at the destination it is unlikely that any form of modern equipment will be available.

The most useful packaging developments have probably been in the standard container fields. Many airlines offer discount rates for material moved in the international standard airfreight containers. Some will even provide a range of suitable containers.

I well remember the shipping manager of one of our well known computer manufacturers bemoaning the efficiency of airport handling facilities and pointing out that his firm had had computer components dropped and damaged in practically every major airport in Europe. The moral is, of course, that accidents will always happen.

ATTITUDE TO AIR FREIGHT

In spite of the potential advantages and savings through the use of air freight there is undeniably a reluctance on the part of the great majority of firms in the country to fully integrate air freight into their company thinking on transport and distribution. It is not difficult to find reasons for this situation.

First, there still exists the belief that air freight is invariably more expensive than surface transport and because of this it should be employed only in the fire-brigade role when something has delayed delivery to an important customer. It was pointed out at the beginning of this section that the old technique of simply comparing transport rates was not acceptable in the total distribution cost concept. Transport is not an isolated function since it will affect other factors within its sphere of activity. Therefore, ideally, when a transport decision is being made these other factors must also be examined. It is fair to say there are many firms not using air freight because they *think* the method too expensive for their organisation, not because they *know* it is.

There are other difficulties. It has already been said that a very large number of firms do not know their total distribution costs and have no coordinating authority responsible for the function. In these conditions it is very often not possible for a company to take advantage of all the savings opportunities mentioned simply because the organisational structure is just not capable of absorbing the requisite techniques. On the other hand it must not be thought that air freight is the answer to all transport problems; it is not. There are many firms not using air freight for the simple reason that their market or their product or their customers are just not suitable for the use of this mode. There is no universally applicable transport method or technique. All have some areas where they are efficient and all have other areas where their effectiveness declines.

The airlines realise that the attitude of industry to air freight can often be one of wanting to use the method but for various reasons finding that the economics of the proposed transaction are not fully to their liking. To help overcome this, some airlines have introduced air-sea links on some of their longer routes.

These operate in the following manner. Say that a particular customer wanted to ship material from London to Tokyo. He feels that the sea journey is just too long and yet the nature of his market and his own internal organisation is such that he cannot take the full advantage of an all-air freight journey.

He can compromise by using one of the air-sea links, and if he does this he will get the best of both worlds. The shipment will arrive much faster than if he had despatched by sea, but the cost will be much less than an all-air journey. His shipment would, for example, be picked up in London and flown across the Atlantic. A further flight would take the load to, possibly, San Francisco, where it would be placed on a ship bound for Japan.

A similar type of compromise can be made with regard to the advantages of air with regard to inventory reduction. It has already been shown how air has the potential to reduce investment in inventory, but as was discussed above, a particular firm may have individual considerations which prevent it from going over to a fully integrated air freight policy. This does not mean, however, that it must forgo all the savings possible in this area.

By combining Exhibits 9.1 and 9.2 to form that shown in Exhibit 9.3 a two-tiered inventory system can be produced. If the normal consumption and replenishment cycle were followed then safety stock would be at the level *AB*. If we have a secondary re-order point, as at *ROPI*, we can reduce safety stock commitment. When the upswing is recognised, a second order is placed. This will arrive by faster transport (air) and have a shorter lead time (*SLT*). The amount ordered would be sufficient to tide the company over the time period *C*, i.e. quantity *A01*. After this the firm's normal shipment would arrive. Even with the possible maximum increase then the service levels decided upon can be kept, saving quantity *010* by using the two-tier method.

If this method of two-tiered re-order points is used it is possible to make worthwhile reductions in the safety stock that would have to be kept if the one re-order point surface transport system were to be used.

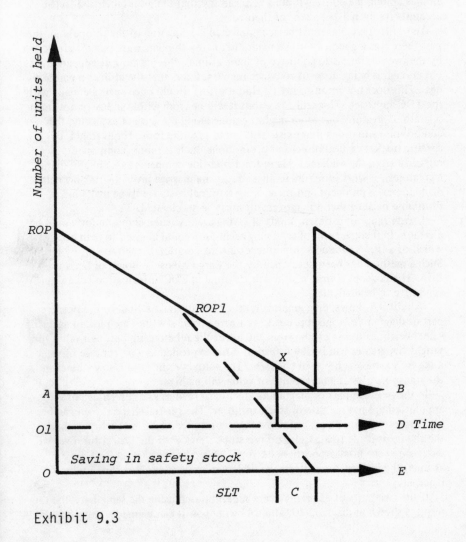

Exhibit 9.3

There is little doubt that the next decade will see increasing use of air freight on a regular rather than a fire-brigade basis. Two things must take place to allow this movement to develop fully. The first of these is that the airlines must break the ground barrier once and for all. The costs of moving freight through the ground terminals are still too high.

The most obvious method of doing this is to increase the average size of shipment handled, and the easiest method to achieve this is the use of containers. At the present time the airlines seem to be saying a great deal about containerisation and doing very little. The maximum discount available for traffic movements in IATA (Internal Air Transport Association) containers is 10 per cent and since the containers have usually to be purchased and maintained by the customer this just does not represent an attractive proposition to many shippers. There are very few airlines among the all-freight lines who can say that their containerised traffic accounts for even 10 per cent of their total.

The other task that must be accomplished is education of the shippers. In the past there was a good case to be made that many shippers were put off air freight by the over-enthusiastic publicity of some airlines; this has now disappeared. Yet not enough is being done to convince manufacturers that the airlines mean business. This does not mean to say an all-out effort should once again be made with the TDC approach. This will come, but it will be from within industry not from operators' pressure, but more might be done along the lines of exploring the compromise situations that exist. This could take the form, for example, of specific market exploitations and promotions, such as motor components regularly from the Midlands. Many foreign airline companies are already doing a great deal of work along these lines, but if the massive investments now being made in new equipment and the soaring terminal costs are to be made into a profitable balance then the movement must be accelerated.

A wide range of different kinds of saving are discussed above and it would be a great help if some form of screening technique could be used to help decide which of a firm's products should receive consideration for movement by air. Such a method has been developed by the Cargo Advisory Board of (as it was) BEA. The concept is simple although, as usual in TDC, information collection can prove to be difficult.

Exhibit 9.4 shows, diagramatically, the basis of the method. In the positive part of diagram *(a)* transport costs (as a percentage of value) are plotted against value/weight ratio. As can be seen, the lower the relationship between value and weight the greater will be the transport costs expressed as a percentage of value. Take for example a block of concrete. The value/weight ratio is low; therefore the transport cost as a percentage of value will be high.

In the negative part of diagram *(a)* technical savings as a percentage of value are plotted against the rate of stock turnover. The general shape shown can be justified as follows. As far as these savings are concerned it is fair to say that as the change is made to air freight those stock items with the fastest turnover will likely show the least proportional savings. This is because (or at least we can assume) the high turnover items would lower levels at any one time in the first place anyway.

If the two parts of diagram *(a)* are superimposed using the same base line the result is shown in diagram *(b)*. The following points can be made. Any item of stock with a rate of stock turnover below X and a fixed value/weight ratio should move by air. Put another way, any items with a fixed rate of turnover of X above a value/weight ratio of Y should go by air. The data for such a screening is easily obtained as far as the value/weight ratio is concerned, and random sampling coupled with EDP simulation should provide the stock turnover information. In practice it would probably be easier to carry out such a survey by class values, thus making approximate data easier to obtain. The screening would then indicate possible products for more detailed investigation. There is, of course, no reason why an individual study should throw up shapes like those illustrated. These were chosen to show a situation where air freight proved desirable. There are product ranges where most lines will go by air and others where costs are uniformly greater than savings and thus nothing will be moved by air, together with all shades of variation in between.

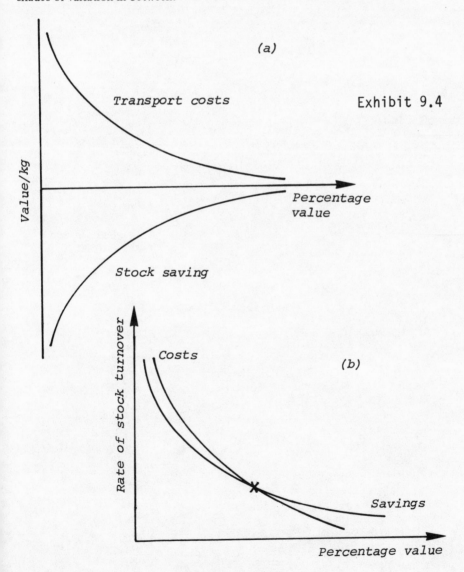

Exhibit 9.4

Part 2

INVENTORY CONTROL

10 Statistical background—an introduction

Given the basic assumption that the role of distribution management is to achieve pre-decided service levels at the minimum cost, then it will be obvious that as soon as the transport decision is taken, it affects the volume of inventory within the distribution system. This is the root of the function of inventory. It acts as a buffer between fluctuations in demand and production levels. In other words, it allows the firm to provide the desired customer service level. Control of inventory levels can make a great contribution to the profit which a firm receives from its logistics system, just as lack of control will reduce its effectiveness.

In the UK inventory levels run at approximately 45 per cent of the national income, in the US 24 per cent, in Sweden 25 per cent and in France 29 per cent. There are many theories put forward for this discrepancy between the UK and other countries, but none of them can fully explain why we should be involved in what would appear to be excessively high inventory levels. The inevitable conclusion must be that large sectors of our distribution management cannot be paying as much attention to the inventory function as they might.

This is not to say that this sector of management is inefficient. There are a great many problems in inventory management that are extremely difficult to answer in the UK context. The most outstanding problem is the one of forecast. Inventory is there to satisfy demand, inventory levels must be set ahead of demand and thus any error in the forecast of future demand for the individual firm will make itself felt in excess, or short, inventory levels.

Distribution planning is also faced with the difficulty of production problems which may affect availability. Moreover, the lack of a definite overall company policy to the problem can often cause coordination difficulties. Nonetheless inventory remains a very important cost centre which must be constantly examined by distribution management to ensure that the levels involved are kept at a minimum consistent with the service policies of the firm.

One of the most common confusions which arises in the management of inventory is cost. It might very well be that this is the chief reason why many members of general management do not accord the problem the attention it deserves. It is a usual misconception that the cost of inventory is the investment which the firm has in that area. It is not at all unusual to ask how much inventory is costing and receive as a reply the level of investment to which the firm has committed itself.

Inventory has a cost other than its purchase price: these costs are normally referred to as carrying costs. They can easily amount to 15-20 per cent of item cost, depending on how efficient a control function operates. Carrying costs will include opportunity cost of capital, insurance costs, handling costs, deterioration (if applicable) and obsolescence costs. It will be obvious that one of the main reasons behind the lack of attention given to these costs is that in the normal firm they are not gathered together in one consolidated account. This means that management is often simply unaware as to the real costs of their inventory. This has its effect on the degree of importance which they will attach to this area. Very often when the real amounts involved are made known there a truly remarkable change in the attitude towards the inventory function.

THE SALES FORECAST

The basis of management inventory is the sales forecast. As with any technique, forecasting can be tackled at a variety of levels of sophistication. The greater the degree of accuracy required then the greater the trouble and time that have to be taken with the forecast.

At the top of the scale many of the methods really require the use of some form of data processing equipment. But it is not a prerequisite to have computer facilities for the more elementary techniques. There are methods available that can be put into operation by any distribution manager who can use a slide rule.

In this discussion it is assumed that there are no forecasting services already available to the distribution manager. For this reason the methods examined are not the most complicated, sophisticated or accurate, in most situations. But it is hoped that their discussion in brief will be of value on two broad fronts. In the first instance they can be used by anybody who wants to build up more manageable estimates of future demand than can be done by hunch alone. Secondly it is hoped that some idea of the relevance of forecasting to inventory problems will be shown, and that this will encourage the distribution manager to delve more deeply into this subject and put into practice the concepts that will be but mentioned in passing at this stage.

There are a great many illusions surrounding the subject of forecasting. The first of these is the habit of expecting the forecast to be a prophecy, 100 per cent accurate. Possibly the most damaging, however, is the convention of looking at the forecast as inflexible. Insufficient attention is given to the forces outside the control of the firm which can produce shifts in the original assumptions. No forecasting method is more accurate than the data which it employs. If incorrect data is used then only an incorrect answer can be expected. If the firm already has some form of machinery for the collection and collation of data, then the task of the distribution manager branching into forecasting is greatly simplified. If not, then his greatest single problem will be the collection of his basic information. This will be obtained from sales invoices, warehouse records and so on. It cannot be emphasised often enough that the forecast will only provide the distribution

manager with the basic building blocks with which he must construct the overall policy for inventory control. The overriding pattern of demand will be affected by influences outside the environment of the firm — even outside the environment of the firm's particular market.

Before any thought is given to the mechanics of forecasting, it is as well that
the distribution executive identify those forces which will be of particular influence on his firm. He must go outside the firm, outside his market even, and look
at these as a segment of the entire economic field. He must attempt to identify
the broad trends in the forces that will affect the future of his firm, for these
can have profound effects on the reliability of any forecast he will make.

One of the most important sources of violent fluctuations in any market's
trends is, of course, politics. A major political decision can alter completely the
course of a firm's fortunes and, of course, any forecast that was made. No forecast in an industry susceptible to political change should neglect a consideration
of future expected policy and the relevance of any change.

Naturally political forces are not the only influences that can, and do, alter the
trend of an industry's forecasts. It is a prime task of any forecaster to identify
those forces within whose framework the movement of his firm's fortunes take
place. These influences will cover items like sales trends in sympathetic industries,
and statistics that can be expected to reflect their movement on some related
industry.

As an example of this type of thinking, a recent government estimate of the
future demand for capital equipment in the UK over the next few years can be
used as an example. Since the government has access to more complete data than
the average firm and since it can also make use of the most sophisticated techniques,
it is reasonable to assume the forecast has an acceptable level of accuracy. Given
this, and also assuming that the firm in question is in some way associated with
the capital goods market, then it is safe for the distribution manager in question
to look to this forecast as a check on how his own firm will be moving.

If, of course, the first is not directly linked to the capital goods area then he
can still use such a guide as the government figures as a basis for other key influences. If, for example, the firm in question is engaged in supplying raw material to a
casting firm which is engaged in the provision of components to the capital goods
field, then the second firm's increase in demand can be expected to be reflected
in the original supplying firm.

The problem with these broad trends is, of course, to gauge their direct influence. This can be most effectively done through the examination of historical
data. You will be able to see that a rise in demand in one industry generated a
sympathetic movement in your own, after a time lag of, say, three months.

The point being made is that the forecast must be looked at as operating within a frame of influences, outside as well as inside the firm. Any change in these
factors will make it compulsory to alter the forecast. In these circumstances it is
more desirable to identify these forces in advance and to try to integrate them
into the original plan.

Obviously the separation and recognition of these influences is of vital importance to the success of the forecasting programme. The main problem is where to
find them. One of the best sources of this type of information is the vast volume
of statistics that are published by the state, trade associations, banks, newspapers
and the universities. Once the factors affecting your firm have been decided upon,
it is likely that information will be available from one or all of these areas.

While on this point it is worth pointing out that the universities are often ignored in this connection; this can often be a great error. All universities have a wide range of research activities going on at any one time and these programmes throw out a great deal of peripheral information that is otherwise not obtainable. When examining your firm's environment and the influences on it, some very valuable information may be obtained from your local university simply for the asking. Most educational institutions are more than happy to cooperate in this way.

Given that the right framework for forecasting has been created what methods are available? There can, of course, be no generally applicable method since demands arise in different ways, each type requiring the application of a new technique or a combination of two or three. One of the most simple types of demand pattern frequently met with in inventory problems and, reasonably easy to deal with, is the spare parts problem. Suppose for the sake of illustration that the inventory problem in question is the spare part for a press in a forge. It is extremely difficult to determine exactly the amount of parts that will have to be kept on hand to ensure the operation of the equipment. But from historical data, available from internal records, the pattern of the demand for the parts should be available. These will take a type of frequency distribution as will be discussed in depth later. By the application of the standard deviation method outlined the desired level of service to the machines can be achieved. It will be noticed that the key characteristic here is that the forecast is simply based on the known pattern of demand. The assumption has been, of course, that workload remains the same. If workload changes it is a simple matter to relate the increase in work to the increase in usage and perform the same calculations as before. Normally this information regarding the increase in usage associated with a known increase in workload will be available from past control information, thus making the problem even more simple. This type of situation where the pattern of demand is known is not at all rare.

The second type of demand behaviour is where the pattern of demand is not known in advance, this being the typical case. Even here, though, there is generally an overall movement to be discerned in the direction of demand. In other words you can say that there is an upward or downward trend in demand. It is this type of problem that causes the greatest concern and it is also here that the identification of outside influences becomes very important.

The calculation of the trend inherent in any demand schedule is the most commonly employed form of forecasting. The basic idea is that demand data is taken in conjunction with time periods, the trend analysed and, provided that no changes take place in the key influences affecting the situation, then a prediction based on the direction of the trend can be made regarding the future behaviour of the demand schedule. Again there are a great many methods used. The more violent the fluctuations in the demand pattern the more sophisticated the technique.

It is assumed that in those firms where fluctuations are great there already exists some form of forecasting. It is repeated that the methods described here are for those average firms where demand is not violent in movement and which have not employed any form of forecasting before.

For products subject to a very steady demand there are two very simple methods of deciding trend. The first of these, the approximation method, is as the name suggests meant to give no more than an indication of the direction in which the demand for a particular product is moving. This is used by constructing

a graph of the historical demand for the item plotted against the sales periods in
which it occurred. A straight line is then drawn, in such a way as to pass through
the greatest number of points — this is the trend. If projected it will give an idea
of the direction in which the demand can be expected to move.

More suitable, even for those products subject to a very steady demand schedule, is the semi-average method. Suppose that the monthly demand for a particular part followed the pattern shown in Exhibit 10.1. Under the semi-average
method the data is arranged, as shown, divided into two and the averages of each
part calculated and noted. A graph is then drawn as in Exhibit 10.2. The horizontal axis represents the monthly periods and the vertical the demand figures. Both
the averages are drawn in the respective (or nearest) periods. The straight line
which joins these points is a representation of the approximate trend of the likely
demand for this part.

Exhibit 10.1

Month	Demand	Semi-average
1	10	
2	20	
3	30	30
4	40	
5	50	
6	60	
7	70	
8	80	80
9	90	
10	100	

To project forward to periods 11 and 12, the line is drawn as represented by
the dotted portion showing that the forecast demand for these two future
periods will be 110 units and 120 units.

These methods are extremely simple to apply and under favourable conditions
can give reasonable results, provided the movement of external influences is remembered. Above all, the demand function must not be subject to violent fluctuations, a condition often present in industrial inventory problems.

They should be used more as an indication of the order of magnitude and
likely direction of changes in demand rather than as prophecies. Whilst these two
methods can be used in a variety of situations they are without doubt far too elementary in the greater number of cases. Few products are subject to such a simple
trends that they can be adequately dealt with in this manner. But nonetheless
such methods are better than guesses.

A very wide range of products do have a marked trend in their demand sche-
dules and there are available more accurate techniques to analyse them. In situations where there is a straight-line relationship the calculation of this and its use
in forecasting are relatively simple.

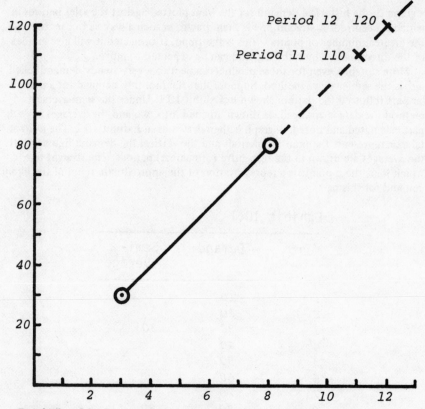

Exhibit 10.2 Moving average forecast by simple
method with limited application

The formula for the calculation of the trend is:

$$y = a + bx$$

where a is simply equal to the average of the sales data, that is in the case 30/5 or
6. The value of b is found by solving:

$$b = (\Sigma xy)/(\Sigma x^2)$$

Here Σxy is the sum of the deviations of y from the origin (period 3) times the
sales. From Exhibit 10.3 this will be seen to be 20. Σx^2 is the sum of the deviations
from the origin squared, again from the table this is seen to be 10.

Therefore in this case b is equal to 20/10 or 2. It is now possible to calculate
all the relevant values of sales simply by starting at the origin period and subtract-
ing 2 units of value from sales for every period prior to the origin or by adding
the same amount for every period subsequent to it.

Obviously the figures used for all the examples herein are very simple. This is,
of course, merely to illustrate the method and avoid confusion by elaborate data.

The method used in the real work environment is identical. To make the forecast for the next period is a simple matter of using the data calculated:

$$y = a + bx$$
$$= 6 + 2 \text{ (3 periods ahead)}$$
$$= 12$$

Although in the simple relationship chosen for the example it is likely that this forecast is 100 per cent correct, in practice there will tend to be an error because of the effect of the outside key influences already discussed. If some estimate of the likely magnitude of this error can be arrived at, it will be of some value in helping the manager concerned to come to the decision required.

The standard error of estimate is just such a method whereby the likely accuracy of your forecast can be estimated. The standard error is calculated as:

$$SE = [\Sigma(y - yc)^2]/N$$

where y is the sales data, yc the calculated sales data forecast and N the number of sales periods.

Because of the simple data employed in this example (and consequently the accuracy of the forecast), the standard error of estimate in this example would be zero. But for the sake of illustration suppose that the standard error of estimate for a similar problem was 0.25. This measure is very similar to standard deviations.

Suppose that using the trend method and calculating the standard error of estimate you arrive at a forecast of 13 units and $SE = 0.25$. This means that you have a 68 per cent chance of your estimate being within the range of 13 ± 0.25. There will be the chance that the forecast $\pm$ 2 standard errors will be 95 per cent correct. That is to say there is a 95 per cent chance that the actual sales figure will be in the range $13 \pm 0.25(2)$ or 13.5-12.5.

Once the trend has been calculated, the forecast made and the standard error of estimate applied, the distribution executive can get down to deciding his inventory policy — with some of the uncertainties reduced. Again the above formula for the calculation of trend can be further modified for those industries experiencing seasonal variations in demand. Seasonal variations are those variations in

Exhibit 10.3

Sales period	Sales	Deviation		Deviation squared
N	y	x	xy	x^2
1	2	-2	-4	4
2	4	-1	-4	1
3	6	0	0	0
4	8	1	8	1
5	10	2	20	4
	30	0	10	10

data away from the trend which can be isolated and applied to future trend expectations, in this way giving a more accurate estimation of the future sales of the product under examination.

The standard deviation of the seasonal variations from their mean can be used as the basis of forming an inventory policy in these situations. To arrive at the seasonal variations for your firm all that is required is the historical sales data. Trend is calculated as already explained and the deviation of the actual sales data from the trend noted. For each period, say quarterly, the deviations are summated and their average taken. Before these averages are taken as the corrections to be applied to trend for seasonal variation their sum should be zero. Suppose you found out that the variations fell out as follows: 19.2, 23.2, −23.7, 15.5 The sum of these is −4, therefore 4/4 or 1 must be added to each value. The corrections to be applied to each trend value in this example where quarterly figures were used would then be 1st quarter 18, −24.2, 23, −17 to be applied to the respective quarterly data.

These figures could alternatively be calculated as percentages of the trend, thus enabling the manager in question simply to calculate his trend and apply the percentage. This approach is to be preferred. His next step is the calculation of the standard deviation of the seasonal variations about their mean.

The trend is calculated and the seasonal index (preferably calculated on a percentage basis) is applied to achieve the corrected sales estimate. This level is used to set the inventory base stock for that period. Safety stock is calculated by the application of standard deviation to the average seasonal index (expressed as a percentage).

For example, suppose your average seasonal variation is 79 per cent for the period in question and the standard deviation is 1.5. Then, to achieve 84 per cent service levels the inventory for that period would be 1.5 per cent of trend after seasonal variations have been allowed for. The level of customer service and its relation to standard deviation is discussed in depth later. For 90 per cent service levels it would be average variation plus 1.28 standard deviations, for 95 per cent 1.68 standard deviations and so on.

The process outlined above is carried out for the appropriate periods always bearing in mind the possibilities of changes in the basic key influences that affect the firm. One of the best methods used for forecasting demand is related to the idea behind the trend methods and is known as *exponential smoothing*. The method has many advantages; it is flexible, the calculations are simple, reliability is high and money records for future forecasts are small.

The techniques rely principally on a monitoring system which can use the information gathered to alter predictions of future demand. The basic equation is:

New forecast = $X\%$ Old forecast + $Y\%$ Latest actual

where $X + Y = 100$ per cent. The idea behind the forecast is a simple combination of what has been predicted in the past combined with what is actually happening. It is obvious that the number that is chosen for the weighting factor (X and Y) will affect the importance that is given in the forecast to the latest actual data.

The higher the weighting factor, then the greater is the importance. Therefore high values for this element will be chosen to reflect a high degree of reliance on the latest actual data, this being an indication that there is thought to be little random fluctuation in the demand for the product under consideration.

The most common values for the weighting element are 0.2 and 0.1. The selection of a value of 0.1 would indicate that there was a belief that there were substantial random characteristics in the demand for the product. When this value is selected it is giving the opportunity for the influence of a great many previous demands to be felt, whereas a 0.5 value places great importance on the immediate past situation. We can restate the basic formula like this:

New forecast = $(1-a)$ Old forecast + a (Latest data)

where a represents a value between 0 and 1. The period chosen for comparison will, of course, vary from firm to firm; the larger it is, the greater the accuracy.

In fact, this simple exponential smoothing can be very useful indeed. It has, however, one important disadvantage; it never quite catches up with a marked trend in the data. To do this, to try to reduce the importance of this lag, a minor change is introduced. Most changes over a *short term* can be represented by a straight line consisting of a constant term a and a variable b. It is this variable term that causes our simple smoothing forecast to lag behind the marked trend that may be taking place in the data.

As before, the forecast for a period is

Simple smoothing = $(1 - a)$ Old forecast + a (Latest data)

there is also a similar forecast for b the variable element:

Forecast = $(1 - x)$ Old forecast b + x (Old actual data)

where x represents the variable element in the data. The actual old x variable element is best measured by the real change in the demand between present and the previous actual demand. Thus, for example,

May forecast for variable =
$(1 - x)$ April forecast + x (April demand — March actual demand)

Therefore the best estimate of true future demand is the one which combines both these elements:

Forecast = Final forecast simple smoothing + forecast for
variable element X number of periods between
end of present period till time forecast is
required for

There is still one further elementary technique, however, that might prove useful in the present context of industrial inventory control. This is correlation. When correlation methods are used in connection with inventory control it is an attempt to codify the relationship between two variables. There may be some relationship, say through salesmen's wages and the demand for a particular product. There will, of course, be a time lag between the operation of these relationships. This can be investigated from past data. If salesmen's wages can be seen to have, say, a 3-week lead over the demand for the material then the correlation between the relevant

Exhibit 10.4

Weekly demand = y; average wages = x

y	x	xy	y^2	x^2
1	1	1	1	1
2	1	2	4	1
3	3	6	4	9
3	3	9	9	9
4	4	16	16	16
12	12	34	34	36

figures is examined. In practice it is seldom that such a straightforward correlation will be noted. The procedure is to examine likely areas to arrive at a measure of their correlation. This is done from a simple formula, much the same layout being used as has been utilised previously.

The maximum degree of correlation is 1. This means that a movement of 1 unit in 1 variable will produce an identical movement in the other. Let us assume that you want to investigate the correlation between the average salesman's wages and the 3-week lag demand for a component. The formula for the calculation of r, the coefficient of correlation, is

$$r = \frac{N\Sigma xy - (\Sigma x)(\Sigma y)}{\left\{[N\Sigma x^2 - (\Sigma x)^2][N\Sigma y^2 - (\Sigma y)^2]\right\}^{\frac{1}{2}}}$$

where y is the component demand and x the average salesman's wages. Suppose that the data in question is as shown in Exhibit 10.4. Then, from the formula

$$r = \frac{5(34) - (12)(12)}{\left\{[5(36) - (12)^2][5(36) - (12)^2]\right\}^{\frac{1}{2}}}$$

$$= 26/(936)^{\frac{1}{2}}$$

$$= 0.85$$

Since this is a high positive correlation it is taken that there is a real relationship between the two variables inspected. If r had been less than 0.80, little real value could be attached to the result. We must now find out the regression equation which shows the details of the movement.

The equation takes the same broad form as that already used, $y = a + bx$, although there is a substantial difference in the methods employed to arrive at values for a and b:

$$a = \frac{\Sigma x^2(\Sigma y) - \Sigma x(\Sigma xy)}{N(\Sigma x^2) - (\Sigma x)^2}$$

The value for b is found from the equation:

$$b = \frac{N(\Sigma xy) - \Sigma x(\Sigma y)}{N(\Sigma x^2) - (\Sigma x)^2}$$

In both equations the symbols have the same values as in the main coefficient formula.

In the case stated above, the value of a from the formula is 0.66 and of b is 0.72. The regression is then:

$$y = 0.66 + 0.72x$$

To apply this to the problem, if it is known from internal records that the average salesman's wage for any one period is 5 then you can calculate the expected demand for the component 3 weeks ahead as

$$y = 0.66 + 0.72(5) = 4.26 \text{ units}$$

Naturally there are no limits on the type of units used. The data is dealt with as before, and the standard error or estimate can be calculated as before.

There is one thing that must always be borne in mind, however, and this is that by far the greater number of forecasts available in the firm have been made by the sales or marketing departments and must be slightly adapted before they can be really used in the distribution area. This is not a very difficult problem in technical terms, but it can frequently prove to be a rigorous exercise in personnel. The sales department will have the raw data in a form similar to that above bit it must be converted. This may involve time, if not much effort. If the sales people will perform the calculations then so much the better; if not the basic material must be obtained and reworked in distribution.

Basically what is required is that the pure sales estimates are reduced to individual components relevant to distribution areas. This is important because very often a firm's sales areas will not correspond with its distribution breakdown. This might prove a useful point for negotiations with the sales department, to attempt to construct sales forecasts in such a way that they can be used by both departments. Very often cooperation will be good, since the extra effort at source is not too much and the mutual benefits can be considerable.

The usefulness of any forecast will depend on the order pattern of the firm's customers. Total sales forecast will depend on the order pattern of the firm's customers. Total sales forecast often cannot easily be broken down into recognisable order patterns and when this is the case their use is suspect. The sales forecast will be reshaped along the lines of the example in Exhibit 10.5. The basic idea is that the requirement for this particular product is calculated for the entire supply territory making use of the individual sales forecasts. When we have completed this procedure for all products and territories the normal inventory routine may take place.

Inventory management is basically a compromise. It is a compromise between the forces pulling the distribution manager in the direction of absolute minimum costs within the inventory system, and external forces from other departments which very often will make him adopt a policy resulting in apparently higher costs.

The most common and obvious factor here is the reaction of the sales and

Exhibit 10.5 Usual sales department type of forecast (top) and the same reshaped for distribution (bottom)

ABC Limited: yearly sales forecast by area

Area	Item 2Ly	Item 4Tx	Item 7 MM
London	500	120	150
South West	90	140	50
Midlands	650	200	100
North	500	196	100
TOTALS	1740	656	400

Reshaped for distribution: Item 4Tx

Accounting period	London	South West	Midlands	North
1	10	10	16	15
2	11	10	16	15
3	17	12	18	18
4	10	11	18	18
5	10	11	16	18
6	10	12	16	18
7	10	12	18	16
8	9	10	18	16
9	12	11	16	15
10	11	11	16	15
11	5	15	16	16
12	5	15	16	16
TOTALS	120	140	200	196

marketing departments. Higher sales are often equated with proportionately higher profits. The attitude is very often met with that greater volume moving through the distributionary systems will result in lower unit costs. This is true in certain cases, but not in all. Many distribution costs (especially in distribution inventory) will in fact increase with increases in throughput.

This situation may cause a great deal of trouble with the distribution manager, but really the setting of operating standards must, in the last analysis, take place outside the distribution department. This is not to say that distribution must remain quiet about the extra cost centres being introduced to the firm's activities; on the contrary it should speak out loudly against them. It must realise, however, that the real job of distribution is to maintain a predetermined level at the minimum costs.

This obviously includes a level which is known to the distribution manager in question to be unrealistic. In certain exceptional circumstances (new product launch for example) exceptional methods may have to be used, at least on a short-term basis. This is fine provided — and this is important — that the other management concerned is made fully aware of the costs involved and adjust their estimates accordingly. If this is done then the distribution man can get on with his job without worrying about how to explain a shortfall in profits.

Now we will assume that all the introductory work has been performed and that everybody is aware of the role that inventory can play, and the extent and type of cooperation that is required. It is worth pointing out here that we are really concerned with the problems of control of inventory in the distributive system of a company not with the problems of inventory and production, at least not directly.

11 Types of inventory– cost and divisions

We must also remember that there are various types of inventory, each with a distinctive role to play in the overall system. In transit, stocks are very important. Any system of distribution warehouses will have a built-in replenishment lead time, i.e. a definite amount of time will be required for orders for replenishment inventory to be placed, packed, transported and made available for use. There will be a tangible pipeline of goods flowing through the system. While this stock is moving its value to the firm must be reduced. This transit inventory is frequently overlooked in the design of distribution networks, and it can be quite important.

We often find that the nature of the product or the service requirements or the location of the market might be forcing a change in distribution thinking within the firm. This might be, for example, towards a greater number of smaller warehouses. While this decision may or may not be the best one to tackle the problem with, the level of in-transit inventory is often passed over and the firm finds that the new system is not as effective as was expected. The same result can come about in the case where the trend of thought is to fewer warehouses, which in its turn will involve the possibility of higher in-transit inventories. The relevant costs must be included in any inventory statistics in either situation. The average amount of in-transit inventory can be calculated from the equation:

$$I = ST$$

where I is the average inventory in transit, S the average sales rate and T the average transit time through the system. It will be noted from this expression that inventory in transit need not be actually being physically moved, and that the general efficiency of the entire replenishment cycle will affect the level.

If, for example, the journey time from supply point to the distribution warehouse is 2 days, but the administrative procedures take 3 then, of course, the time to be remembered is 5 days not 2. This is important when considering numbers of distribution points. Movement either to a greater number or a smaller will involve changes in administrative procedure. It is well to ensure that the change does not involve large increases in the in-transit inventory levels. If a field depot sells some 200 units per week and the average transit time through the system is 2 weeks, then their in-transit inventory will be 400 units.

Alternatively suppose we have a firm with approximately £5 million sales per year, with about half of its revenue devoted to direct unavoidable costs. It will, if it has an average through-system time of 2 weeks, have some £500,000 in in-transit inventory — a significant figure.

This is, in fact, an area of distribution management within which savings can often be made without major changes in the overall system. Take the firm mentioned above; obviously the 2-week through time is very large. This will be absorbed chiefly by administrative procedures. If these could be rescheduled with the through time in mind, significant economies could result.

Say, for the sake of illustration, that the through time was reduced by half. This, in its turn, would reduce the in-transit inventory from £500,000 to some £250,000, an economy no-one could afford to ignore; remember that this is a positive saving, and worth a great deal more if turned into an increase in sales. Say, for example, that the firm had a 10 per cent margin on sales then this saving through administrative procedures would be the equivalent of approximately some £2,500,000 or 50 per cent. The implications are obvious.

This example, of course, is an extreme situation and in the real work environment such spectacular results are extremely rare to say the least. But the lesson is there — inventory savings can be made by reducing through times.

Included in the areas to be studied are, of course, such considerations as materials handling efficiency. This is an area for the application of work sampling, a subject to be discussed in the warehousing section.

The next and by far the most widely recognised inventory type is cycle inventories. These perform the essential decoupling service between variations in demand and production.

Cycle stocks follow the basic pattern shown in Exhibit 11.1, although their location can vary a great deal. Point of production will almost certainly find that the economic load for movement between *A* and *B* will not be the same as between *B* and *C*; and certainly rarely will it be the same as the final customer wishes to purchase at the point of sale. Therefore, cycle stocks must be held at some or all of these locations to allow some rationalisation of production quantities, economic movement loads and demand. Just exactly where they will be located varies. But somewhere along this line they must be held — and the cost met.

In this situation there is always the chance that the customer will make a surprise change in the size of his order, or that new customers will be attracted and so on. The essential point is that there is a risk factor which must be taken into

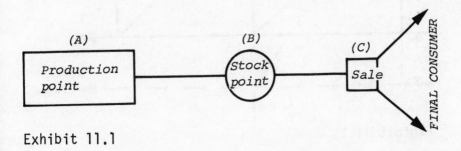

Exhibit 11.1

account. This is the next type of stock of concern to us, namely safety stock.

The level of safety stock is of great importance and will be looked at in greater depth later, but at the present time we will briefly examine the major factors which affect its size.

These will obviously start with the degree of variation in the likely demand schedule. The greater the vagaries in demand then naturally the higher will be the safety stock requirement. Directly linked with this is, of course, the service policy of the firm. If it has been decided that there will be a high service level and the variations in demand are difficult to forecast, then the cost of maintaining the high safety stocks needed must be very carefully examined. This is always important – the higher the service level demanded then the greater will be the cycle and safety stocks needed to meet the policy.

The replenishment lead time will also have an important effect on safety stock. The greater the lead time the greater will be the stocks held, that is over and above inventory in transit.

Finally we have seasonal stocks. This is inventory that is held as a direct result of some strongly pronounced seasonal variation in the demand for the product. These are problems that come more within the production department's sphere,

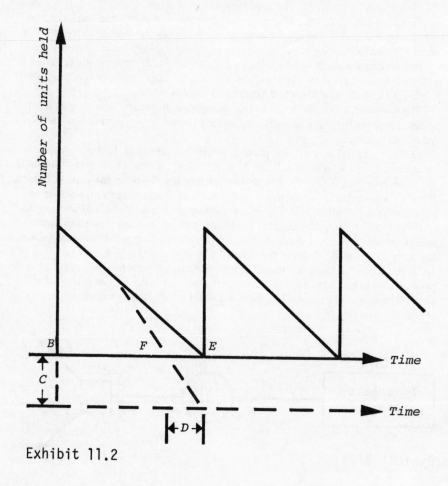

Exhibit 11.2

because the most important decision to be taken is in patterns of production. For this reason they are best left to more specialised works in that field.

The greatest amount of time and effort is usually devoted to cycle and safety stocks. This is not a bad thing because in the vast majority of distribution systems these two account for the largest share of the investment in inventory. However, the importance of in-transit inventory must always be remembered.

Exhibit 11.2 shows the role of safety stock. When demand is known and lead time is certain there is no need for safety stock. Usage and replenishment cycles are all the same, following the path of the unbroken line. A maximum level is decided upon, A, which will maintain service levels over the certain lead time. Inventory will be depleted until there is zero stock left at B, time E. At this point the replenishment shipment arrives bringing levels back up to A and so the cycles continue. If demand fluctuates as shown by the broken line then inventory would be 0 at time F and a stockout occurs over the period FE. To prevent this an estimate is made of the fluctuations expected and the demand over the period FE and this becomes the safety stock. How comprehensive this will be depends on the costs and benefits involved.

INVENTORY COSTS

Irrespective of the classification which a particular type of inventory receives and the attitude of general management towards it, there will be costs associated with the retention and replenishment of the required amounts within the distribution system. These costs are the basic point behind inventory control, the whole purpose being to reduce them to the minimum consistent with the operating specifications laid down by the distribution department in consultation with other management areas.

ORDER COSTS

The amounts referred to here are the sums which must be incurred for every repeat order. These costs will include items having a direct effect on in-transit inventory as well as the other classifications. The order processing system must be costed and such action as unpacking, inspection and movement to store will also be included. The question of the most efficient order processing methods will in the vast majority of cases be outside the control of the distribution department, this being the realm of O&M. It is worth remembering, however, the effect that a sluggish system can have on in-transit inventory levels.

DELIVERY COSTS

Usually delivery costs are included in the general prices agreed between delivery subsidiary (in the larger groups) or it will have been already decided to include them in order costs. Sometimes, the one order may cover a number of deliveries and in these circumstances it is useful to extract the individual delivery costs concerned for inclusion as required.

These are of crucial importance in distribution. They are normally broken down into two broad divisions, direct and indirect. The direct costs involved with a stockout are those costs which are due to a halt in procedures or a change in location of activities. For example, if a particular category of merchandise falls short in a warehouse then it might be necessary that a section of order pickers may have to be halted until replacement.

This need not happen, of course. They may be moved on to a different area within the warehouse. Nonetheless a disruption in the normal routine has taken place; this costs money. Another method of dealing with the stockout situation (depending on the order-picking discipline used) might be to allow the flow of orders to continue uninterrupted, the missing product being placed in the respective orders at a later time.

It does not really matter which course is adhered to; there will still be an increase in costs at the warehouse. The fact that such stockouts might result in automated equipment being stopped is yet another potential source of diseconomies caused directly by a stockout.

By far the most important area in stockout costs are the lost sales which can result from lack of a particular line. The importance of these lost sales depends to a great extent on the type of market which the firm is operating. If it has a dominating position and a highly desirable brand image, then its consumers may be prepared to wait until the stockout situation is remedied. One just needs to look at the time certain people are prepared to await the arrival of a new model car, but these are the exceptions. The normal situation is that the firm is in competition, and that there exists a close substitute for its product. Where this is the case then the occurrence of a stockout will mean that the consumer will simply go elsewhere to have his demand met.

It is not only the direct costs of the lost sales which must be reckoned with but also the indirect costs like the loss of goodwill. While it is reasonably easy to come to some estimate of the cost of lost sales, goodwill is another matter. When a customer finds that his request cannot be met, it is not only that specific sale that he will make elsewhere. It is possible, indeed likely, that his future purchases will be made somewhere where he feels the efficiency and service are greater. Moreover he is unlikely to keep his views to himself. It is at this point that the already mentioned conflict between sales and distribution will arise — to what extent customer service?

CARRYING COSTS

Carrying costs are one of the most important areas of interest in distribution inventory management. They are also one of the most difficult to quantify accurately.

These are the costs incurred by simply holding inventory and include: the opportunity cost of capital tied up in inventory, cost of storage space, handling costs, the cost of deterioration and protective packaging, damage incurred in storage (including pilferage, if any), obsolescence and insurance.

Most firms can tell you very quickly the value of the inventory which they are carrying. This figure is usually fairly accurate given the limitations of the

various valuation methods in common use. It very often comes as a surprise to
them that the cost of carrying such inventory can be as much as 30 per cent of
item cost, and in any case is likely to run out at an annual average of between
15-20 per cent of item cost. The reason behind this is that many of the costs included above as carrying costs are not usually gathered in a consolidated account
and even when they are, a great deal of argument is likely to surround the true
values involved. Be this as it may, the basic fact cannot be hidden: carrying costs
can be substantial.

ADMINISTRATION COSTS

It does not really matter how important or how unimportant a particular block
of inventory is to the effective operation of the firm. As soon as it has been included in the total inventory capacity of the organisation, certain administrative costs
must be incurred. A check must be kept of quantities received and despatched, of
where it is located in the warehouse and so on. These costs, while they concern
the distribution manager, are best looked after and investigated by the O&M department.

The above is a brief description of the types of costs which the manager of a
distribution inventory must keep to the minimum. It will be noticed that they
can be very conveniently divided into those that are likely to decrease per unit as
the volume of throughput increases and those that may in fact involve a greater
burden as the volume increases.

Order costs, delivery costs and stockout costs will decrease per unit as the volume increases, but carrying costs will increase. This relationship is basic in all
inventory control and will be dealt with in greater depth later.

COST OF CONTROL

Before going on to discuss methods of controlling these costs, it is as well that we
look at the cost of control. It is essential to adopt a reasonable attitude to this
problem. Control costs money, and the more elaborate and exact the form of control discipline, then the more expensive it becomes. A careful check on the benefits from exact control must always be kept. A balance must be struck between
the costs of introducing and maintaining a control system and the costs involved
with not having the system. This is especially true in the control of distribution
inventory where the optimum result from a sophisticated control method is often
not worth the cost because the marketing or sales people, or both, may be pressing
ahead regardless, at least in the short term.

This ignores what the distribution management might have to say on the real
costs associated with a particular project. Where this is the situation there is really
little point in devoting the extensive time required for many of the more expensive
control systems to an end which is often met just as effectively by a less sophisticated and cheaper method.

In a number of cases a very high degree of precision is not worthwhile because
the source data from which we would be working is itself inaccurate. We are not
saying that simply because source data is not 100 per cent accurate subsequent
processes can be slipshod. What we are saying is that, given the original accuracy,

the costs involved with the subsequent treatment should be carefully weighed against the real tangible revenue benefits likely to accrue from pinpoint accuracy. Put simply, benefits must always justify costs.

Bearing the foregoing in mind, the first question which is likely to spring to mind is, how do we decide which areas to devote the most attention to? If we can examine the relationships between each category of inventory and the benefit which the firm derives from holding it then this should give us a basis to work from. It is, of course, very difficult to generalise on this problem, but experience has shown that there are certain basic guidelines which, if not accurate all of the time, are reliable enough to warrant some attention most of the time.

ABC METHOD OF CONTROL

The most simple of these is the 80-20 rule sometimes applied as the 70-30 rule. This is very old, in distribution management terms, and says simply that it is not uncommon to find that 70 per cent by number of the items carried in a warehouse account for only 30 per cent by value of the turnover from the same location. It can be looked at the other way, of course, namely that 30 per cent by number of the items carried account for 70 per cent by value of the business done, the same allocation procedure applying to the 80-20 variety of the rule.

This concept is of value only because it is very often approximately correct. Not that we are recommending that it be adopted as a basis for inventory control. There have been, however, several developments based on the idea behind the rules, i.e. that a small proportion by number of the items carried in a warehouse account for a much larger proportional value of the turnover involved. If, in fact, this situation obtains in any system the importance is clear. We devote more of our time and money to the management of the inventory which contributes most to the firm's wellbeing, and correspondingly less effort to the less active inventory groups.

These refinements of the older rules of thumb have become known as ABC systems of inventory management. Certainly, they can be used as a form of control discipline in the smaller firm (as illustrated later), but the chief use to which the larger organisations put them is identification.

They usually operate on a basis of classification, putting all items held into three groups (or more). These groups represent the relationship between the numbers of items held and their share of the turnover or value usage. The most common categories are 70-20-10 and 60-30-10, although any particular classification can be used.

Once the ABC programme has been carried out, basic inventory control decissions can be taken. For example frequency and order lot of the various items can be decided upon, but more important the revenue earning product groups have been identified. Cost of control and the lack of it can be examined and the most important priorities established.

The ABC system is extremely simple to apply in practice. The only likely problem is that as the number of items held increases the volume of calculations involved becomes correspondingly large. This is however a question of time allowance, not difficulty.

The steps are as follows. First, for each item that is held in stock, a list of usage values must be made in the most convenient units, pounds per week, per

month and so on. Next a list of all the items held by number is made in descending
order of usage values. Thirdly, the respective usage values are placed beside each
item. Then cumulative totals of both the number of items and their usage values
are made. Finally these are turned into percentages of the total number of items
and the total usage values. These are often then plotted on a graph to give a
pictorial impression of the breakdown that has been made.

The major problem is to decide where the cut-off points between the various
classifications will be made. A completely accurate cut-off point can only be
found by examination of the individual situation, a constant monitor being kept
on the items under consideration and the alterations which show themselves as
being required being made when discovered.

This may be the only fully accurate method available but Thomas (in *Stock
Control in Manufacturing Industries*) has given the following approximation
which has been found extremely useful as a first step. First determine the average
usage value per item; multiply this average by six. This will give the cut-off point
between A and B items. Half the average is taken as the cut-off point between B
and C items. This will give a good indication of the values of the items to be included in the categories in question. If, for example, on carrying out the method
described by Thomas we find that the cut-off point between A and B items is a
usage value of £80 a month, then all items with this usage value or above will be
included in the A classification and will remain there until the usage value falls
below a predetermined level for an accepted number of weeks, say to £70 for 6
weeks. Similar rules are made for the items falling within the C classification.

When the study has been carried out and the rules for determining the cut-off
points have been agreed upon, greater attention can be paid to the operation of
the most important inventories, namely the items coming under the A classification.

Let us look at a simplified example. Suppose we are looking at a distribution
warehouse that has never been appraised before; up to this time inventory has
been looked upon simply as a means to an end and not worthy of much attention.

Let us assume that we hold 20,000 items at this point, having an annual inventory value of £200,000 and experience has resulted in the safety stock being set
at some £20,000. Orders are placed every 4 weeks, the normal order quantity
being valued at £15,000. A stockout of any item is considered as disruptive as a
stockout of any other item.

We will assume that an ABC attack has been made on the inventory held and
that this shows that 70 per cent by value of the turnover is accounted for by 10
per cent by number of the items held, 20 per cent by value going to 20 per cent

Exhibit 11.3

Item	Total,%	Number	Total value,%	Value	Minimum stock
A	10	2,000	70	140,000	14,000
B	20	4,000	20	40,000	4,000
C	70	14,000	10	20,000	2,000
TOTAL	100	20,000	100	200,000	20,000

by number and that 10 per cent usage value is accounted for by 70 per cent by number of the items held.

Under a non-selective approach at this depot average inventory would cost £27,500 per annum, i.e. minimum inventory (safety stock) plus half of the order quantity.

Exhibit 11.3 displays what we now know about the inventory situation at this warehouse. We have assumed that the share of the various classes of items in the total safety stock figure is proportional to their share of the total value of inventory. The same supposition is made about the share which each class of products has in the order placed every 4 weeks thus:

A items   £10,500
B items   £ 3,000
C items   £ 1.500

On examination of the existing position it is obvious that the old method of considering inventory as a homogeneous unit and allowing £20,000 of inventory as safety stock is too expensive a precaution for some of the classes now thrown into the light.

The first possible step is to concentrate more effort on the management of the A class items, for after all they account for 70 per cent of the value usage. They are therefore very important for the profitable operation of the depot. Because of their relatively small numbers (10 per cent of total) it will not be prohibitively expensive to introduce tighter control. C items do not contribute a great deal to the profitability of the warehouse but it will be remembered that we decided that a stockout of one item was as important as a stockout of any other item. Therefore, we must still keep the safety level at an acceptable point, but at the same time lower the costs associated with the holding of these items. The B class merchandise we can leave alone in this situation. The reason is that as always the cost of introducing a control discipline must be weighed against the cost of not using it. We assume in this situation that the relative advantages and disadvantages are such as to persuade us to refrain from changing the situation in the C category.

Therefore the following initial steps will be taken. Items in class A will have their reorder cycle reduced from 4 weeks to 2 weeks. Safety stocks will be reduced accordingly, as will the reorder quantity. B items will remain as before. C items will be reordered only every 2 months; little attention will be paid to them, but safety stock will be doubled to maintain service policies.

If all of these recommendations are followed the results we would expect are:

1   *A items*   The safety stock is reduced to £7000. An order worth £5250 is placed every 2 weeks. Average inventory will be safety stock plus half order, i.e. £9625.

2   *B items*   Continue as before: safety stock £4000, order £3000. Therefore average inventory will be £5500.

3   *C items*   Safety stock doubled; order quantity also doubled. Therefore average inventory will be £5500.

4   *Total inventory*   £20,625.

It can be seen that the annual average inventory held at the warehouse under examination has decreased from £27,500 to £20,625, a saving of some £6875 or approximately 25 per cent. Notice that this saving was brought about primarily through organisational changes, no sacrifice of service policies being involved.

Not only does the ABC method prove useful for basic savings in inventory, it is also very useful when deciding upon the location of stock within the warehouse. This is an important part of warehouse management, and more time is spent on the subject in the next section which in fact deals with the whole question of the place of the warehouse in distribution management. If the inventory of a particular firm lends itself to an ABC breakdown, then the location of the various categories of merchandise should take place on the same basis. This would allow the operation of the different control disciplines and would also give the chance for more sophisticated equipment to be utilised on the A item locations. What has gone before will obviously have some bearing on the material on stock location in the next section. The techniques described there are designed for full use only in those situations where there is not a direct easy breakdown along the ABC method. When this is available, then the methods mentioned for location need not be ignored. They can be used as a subdivision to allow for the more accurate and effective placement of items within each class. The greater the area concerned then the more important will be the location of individual product lines within the overall class location.

In conclusion, the ABC analysis of an inventory point is not at all difficult to carry out, and the results can be most rewarding. It must be remembered that the ABC system is best regarded as a jumping-off point. Strictly speaking, only broad policy decisions can be made on the basic information obtainable from this type of study. The next important step is to examine carefully the possible control disciplines that might be introduced to control the costs of A items and possibly B and C items as well.

12 Control disciplines: conditions of certainty

Once we have decided on the types of inventory we are going to spend the greatest time and money on, we must begin thinking of the type of control discipline which we are going to use. Needless to say the use of the standard disciplines discussed below is not limited to any particular class of item, but the relative costs involved must be examined carefully before it is decided to extend expensive control systems to all classifications of items held. There are basically two types of control method:

1 Fixed order quantity.
2 Fixed order period.

These are extremes, of course, and in practice a great many compromises between the two systems exist. We will examine the fixed order quantity scheme first.

FIXED ORDER QUANTITY CONTROL

As the name suggests, this system relies on the order placed being the same quantity every time. If this is the case then it is obvious that the variable factor is the period between the orders. The amount of inventory on hand and on order and the estimated demand over the replenishment lead time are continuously analysed, i.e. the current supply situation is always known *vis-a-vis* expected demand. The system operates simply. Whenever the expected demand over the time estimated to elapse before another order is received exceeds the level of inventory on hand and on order, a new order is placed for the predetermined quantity of materials.

FIXED REORDER PERIOD

Under a system of fixed reorder period the situation is similar. The basic difference is that the period between orders is always the same, the factor which alters being the quantity ordered at each period. At each order point an amount is ordered which will bring the stock on hand and on order up to the expected maximum consumption over the time between placing the next order and receiving it. Under this system the most suitable types of inventory are those where the costs of monitoring (as required in fixed order quantity methods) are high. In fact each of the pure forms of these systems have their advantages and disadvantages.

FIXED ORDER QUANTITY VERSUS FIXED ORDER PERIOD

In the first instance the fixed order quantity method can be extremely expensive to operate. This is because of the continuous monitoring of inventory on hand and consumption which must occur. This may not be too high a cost when the number of items is small. When we move on to what is virtually a small to medium warehouse carrying a few thousand items then the size of this particular problem will be realised. Where there are electronic aids available the cost is reduced. These can only be justified where the volume and savings involved are considerable. Another major difficulty is in forecasting demand over the replenishment lead time. This difficulty applies to both control methods in fact; the more violent and unpredictable the variations in demand, then the more expensive will be an accurate system of either type.

Even if we assume that these basic faults in the mechanics are acceptable, some further problems remain. In the fixed reorder quantity method the amount may always be the same, but the fact that the timing of orders will vary can cause a great deal of difficulty.

If the warehouse in question is part of a larger warehouse network then the central stockholding point might prefer a general agreement on the timing of orders. It is quite possible for the central depot to find that an individual depot warehouse varies the timing of its order practically on every occasion. This might result in a higher level of efficiency for the individual depot, but in the long run it might very well work against the overall effectiveness of the entire distribution network.

It will do this simply by disrupting the schedule of the central order processing point. It is very unlikely that the head office will be able to organise a random processing method. So when, because of an unexpected increase in demand, an individual depot places an unforeseen order, two things must happen: whether this order is given priority or it is pushed further down the line.

No matter what actually happens either of these two actions is going to increase the level of somebody's inventory in transit.

On the other hand where the fixed reorder quantity method is held to, there are certain advantages. It will be possible, for example, to develop a standard module for each demand point. This will consist of the fixed order quantity. This might be used as a standard unit all the way from the end of the production line to the final storage point.

The final decision about fixed order quantity will depend on making an estimation of the costs and advantages involved and deciding if the benefits outweigh the disadvantages. Basically it will most likely develop into a comparison between the savings possible through the development of a standard (or nearly standard) module for the individual depot against the costs of constant monitoring (which can be reduced on a per unit basis by using a central computer with the depots on line) and the diseconomies brought about by the likelihood of unforseen orders arriving at the next stockholding point further down the line.

The fixed reorder period has some advantages over the fixed order quantity but neither is perfect. It suffers from the basic problem of having to forecast the demand it can reasonably expect over the replacement lead time for the particular organisational system within which it is used.

If the depot concerned is once more seen to be part of a much wider network then the central point can achieve some distinct advantages from the fixed order period method of control. The first of these is standardisation of ordering times. If the central stockholding point is dealing with large numbers of depots it is likely that there would be savings available if it could rely on receiving the individual orders in some sort of predictable order and interval. This would allow an effective order processing and despatch method to be built up. Moreover, it might be possible to introduce economies in transport costs as well. Under the fixed order quantity method an order must be despatched to the depot that requested it within the pre-agreed time, otherwise stockouts would occur at the depot. This can often involve underutilisation of transport capacity.

On the other hand, where there is a fixed order period in operation, it might be possible to arrange geographical areas with sympathetic periods in such a way as to allow consolidation of orders, i.e. assuming that they will not always be of sufficient size to demand full vehicle loads individually. As before, the final choice will depend on a comparison of the costs involved for each individual situation.

DECIDING QUANTITIES AND PERIODS UNDER CONDITIONS OF CERTAINTY

The next problem we will examine is in a way independent of the decision made between the two systems discussed above, or a combination of them. In both cases there are crucial points to be decided upon. These are, in the fixed order quantity method, first the order quantity and secondly the reorder point. In the fixed order period method the most important decision is obviously the number of orders to be placed over a given period thus establishing the order period, and secondly the quantity to be ordered. It is a reasonably simple matter to derive formulae for these calculations in a textbook, but in practice other difficulties will appear. Therefore the approach which will be taken is firstly to decide the formula under textbook conditions, then to try to discuss the alterations that will have to be made if the results are to have a practical significance. Take the fixed reorder quantity first. Many years ago the solution to the quantity problem was developed by Camp. The name which he gave to the quantity to be ordered each time was the *economic order quantity* (EOQ). The derivation of this quantity really relies on the basic characteristics of the costs associated with inventory. If we return to the outline of costs dealt with at the start of this section, we will remember that they could easily be divided into two broad groups: those costs which tended to decrease per unit as the volume of inventory being dealt with increases, and those which tend to increase as the volume of inventory increases. Broadly speaking we might say that those costs associated with ordering the inventory will decrease per unit as the quantity of inventory increases, while those associated with carrying the inventory will increase as the volume of inventory increases. We will now examine the implications of this, in the first instance under conditions of certainty (textbook conditions), then look at the effect of uncertainty on the result.

From Exhibit 12.1 the general position will be seen. Order costs are decreasing with volume of carrying costs increasing; the total costs are moving in sympathy with the two factors. The EOQ will be the amount that reaches the best compromise between these opposing forces. In the diagram this quantity is represented by the point Q, i.e. where total costs are at their lowest.

The cost of carrying inventory will be equal to the order cost per unit purchased at S/q at the intersection of the two cost lines in question, namely at the point x. At this point the average annual unit cost will be equal to half the carrying cost (I) as a percentage of unit cost times the price per unit (P) times the quantity ordered per year (q), i.e.

Annual average cost (at x) = $\frac{1}{2}IPq$

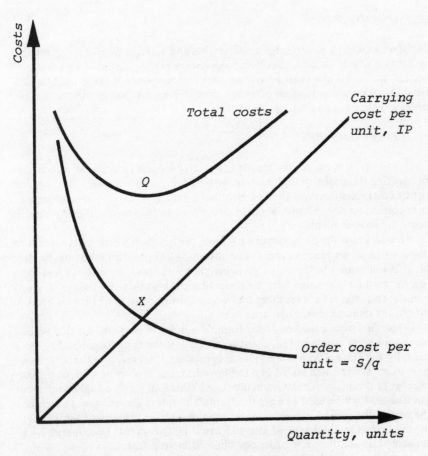

Exhibit 12.1   Determination of EOQ

The order cost at point x over a time period the same as that used for carrying costs (1 year) will be equal to the annual rate of inventory depletion, i.e. sales times the fixed costs to place an order divided by the number of items ordered:

Order cost at $x = DS/q$

where D is the sales, S fixed costs per order and q the quantity ordered.

We are simply saying that the unit cost per order, S/q, multiplied by the amount actually ordered, which is sales, will give us the real order costs at point x. Since these two costs are equal at point x we can say:

$\frac{1}{2}IPq = DS/q$

Multiplying both sides by $2q$ we obtain

$IPq^2 = 2DS$

$q^2 = 2DS/IP$

$q = (2DS/IP)^{\frac{1}{2}}$

But if we look back to our original statements and diagram we will see that the quantity q which we were calculating was always at the point x. If we draw a vertical through q at x then we will see that it corresponds to the point Q which we said is the economic order quantity; therefore we can say that the economic order quantity is also given as

$EOQ = (2DS/IP)^{\frac{1}{2}}$

That is to say, if we order the amount calculated by this formula, we will always be ordering the quantity that reaches the best compromise between the two competing costs classifications that we mentioned earlier. When we have calculated the economic order quantity we have also moved to help solve another point, this being the reorder point.

We now know the best quantity to order; the question which must come after this is when do we place an order. The answer to this problem is also easily arrived at. This will simply be the expected demand over the period which it takes to receive an order, i.e. usage over the replenishment lead time. By fixing our reorder point at this level we are ensuring that we will always have inventory on hand to satisfy any demand that might arise.

Before illustrating the use of the formula it is worth pointing out that while there are a great number of different statements of the EOQ formula, they are all basically the same. There is one type of exception, however, as it is not uncommon to see the formula stated in a fashion which has as its denominator the carrying cost of inventory for the particular firm. This is, of course, a valid statement but it should not be used as a general formulation. It is always wiser to include the cost of the unit of inventory under examination, as failure to do this could possibly result in arriving at what are identical EOQ figures for products having the same rate and the same order costs but different prices.

As an illustration let us look at a simple example. Suppose the following information is known for a particular product: the cost of the item is £16 and the inventory carrying costs are estimated to be 25 per cent. The incremental cost of placing an order is estimated at £2 and we will assume that demand is constant at 2 units per day on the basis of a 6-day week. The annual demand for this product will be 12 time 52 units or 624 units per annum, therefore

$$EOQ = (2DS/IP)^{\frac{1}{2}} = (2 \times 624 \times 2/0.25 \times 16)^{\frac{1}{2}}$$

$$= (2496/4)^{\frac{1}{2}}$$

$$= 624^{\frac{1}{2}}$$

$$= 24.98 \text{ units}$$

Since we cannot order 0.98 of a unit, we can say the economic order quantity for this particular product is 25 units. The next problem is to establish the reorder point which is done as described above. Let us assume a 1-week replenishment lead time. Then there will be a demand of 6 working days at 2 units per day; therefore we will place an order for the EOQ whenever the inventory on hand reaches 12 units.

OBJECTIONS TO EOQ

There are many valid objections that can be made to the EOQ method developed above. Many of these or ramifications of them have already been looked at in the discussion of the advantages and disadvantages of the fixed order quantity method above.

The most important is that we depend on conditions of certainty. It is obvious from the derivation of the formula that we assume that demand over the reorder cycle is constant. In the application of the formula, and indeed in the arrival of the reorder point, we assume that the demand for the product is known. In the real situation, of course, this is very seldom the case. We also assume that there is no likelihood of the replenishment lead time varying, which again is very seldom so in the real world.

Again, we take it for granted that there will be available accurate figures for the costs of placing an order and carrying costs. As we have seen before, these two cost categories can have a fairly wide interpretation. All of this may be true but the case was made at the start of this section for the use of approximations in the inventory field. It is probably the wisest course to choose a range of estimates for the disputed values and to make the appropriate adjustments in the light of subsequent experience.

It is often said that a rigid adherence to the exact amount given by the application of the EOQ formula can result in a variety of inconvenient quantities being ordered over the entire range of products held. This is perfectly true, but again alterations can be made in the light of experience to reduce these inconveniences to the minimum. The last problem to be considered has already been dealt with as mentioned, namely that the use of an EOQ will result in orders being pushed through the system at varying times.

The question of uncertainty will be dealt with later. We will now turn to the derivation of the same critical points for a policy of fixed reorder interval operations. The formula for the fixed reorder period can, in fact, be arrived at from our original order quantity formlae as follows.

If we represent the number of orders which we need place over a given period of time as N, then if we can calculate the optimum number of orders placed we can derive the oprimum reorder period. We know that

$$Q = (2DS/IP)^{1/2}$$

and we can also say that N will equal D/Q, that is the optimum number of orders to be placed will equal the sales divided by the economic order quantity. Therefore we can proceed:

$$Q = (2DS/IP)^{1/2} \text{ and } N = D/Q$$
$$Q = D/N \text{ also } D/N = (2DS/IP)^{1/2}$$
$$D^2/N^2 = 2DS/IP$$
$$N^2 = D^2(IP)/2DS$$
$$N = (DIP/2S)^{1/2}$$

As long as we know the length of the period over which we must place this number of orders, normally a year, we can then calculate the reorder period. At the same time, however, we must also decide on the optimum order quantity if our system is to operate to its maximum effectiveness. This is based on the expected rate of demand between orders, that is to say EOQ is sales/number of orders made.

Let us look at our example again, only this time supposing that we are to operate on a fixed order period basis:

$$N = [DIP/2S]^{1/2}$$
$$= (624 \times 0.25 \times 16/2 \times 2)^{1/2}$$
$$= 624^{1/2}$$
$$= 24.98 \text{ times}$$

Thus, we would place an order for this product every $312/24.98 = 12.46$ business days, say 13. We now know the fixed order period over which we will operate, and we must determine the amount which we will order on each occasion:

$$Q = D/N$$
$$= 624/24.98$$
$$= \text{say 25 units}$$

Therefore, for this set of conditions, we will place an order for 25 units every 13 business days.

This is the situation, as we said earlier, in conditions of certainty. This proviso cannot be guaranteed in the real environment as indeed the opposite is usually the case. We must now attempt to introduce uncertainty into the formulae for deciding the amount to order and the time to place the order.

13 Control disciplines: conditions of uncertainty

While we will now look at uncertainty we must be careful to remember just exactly what we mean here. We do not mean complete randomness, for if we were to work up an approach to inventory trying to introduce an element of absolute randomness we would find it very expensive indeed. It must be assumed that the randomness effect is limited, i.e. we assume that future experience will resemble past and present experience. We find ourselves trying to predict probability of past experiences reoccurring rather than complete stabs in the dark at targets we have no way of knowing if we are likely to meet.

Bearing this in mind we move in the manner outlined below: First we establish from past knowledge the spread of the various variables we must handle, namely the range of demands and the variations in lead times. We must then try to estimate the likelihood of the same magnitudes from the past reoccurring in the future. If we do this we can arrive at an estimate of the costs involved. When we have accomplished this, two actions can be completed, we can revise (if required) our reordering quantities and our reorder points, and we can decide the costs involved if these actions were not carried out, i.e. we can examine the costs of customer service and decide at what level it should be set.

As always there is here the problem of accuracy and costs. Very often we find in textbooks on this subject extensive discussions of methods of calculating probabilities and costs. These are all accurate and correct as far as they go. But they usually have in common one disturbing feature that they tend to deal with the problem at the textbook level. This is not a criticism of the method of reducing problems to their simplest components, indeed extensive use has been made of the method throughout this volume. Rather it is an attempt to point out that while the method has great value, we must always be careful to draw the comparison between costs and effectiveness that was made at the very beginning of this section.

As will be shown below, it is very easy and relatively cheap in terms of time to illustrate the calculation of probabilities and costs for various demands when we can limit the product range to one or two types and where the past variations in demand have been slight. On this basis very accurate and sophisticated formulae can be built up to overcome the problems already mentioned above in the calculation of economic order quantities and reorder points. When the attempt is made to translate the same techniques to the real work environment it is not simply (as is the case in many situations) a slightly more complex form of the same method that must be used, but a vastly more complex and much more expensive technique.

This would be of little real importance if the benefits that could be expected from the extra expense would justify the outlay, but in many cases the costs of introducing the method and of continuing it do not produce proportionate results. Does this mean that we do nothing by way of trying to solve the problem of uncertainty? The answer is no, for two reasons. It is possible that the firm concerned may be large and that the processes mentioned above could simply be a small part of the utilisation programme for a computer complex justifying their cost in this manner. Or, alternatively, and the answer for the widest majority is that a compromise is reached.

In fact we return to that old law of inventory control where accuracy and sophistication are pushed to the point where diminishing returns set in. Let us now illustrate the general statements made above. The maximum accuracy approach will be dealt with first.

QUANTITIES AND PERIODS

It will be remembered that the simplified example we chose to look at for deciding EOQ and ROP has the following characteristics: that average demand was 2 units per working week and that the replenishment lead time was 7 days, that is under considerations of certainty. If we assumed that a firm with this demand and order patterns really did exist, then we would expect certainty to be rare. Remember, not impossible, only rare, for there are a surprising number of firms which do in fact have what can only be called a certain demand schedule. These would almost surely be suppliers of components to large consumers, e.g. a supplier of basic components to the car industry. They can be reasonably sure of long-term demand patterns very similar to those of the past; furthermore any likely changes in specifications are likely to be known well in advance. For the moment, however, we will assume that for our purposes that variations in demand and lead times are common. Let us suppose that if the firm's lead times for an 80-day period were that out of a total of 4 orders placed 2 arrived in the 7-day period and that 1 arrived in 6 days and 1 in 8 days. Let us also assume that demand over the same period was as shown in Exhibit 13.1. From this we can build up an

Exhibit 13.1

Demand	Units	Days	Frequency, %
0	0	10	12.50
1	5	5	6.30
2	80	40	50.00
3	75	25	31.20

occurrence table of probabilities thus:

Probability of demand for 0 units 0.125

1 unit	0.063
2 units	0.500
3 units	0.312
	1.000

What this says is that in the future the likelihood of the firm finding a day with a demand for 1 unit is approximately 6 out of every 100 times, and so on. We also know that there is a 50 per cent chance of a lead time of 7 days occurring and 25 per cent each for one of either 6 or 8 days.

From what we have said above it is obvious that we have taken the 80-day period as typical. Even if such a firm existed we would naturally like to see the same type of calculation performed on data for a much longer period; nonetheless the calculations would not be more difficult, only longer. We can take our analysis a step further. Suppose we wanted to calculate the probability of meeting a 6-day lead time followed by a weekly demand of 10 units, being composed of 5 days when the demand was 2 units and one when it was nil. It would be calculated as follows. The probability of meeting a demand for 2 units is 0.5 and the probability of meeting a demand for 0 units is 0.125, while the probability of meeting a lead time of 6 days is 0.25 since at the same time we have said that the basic pattern is of 5 days demand for 2 units and 1 of 0 units. There are 6 ways this might be satisfied, therefore the probability of such an event taking place is found by multiplying the individual probabilities concerned. Thus, probability of usage equal to the pattern we mentioned is:

$$6 \times 0.25 \times 0.125 \times 0.5 \times 5 = 0.46875$$

(or about 4 out of every 10 cycles). Again the possibility of meeting a 6-day lead time followed by a working week with zero units demanded is again the product of the individual events concerned:

$$0.25 \times 0.125 \times 0.125 \times 0.125 \times 0.125 \times 0.125 \times 0.125 = 0.0000009535$$

i.e. about 9 out of 10 million times.

Or again of meeting a 6-day lead time and a weekly demand of 1 unit: this could be achieved by a demand for 0 units on 5 days of the working week and 1 demanded on the sixth. There are six basic patterns this event could take thus:

$$6 \times 0.25 \times 0.063 \times 0.125 \times 0.125 \times 0.125 \times 0.125 \times 0.125 = 0.000002883$$

i.e. about 2 times out of a million.

This basic process of multiplying the individual probabilities and the pattern types can be carried on to give a complete range of probable demand chances from zero up to the maximum of 18 units (0.0002009 or about 2 in 10,000 times). A cumulative table can be constructed to give the probability of any demand week being less than any given figure. From this table it is possible to proceed to recalculate the formulae for our vital points in inventory control. We will examine the fixed order quantity method first or, as it is sometimes called, the fixed reorder point method. It should be obvious that one approach is available with little cal-culation. This is to look at the maximum possible demand and alter EOQ and ROP accordingly. If this was done then it would undoubtedly put the firm in a position of always being able to satisfy any demand made on it; that is service levels would be at 100 per cent. The decision here is uncomplicated: it is to decide if the costs involved in holding the extra inventory are made worthwhile by the extra profits received.

OPTIMUM ORDER QUANTITY UNDER UNCERTAIN CONDITIONS: FIXED ORDER QUANTITY

We have already said that it was extremely unrealistic to assume conditions of certainty. We must also remember that only a proportion of people who cannot be satisfied from stock will, in fact, go elsewhere for their purchase.

This is important when setting order quantities and reorder points under con-ditions of uncertainty. If everybody went elsewhere then the cost of not having 100 per cent service levels would be easy to calculate; they would simply be the margin on the lost sales. Since the normal situation has people prepared to wait, we must arrive at an estimate of the cost of running out of inventory. Under these conditions this can be related to probability of experiencing such situations and the decision regarding service levels is made more easy.

Heskett Ivie and Glaskowsky in *Business Logistics* developed the following formula to deal with the conditions outlined above:

$$EOQ = \{2D[S + xE(u > R)]/IP\}^{1/2}$$

where EOQ is the optimum order quantity, D the demand, I the inventory carry-ing cost, P the cost of unit inventory in question, S the incremental cost of placing an order and x the penalty of not satisfying an order (stockout cost). Unexpected excess of usage is associated with x; $u > R$ is the usage over reorder point.

The optimum reorder quantity is thus given by the square root of the factors introduced by uncertainty. The old formula for conditions of certainty was

$$EOQ = (2DS/IP)^{1/2}$$

What has been introduced are the costs associated with the probability of a stock-out occurring.

We must also arrive at an estimate of our reorder point. It is assumed that management will continue to add inventory until the point where the costs of adding another unit will equal the benefits from so doing. Let us look at the situation in Exhibit 13.2. It can be seen that as the number of units held increases the cost of adding successive units increases, while at the same time the costs arising out of stockouts will decrease. There is less chance of a stockout occurring because of the greater service levels. The two costs intersect and where they do so they will be equal. This is the optimum reorder point, hence the optimum safety stock and also the optimum service level over the replenishment lead time.

The costs of adding another unit of inventory will be the carrying costs times the price of the unit times the quantity ordered divided by the demand (the number actually used). i.e. IPQ/D.

The cost arising through a stockout will be the costs of the stockout times the probability of the situation happening, that is $P(u > R)x$. Therefore if we set

$$P(u > R)x = IPQ/D$$

we are describing the position when the cost of a stockout occurring equals the cost of adding another unit of inventory:

$$P(u > R)x = IPQ/D$$
$$P(u > R)x = IPQ/xD$$

When this is done we can calculate the value for IPQ/xD. This will give us our usage value which can be read from the $P(u)$ table that has been drawn up. This is our reorder point.

Using the method developed by Heskett Ivie and Glaskowsky we could now proceed to calculate our critical points as follows. Looking back at the past records of our firm we can arrive at an estimate for the stockout penalty (x). This will be made up of two broad types of costs — the cost of actually making the back order and the profit lost on the proportion of non-satisfied customers who go somewhere else to make their purchases. From the records we find that approximately 75 per cent of the customers go elsewhere and the cost of a back order is £3. Assume that the profit on the item in question is £4 then

$$x = 3 + 3 = \pounds 6$$

Using our original estimate under certain conditions for the value of Q, i.e. 25 units, we can proceed as follows. Remember what we are calculating is the point

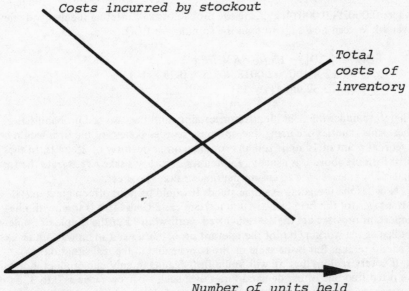

Exhibit 13.2

at which the cost of carrying an extra unit of inventory is equal to the probability times the cost of a stockout occurring, i.e. we will decide the level at which the cost involved with extra service levels is just worthwhile and no more. As above, this is given by the formula IPQ/xD. The period which we drew our figures for the example in probabilities from was a short one of 80 days, representing approximately 4 order periods from a possible of approximately 16. We must therefore make the same adjustment to our carrying costs in the final formula as below:

$$P(u) = IPQ/xD$$
$$= 0.25 \times 0.25 \times 16 \times 25/6 \times 80$$
$$= 0.02115$$

We would then turn to the cumulative table of probabilities that we had constructed as mentioned above and find the figure for usage, which would give us the value 0.02115.

What we are doing is saying that for the figures used in this example we will push service levels to the point where we will accept a stockout 2 times out of every thousand, or 98.8 per cent service levels. Let us assume that we have constructed our table and we find the value to be, say, 14.

The next step in the Heskett Ivie and Glaskowsky method is to find out the costs which would be incurred by setting out reorder point or safety stock at 14. This is done by calculating the cost obtained by the product for the stockout penalty and the probabilities of meeting demands greater than could be met with this safety stock level, i.e. demand from 14 up to the maximum possible of 18. Therefore:

$$\text{Excess cost} = 6[4(0.00020) + 3(0.00014) + 2(0.00016) + 1(0.00029)]$$
$$= 0.00183$$

where 0.00029, 0.00014, etc., are the probabilities of meeting the demand relevant over 14. We can now substitute in the formula for EOQ:

$$EOQ = \left\{ 2D[S + Ex\,(u > R)]\ /IP \right\}^{\frac{1}{2}}$$
$$= (2 \times 160 \times 2.00183/0.25 \times 0.25 \times 16)^{\frac{1}{2}}$$
$$= 25.32 \text{ units (say 25)}$$

Therefore under the conditions of uncertainty and the assumed probabilities of these uncertainties occurring, the optimum reorder policy for the firm would be a reorder point of 14 units and an economic order quantity of 25 units. In the final formula above it is usually required for accuracy's sake to reiterate the formulations at least once to ensure the final answer is correct.

Now, as the foregoing example stands it would seem to offer a great many advantages for the firm faced with uncertain conditions. This is true, with one important proviso: are the costs involved worthwhile? For the simple example we looked at the working out of the relevant probabilities and so on was not an extended exercise. But is the same method applicable to the real situation?

It is very seldom that we will find a firm dealing in only one product, nor will we often find one whose demand varies over such a narrow range as 0 to 3. As the numbers of products carried and the variations in demand extend, then so also does the calculation of the various probabilities become more complex. Further-

more the range of lead times was also extremely small in the example. It will be
noticed that the example was worked out for only one of the obtainable lead
time variations. To be more accurate the entire range should have been dealt with,
and then sub-class probabilities introduced between the range of lead times and
demand variations possible.

In other words as the scale of the problem is taken closer to what could reasonably be expected in a real situation, the method of calculating the probabilities
and so on required for a high degree of accuracy becomes very cumbersome. It
might easily fall into that category of techniques where diminishing returns set in
very early, unless electronic data processing equipment is available at low cost, in
which case there is no problem. Let us now look at a compromise method between the low cost but unrealistic conditions of the uncertainty method, and the
more realistic but cumbersome method described above.

The method here is not to look at the vast number of individual probability
calculations, but to deal with ranges of likely demands, i.e. in a more realistic
situation the demands being dealt with are not twos and threes but likely to be in
tens and hundreds. Since this is the case then the most simple method of dealing
with the question is to arrange the possible demands in ranges, as shown, for
example, in Exhibit 13.3.

Exhibit 13.3

Number of units per week	Frequency	Probability	Cumulative probability
40–50	3	0.05770	
30–40	12	0.23070	0.28840
20–30	20	0.38461	0.67301
10–20	14	0.26930	0.94231
0–10	3	0.05769	1.00000
	52	1.00000	

It is obvious that this approach is very much easier and simpler to put into
operation in a more realistic workload situation. It is not as accurate as the
method using all individual probabilities, but it is likely that the cost savings will
more than compensate for any minor errors here. The technique can be made
more accurate by narrowing the class interval used. In the example above a yearly
period has been used and naturally the longer the period that the data is based
on the more accurate the prediction. The method is used as before except that
when the reorder point and the stockout costs are being calculated the class
probability is used.

FIXED ORDER PERIOD

We will now examine the situation with regard to the fixed order period method

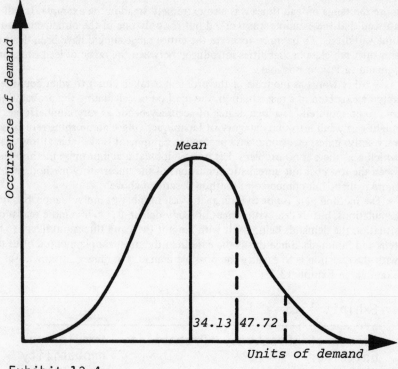

Exhibit 13.4

of control. In this discussion the first step in the development of a compromise solution will be made. If the demand occurrences for our previous example were to be plotted in the form of a graph then we would get the shape shown in Exhibit 13.4. This bell pattern is the normal distribution and is the one most commonly met with in the distribution function. It is not, needless to say, the only pattern. Binomial and Poisson distribution also frequently occur, but these also have certain characteristics similar to the ones which will be looked at in the normal distribution and these can be used in a like manner to that described below.

One of the most useful measures in the normal curve, at least for distribution control, is the standard deviation. In Exhibit 13.4 we have a normal distribution. The mean, as shown, will have 50 per cent of occurrences on one side and 50 per cent on the other. The standard deviation is a type of average measuring deviation from the mean. On the diagram the usefulness can be seen. The perpendiculars represent the mean and standard deviations. It will be seen that the mean +1 standard deviation will cover 84.13 per cent of the range of occurrences under the normal curve. This can be used in estimating the inventory levels required to service future demand, provided they keep to a normal distribution.

Very similar measures can be used in other distributions. For the standard deviation, tables are available to give the area (and hence the occurrence) that will come under any number of standard deviations.

For our purposes we are not really interested in the demand frequencies below the mean, only in those above the mean. That is, if we are going to use the standard deviation as a measure for helping us to forecast inventory levels we are not concerned with those demands below our inventory holding, only with those above it − the ones we might not be able to satisfy. With this in mind, examine the standard deviation again. It will be seen that if we take the arithmetic mean +1 standard deviation, we would be able to cover 84.13 of all demand likely to occur. This is composed of 50 per cent (arithmetic mean) + 34.13 (1 standard deviation). In the same manner, the mean +2 standard deviations would allow us to cover about 97 per cent of demand and the mean +3 standard deviations would allow us to cover 99 per cent of demand.

We can then say that if we kept a safety stock at any of the above combinations of arithmetic mean and standard deviation we would have set our service levels at the corresponding coverage of likely demand occurrences.

For quick reference some common combinations are given below. The service level given could be obtained by setting the reorder point at the mean plus the given number of standard deviations.

80 per cent service levels: arithmetic mean + 0.84 standard deviation
85 per cent service levels: arithmetic mean + 1.4 standard deviations
90 per cent service levels: arithmetic mean + 1.28 standard deviations
95 per cent service levels: arithmetic mean + 1.65 standard deviations

It should be noted that more accurate data can be obtained from the tables already mentioned, although for our purposes the accuracy is of doubtful value. Only in exceptional circumstances will any firm want to set its service levels at say 83 per cent (mean + 0.95 standard deviation).

In practice, the pre-setting of service levels will very often relieve the management of the distribution function from the task of calculating the key points we discussed earlier in any detail, because their reorder point is already set for them and the maintenance of this level becomes the most important target of the inventory function. The more competitive the industry, the more this will be the case.

If this is the situation, it is likely that the general management of the firm will be prepared to accept a cost for service levels other than the normal ones of carrying the extra inventory. These other costs are really penalty costs. They arise out of the extreme competitiveness of the industry forcing management to remove the economic order quantity and reorder interval factors developed when it was assumed that conditions were certain.

If we look back at the calculation of our reorder interval under certain conditions it will be noticed that the key factors included demand carrying costs and order costs. In the extreme conditions we are now looking at these might be ignored and service made paramount. If a management has said that they must have 95 per cent service levels for a particular market then it is up to distribution to provide this − once the costs have been pointed out and accepted. When this happens there is little difficulty in deciding the reorder interval. Suppose that it has been decided that service will be at the 95 per cent level and that for a particular market this arithmetic mean plus 1.65 standard deviations has a total of 200 units.

If we make the reorder point for our control system at 200 units, we are keeping a safety stock level of 200 units and this can be expected to meet 95 per cent of all demand made on us. In this set of circumstances the number of times we will place an order is simply the total expected demand divided by 200. If this was 2400/200 we would have to place an order 12 times a year or approximately every 26 days.

In this set of conditions everything has been subjected to the criterion of maintaining present service levels. Obviously this type of approach can result in higher costs being incurred for a given set of service levels than is absolutely necessary. We must try to develop a method between the very costly idea noted above and the other extreme which would once again involve us in extended probability calculations. The key to this method is standard deviation. The following discussion again uses the methods of Heskett Ivie and Glaskowsky.

It will be remembered that the chief benefits that can arise from the use of a fixed order period method of control are the standardisation of procedures used throughout the organisation, the opportunity for consolidation and so on. Let us assume that the situation is this, that because of the advantages that general management feels the firm can obtain for a movement towards standardisation of procedures distribution management in the firm we have been looking at all along is informed that in the future it will have to place an order every 20 days. This means that there are certain points in the old inventory control method (under conditions of certainty) that will have to be re-examined. The quantity that must be ordered now every 20 days will have to be enough to bring the level of stock on hand and on order to a quantity sufficient to provide the predetermined service level coverage during the period of 1 order level plus 1 order cycle. This is in fact the replenishment lead time for the fixed order period system.

Therefore the amount to be ordered at each order interval will be $Q = R - q$ where q is the amount on hand and on order before Q is decided and a new order placed, R being the reorder point at the beginning of the replenishment lead time.

As before we will continue to add inventory to our stock until the costs of providing the extra service was matched by the likelihood of a stockout occurring.

$$P(u > R) = IPQ/xD$$

But we know that $Q = D/N$. Therefore by substitution:

$$P(u > R) = IP/xN$$

We can then determine the quantity required on hand and on order (that is over the replenishment lead time) to meet average usage plus the number of standard deviations to meet the possibility that average usage might exceed the inventory on hand.

Let us look at a simple example of this compromise method. Let us assume that our order cycles are distributed as before, i.e. 50 per cent on 7 days, 25 per cent on 6 and 25 per cent on 8 days. Suppose that for reasons already discussed the distribution manager has been informed that he will place an order every 20 days, which gives him a replenishment lead time of 20 + 7 or 27 days.

We must now calculate the standard deviation of order cycles and demands (see Exhibit 13.5). The formula for so doing is standard deviation:

$$c[(\Sigma fd^2)/N]^{\frac{1}{2}}$$

where c is the class interval, f the frequency, d the deviation from the mean and
N the number of occurrences.

We have then a situation where the average replenishment lead time is 27 days, an order cycle of 7 days with a standard deviation of 0.707, and where the average demand is 2 units per day with a standard deviation of demand of 0.935. It can be shown that the deviation of demand during the replenishment lead time is equal to

$$[L_t(SD_t)^2 + d^2(SD_d)^2]^{1/2}$$

where L_t is the average replenishment lead time, SD_t is the standard deviation of order cycle, d is the average demand per day and SD_d is the standard deviation of daily demand. Thus:

$$[27(0.935)^2 + 2^2(0.707)^2]^{1/2}$$
$$= 5.05 \text{ units}$$

As pointed out by Heskett Ivie and Glaskowsky this can now be used to determine our key points. We have already decided the number of orders that must

Exhibit 13.5

(a) Order cycle

Days	Frequency	Deviation from mean d	d^2	fd^2
6	2	-1	1	2
7	4	0	0	0
8	2	1	1	2

$N = 8$ $\quad \Sigma(fd^2)$

Standard deviation $= c(fd^2/N)^{\frac{1}{2}} = 1(4/8)^{\frac{1}{2}} = 0.707$

(b) Demand

Units	Frequency	Deviation from mean d	d^2	fd^2
0	10	-2	4	40
1	5	-1	1	5
2	40	0	0	0
3	25	1	1	25

$\Sigma N = 80$ $\quad \Sigma(fd^2) = 70$

Standard deviation $= c(fd^2/N)^{\frac{1}{2}} = 1(70/80)^{\frac{1}{2}} = 0.935$

be placed. What we have been calculating above is the adjustment in terms of units that must be made to reorder points and reorder quantities to take account of the directive that has been given by general management, namely that an order will be placed every 20 days. The period which we have been taking all our figures from is an 80-day one, and the number of orders that would be placed in that time would be 4. Using our values employed in the calculation for the fixed order period points under conditions of uncertainty we can substitute in the equation:

$$P(u > R) = IP/xN$$
$$= 0.25 \times 0.25 \times 16/6 \times 4$$
$$= 0.0411$$

This is in fact the ideal point at which to set our service levels for our assumed conditions. If we are to allow a stockout on only 4.12 per cent of occasions we must add to our average demand the complementary amount to make sure that we always have enough inventory on hand to meet the 45.8 per cent of the demands that will exceed average demand. We must look up the standard tables available giving areas under the normal curve to find the corresponding value for the 45.8 level; this is 1.73 standard deviations.

Therefore to the average demand expected we must add 1.73 standard deviations, thus bringing the stock held in safety (reorder point) up to the required level:

$$R = u + 1.73 \text{ standard deviations}$$
$$= (27 \times 2) + (1.73 \times 5.05)$$
$$= \text{say 63 units}$$

If at the beginning of a particular order interval the amount on hand is, say, 12 units then the quantity ordered is $63 - 12 = 51$ units. Or, using the formulation developed earlier:

$$Q = R - q$$

It can be seen that the above method, if dealing with the direct selling of a fixed reorder period, is a compromise. The elements that have been introduced making it different from the simple method first discussed, chiefly in a question of degree. In the basic method everything was sacrificed to the maintenance of a given service level. This had been set by general management, probably with little reference to the distribution costs involved, hence the mention earlier of penalty costs. In the second more detailed method this situation had changed.

What has been set this time was not service levels but the length of the reorder period. What was then done was to try to calculate the optimum service level under the conditions of existing known variations in demand and order cycles. This was completed by setting the service level at the point where the probability of a stockout equalled the cost of maintaining the related level of inventory. Once this is done, a compromise probability is reached, i.e. instead of calculating each individual probability as was done for the fixed order quantity example, a normal distribution was assumed and the standard deviation measure used to give us the size of the reorder point corresponding to the calculated optimum service level.

There can be little doubt that the second method would prove the more accurate. Moreover through the use of compromise measure instead of individual probabilities it is not too involved for easy application in a realistic situation. There is, however, one major objection to this method of tackling the problem; it depends on the distribution management being free to set customer service levels at the 'money optimum' point. This can very often not be the real situation, and where not, then the old method involving penalty costs, or assuming conditions of certainty (then compromising on the results obtained), will probably be employed.

Throughout this discussion of the major points of an inventory policy under conditions of uncertainty one element has consistently been of major interest, namely the service levels to be met. The basis of the techniques examined above has always been the setting of the probability costs of a stockout equal to the cost of carrying an extra unit of the inventory.

Throughout the function of distribution in the real work environment it is extremely likely that the questions of service levels will be of the greatest importance to management. At the same time it is also likely to cause an unreasonable amount of conflict with the other areas of management on this side of the firm's business, namely sales and marketing.

This conflict has already been examined, but at this point the attention is to focus interest on the costs involved. It is usually through lack of knowledge of these costs that the original problem arises. It is not at all common to find that the sales and marketing side of the firm will set a service level which they feel will result in a better performance by the firm in its markets. Nobody would disagree that high service levels are a desirable objective, but very often the levels that are set bear little relation to the profits coming from the increase in performance. Management outside distribution often holds the opinion that the unit costs involved will decrease with increases in the volume passing through the network. We have already seen that this is a valid assumption for only a few of the total costs involved, as some will increase. We are not saying that the service levels set must be dictated by distribution effectiveness, but we are saying that when the economic levels are to be bypassed then the management responsible for this decision must be fully aware of the true costs incurred.

In the course of the development of the formulations under conditions of uncertainty, the optimum service level is automatically built into the operating points developed, but to illustrate the importance of the concept let us look at an example under the following conditions: that any customer not satisfied from stock will go elsewhere, that a good forecast of total demand is available, but its incidence is not known and finally that normal distribution is present. We will also suppose that inventory carrying costs are 25 per cent of item cost and that each unit costs £100; further we assume a profit margin of 1 per cent. If the latter figure seems low, it is not at all uncommon in certain areas of distribution and, for example, the wholesaler with this margin is not rare.

Exhibit 13.6 gives the information we have available. The formula for the calculation of the standard deviation was

$$SD = c(fd^2/N)^{1/2}$$

where f is the frequency of the various demands, d the deviations of the demands from the mean and N the total number of frequencies. Substituting, we have:

Demand	Frequency	Total demand	Deviation d	fd^2
100	1	100	−6	36
200	2	400	−5	50
300	3	900	−4	48
400	4	1600	−3	36
500	5	2500	−2	20
600	6	3600	−1	6
700	10	7000	0	0
800	6	4800	1	6
900	5	4500	2	20
1000	4	4000	3	36
1100	3	3300	4	48
1200	2	2400	5	50
1300	1	1300	6	36
Totals	52	36400		392

$$SD = 100 (392/52)^{1/2}$$
$$= 275$$

Now that we know the standard deviation of demand for our occurrences we can look at the effect of the various service levels that can be decided upon.

Let us look at the situation where the general management decided that an 80 per cent service level is desirable for this firm, and this product. To reach this level it will be remembered that the safety stock required is the average usage plus 0.84 standard deviation. This will be 700 + 0.84(275) or 231 units must be added to average usage. Let us examine the effect that this would have, assuming that in the past average demand was carried allowing approximately 50 per cent service levels, and a sales figure (at cost) of £1,820,000 (18,200 units).

By increasing the service level to 80 per cent there is naturally an increase in sales from the figure above to £2,912,000 (29,120 units), i.e. there has been an increase of some £1,092,000. To achieve this increase we have had to add to inventory an extra 231 units at a cost of £23,100. Since the carrying costs have already been decided to be 25 per cent the extra cost burden of these units is 0.25 (23,100) or £5,775. Now let us return to our sales cost figure, which was an increase of £1,092,000. There is a mark-up of 1 per cent therefore the incremental profit is £10,920. To reach the true profit figure we must subtract the extra cost of inventory − £5775. Therefore the true increase in profit is £5145. This is fine and there is little doubt that the policy of increasing service levels has paid off. This success might tempt further increases in service levels. Suppose that the level of 90 per cent is decided upon. To reach this level we must add to our average demand 1.28 standard deviations, i.e. 1.28(275) or 351 units. This is 351 − 231 or 120 units greater than that required for the 80 per cent service level; thus the extra cost for the 90 per cent service levels is £12,000. At the 90 per cent service level there will be another increase in sales to 32,760 units or 3,276,000 at cost. Therefore there has been an increase in sales of £3,276,000 − 2,912,000 or some £364,000; remembering our mark-up of 1 per cent this gives us an apparent profit of £3640. To achieve this we have had to carry an extra £12,000 of inventory that costs 25 per cent or £3000 therefore the true profit is £640, still an increase. What would the position be if we moved to 95 per cent service levels? This would mean adding 1.65(275) to our average usage of 453 units, i.e. 453 − 351 or 102 units greater than that required for the 90 per cent service level. The extra cost is £10,200. At this service level the sales achieved would be £2,458,000 (at cost). With our 1 per cent mark-up on the increase in sales the apparent profit is £1820. But to achieve this we have to carry £10,200 extra inventory at 25 per cent or at a cost of £2550. Therefore if this firm took its service level to 95 per cent the result would be an overall loss of £730. If it were to be taken higher the result would be a great proportionate loss. The example above is oversimplified but it serves its purpose, namely to point out that increased sales through increases in the service level of the firm will not always result in related increases in profits. In the real situation, of course, it is unlikely that there will be such steep diminishing returns except under special circumstances, such as very wide fluctuations in demand. The important point is that when distribution management has set

$$P(u > R) = IPQ/xD$$

then this is the optimum reorder point, hence the optimum safety stock and from this the optimum service level. This figure will give the level of inventory which if adhered to will allow the firm to satisfy that part of its demands which will prove the most profitable − although, as pointed out several times, other considerations might overrule this decision. If this happens then distribution management must construct an example similar to the one above to calculate the penalty costs as above. This would be tackled in the following manner. Firstly a list of all possible reorder points is drawn up, then the service levels associated with these points are calculated. This might be obtained from the probability calculations that might have already been completed. Additional inventory which might be required for these various service levels is calculated. The relative carrying charge is obtained and noted. Then the cost of the lost sales is calculated. This time we cannot assume that the unsatisfied customers will all go elsewhere, unless, of course, this is the actual situation. This is completed in the same manner as when calculating the fixed order quantity under conditions of uncertainty. The total costs, i.e. the extra carrying costs and the costs of lost sales, are then totalled and this is subtracted from the apparent profit. If this procedure is carried out then at least the other areas of management will have the true costs for their service level decisions before them.

To sum up, the inventory function is extremely important for the efficient operation of the distribution network. A great many control disciplines are available to management in this area. They are, however, likely to be expensive if applied to all items carried by the firm. The first step is then to see if the product range under consideration shows a marked tendency to the ABC type of breakdown. If this is in fact true then make the delineations required by the methods described. Once this has been completed and the break points between the classes proved satisfactory the next step can begin. Any possibility of savings through simple changes in routines must be investigated first. The role of in-transit inventories and the effect that clerical procedures can have on the investment here must not be overlooked. Lengthening or cutting the reorder cycles of the various classes must also be examined.

If this has been done then greater attention can be paid to the A class items. The more accurate forms of controls described can be introduced, for all or a few of this type of item. Individual circumstances can be easily met by alterations and combinations of the basic control disciplines described. The most important thing to remember in inventory control is that very often extreme accuracy is not worthwhile in terms of return for expenditure. The cost of maintaining a control system must never outweigh the benefits that are being received from the method.

Part 3

WAREHOUSING

14 The location of fixed facilities

The problem of selecting the location for fixed facilities, be they for production or distribution, is one of the most important for the future cost structure of the firm. In spite of this, locational studies have long laboured under many difficulties. One of the most influential of these factors has been attitude. It is possible to classify attitudes to location into two broad areas: industrial managers and the quasi-academic. The first of these developed over a long period with its roots steeped in 'experience' and to a certain degree apathy. The second approach really has come about through the interaction of the purely theoretical approach and the growing liaison between the more realistically bent academics and the more aware industrial managers. It is, in short, characterised by attempts to modify theoretical ideas with practical requirements.

In the past there has been little evidence from industry that more than a very few were interested in optimising the locational decision. This is exemplified by the remark made by W.F. Luttrell in *Factory Movement and Industrial Location* that he 'would have liked to have given an example of a classic case of location choice in which operating cost estimates were made for two or more places, all imponderables or non-cost factors assessed and then a way found for comparing the good and bad points of one place with those of another. Unfortunately we have not been able to find such a case.' A remark of this nature as a result of what was, most likely, the most comprehensive studies of locational decisions undertaken in the United Kingdom is to say the least unpromising. This survey was carried out in the fifties, however, and the situation has improved since then, but there is little doubt that the kind of attitude met with still exists. One of the main reasons why this is so is the fact that many firms in this country have grown, not so much through a policy of internal growth, but through takeover and merger. The economic reasons behind this do not concern us here, but what does are the possible consequences for distribution and transport. The major consideration here is that the new company is faced with an already existing distribution network and there is little scope for variation and improvement, except in new markets. In many cases management have been more pre-occupied with other areas of activity such as production marketing and finance, and for most managers in this country the locational decision is usually thrust upon them by negative forces, e.g. government, rather than by a concientious desire to move to improve operational effectiveness. Thankfully, however, this attitude is changing and more and more managers are taking a much more positive approach to the effect of location on total performance. This is, of course, especially true with regard to the location of distribution facilities.

It is to the economic theorists that we must turn for further discussions on the relationship between methods of locational decision-taking and what industry seems to do in practice. Luttrell believed that the lack of attention was due to the difficulty in measuring non-cost attributes of alternative sites, and the fact that the choice of location did not seem to be the crucial decider on the success of the firm. This, it was felt, was due more to the way a new factory was operated rather than where it was operated. There also appeared to be a strong school of thought that within the UK most industries were of the footloose type, i.e. operating costs were not substantially different in any of the major industrial areas. This idea received some backing. The Toothill Report on the Scottish Economy made a great deal of the results of a survey which they carried out among firms who had moved to Scotland. The aim was to gather information regarding increased operating costs which firms had experienced as a result of the move. The majority said that these had increased by 2% or less. Since most economic theories concerning location lean heavily on the influence of transport costs, then this result and more like it tended to confirm for many people that by and large almost any location will do. This resulted in much greater weight being given to non-transport-related factors such as labour relations. This situation was changing even in the fifties for whilst on the one hand some studies seemed to show a predominance of footloose industries in the UK, many of these self-same industries were complaining of government regional policies which they said were forcing them to locate in high-cost areas. The reason given as to why the firms saw their possible new locations as high cost was often said to be distance from the market. This apparent confusion was an important influence in developing the modern attitude to the location problem — one where investigative techniques and model building are given as much if not more credence than hunches, or regional likes or dislikes. This is especially so in the location of distribution facilities where it is often possible to build a cost model of the system under consideration and take a decision on this basis. This approach can often be adapted for productive locations and, coupled with regional analysis, can provide a very comprehensive aid to management.

This is not to suggest that all the risk and argument has been taken from this particular area of management activity — far from it; indeed there are some people who maintain that the process has simply become more jargonised and the real decision will be most influenced by the sporting predilictions of the managing director.

THEORIES OF LOCATIONAL FORCES

The first attempts at producing theories dealing with the locational decision are bound up with the names of Johann Heinrich Von Thunen in the late nineteenth century and Alfred Weber in the early twentieth. It is usual to refer to Von Thunen and Weber as belonging to the least-cost school. They were characterised

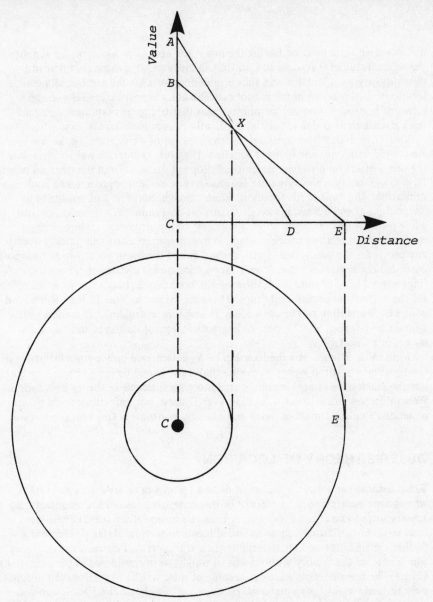

Exhibit 14.1 Von Thunen's Rings. If there are two crops,
A - turnips and B - wheat, and C represents the city
demand, then near the city turnips yield CA and wheat
CB; CA>CB. As the distance from the city increases,
turnips become less attractive. Higher transport costs
for turnips make AD steeper than BE. At X transport
costs have absorbed the value advantage and from X on
wheat becomes the more attractive crop. The same reasoning
can be applied to manufactured products, AD and BE being
known as the net profit/distance gradients. The steeper
the gradient, the less able is the product with higher
transport costs to bear manufacture away from the centre
of demand

by the search for a location having the minimum cost of production. To simplify the original studies it is usual to find that an assumption is made that demand does not vary with location and that production costs are the same at all possible locations. This resulted in the school concentrating almost exclusively on the effect of transport. Another assumption was that transport costs were constant for a given weight and that they were directly proportional to distance.

Von Thunen based his approach on the concept of a city state, i.e. he was concerned with only one demand location. His primary interest was to formulate the likely effect on different agricultural crops of distance from the demand point. He was in fact arguably laying the foundations of modern approaches to land utilisation. The basis of his theory is simple enough. Since he had assumed one demand point and a constant weight/transport cost ratio, then those crops with a low price/weight ratio will be grown closest to the city because since their market price in relation to their weight is low, transport costs will quickly absorb any profit for the cultivators if they move beyond the break point where transport costs just equal market value. Von Thunen constructed a series of concentric rings around his city state, each showing the boundary between the areas suitable for the cultivation of different crops. These are known as Von Thunen Rings, and with a little adaption can be used today in assisting in deciding the market boundaries between warehouses. A diagramatic representation of the theory is shown in Exhibit 14.1.

Whilst Von Thunen saw the location being determined only by the influence of transport costs, Alfred Weber envisaged that these would be joined by labour costs and the economies of agglomeration in a more comprehensive theory of location. Weber deserves greater discussion than Von Thunen, but unfortunately in practice, he tended to place almost as much emphasis on transport costs as his predecessor.

WEBER'S THEORY OF LOCATION

Weber assumed an infinite number of demand points in an area with a constant weight distance transport cost. Some of the materials required for manufacturing activity were to be found everywhere. These he termed ubiquities. Others were local in their distribution; these he called localised factors. Materials received a further classification to help determine their transport cost characteristics. Those which entered the factory without loss of weight were considered as pure materials. Others, like raw materials which gave some of their weight to the finished product, were termed weight-losing material. He then used this basic classification in conjunction with his assumption on transport costs to explain the choice of location for a firm somewhere between the source of a localised raw material and its final market. Today we tend to use a similar classification when speaking in broad terms of location. Thus a raw-material-oriented firm would be one where the chief product tends to require weight-losing materials and we would normally expect to find that such a company feels its raw material (or a good port location for its importation) as exerting more pull than its market. There would be little point in paying transport costs for our raw material when some of its weight was going to disappear in manufacture. In the same vein we can refer to market-oriented companies where the pull of the market is greater — or indeed to footloose firms the use of ubiquities to a large extent is assumed and where location can be almost anywhere provided basic utilities are present. These choices are best seen in a

Exhibit 14.2 Weber's problems   *207*

Type	Type and location of raw materials	Pull on production location
A	*Localised pure*	*RM* ← *No opt.* → *MK*
B	*Ubiquities*	*MK*
C	*Localised pure + ubiquities*	*MK*
D	*Localised weight-losing*	*RM*
E	*Localised pure + localised weight-losing + weight-losing ubiquities*	*RM*

formalised list as in Exhibit 14.2 where we move from the position where the firm under examination is faced with the simplest problem from Weber, i.e. uses only localised pure materials to the situation where it is faced with localised pure plus localised weight losers plus weight-losing ubiquities.

If we look at Firm A, then since it is using only pure materials, the relative weight of the materials in the finished product will be the same as for the movement of materials to the production point. Since we have assumed a constant weight distance transport cost then neither the source of the materials nor the market will have the decisive pull on location. There will be no optimum location since the total distance to be travelled will always be the same and consequently total transport costs will be the same.

Firm D is in a different situation. Here we are using localised inputs but this time they are weight-losing. In this situation we would expect the source of materials to have a stronger pull than the market. The reasons are obvious: since the transport rate will be less for the processed material than for the raw, location as close as possible to its source will reduce total transport costs. Remember, it is assumed that we are faced with constant weight distance costs, i.e. for a given weight the cost will be proportional to distance of movement. Thus weight is the chief variable factor with relation to costs.

Company B utilises ubiquities. It does not matter if they are pure or weight-losing. The effect here is again to pull towards the market. If they are not weight-losing the firm will try to reduce its transport costs to a minimum. This can best be done by locating at the market. Since the firm uses ubiquities these are available everywhere. Likewise if they are weight-losing, location will still be at the market since the materials will be available there anyway.

Next we have localised pure plus pure or weight-losing ubiquities. The pull of the market is the strongest here.

Finally we have Firm E where we have localised pure, localised weight-losing plus ubiquities. This particular combination is the one closest to the real situation. The net effect in this situation may vary. If the ubiquities are weight-losing then if this is more than counterbalanced by the proportion of weight-losing locals there will be a pull to the source of the weight-losing material. If on the other hand the weight-losing ubiquities are used in much greater proportions than the local weight-losing material there may be a case for moving closer to the market. The relative cost of moving small amounts of weight-losing local material plus the local pure material to the location where the very large quantities of ubiquities and the market are to be found is less. If in this situation we located at the source of local weight-losers then we would simply be paying for the transport of greater weights of material (the ubiquity) to a market where they could be found and used anyway. From this it can be seen that ubiquities only play a part in the locational decision insofar as they enter into the weight of the finished product. Some ubiquities do not, of course, do this on many occasions. Think for example of fuel or power. These are available at all major industrial locations in the United Kingdom.

From the simple example discussed above it will be obvious that in Weber's theory the really important factor is the relative weights of the raw materials used and the finished product.

To allow an attempt at more rigid treatment of this fact he formulated the 'material index'. This was the ratio of the weight of localised raw material to the weight of the finished product. From this he laid down three general propositions. First, that those industries with a material index of less than 1 will be located at the market. Given our examples above this is fairly obvious. In this case there is less proportionate weight to be moved to the point of production at the market. If we did not produce at the market then we would be moving greater weights longer distances. Secondly, pure materials will not exert a decisive pull to these locations. If the material is not going to experience a change in transport cost at any location, why move towards it? Thirdly, weight-losing materials may pull firms to their locations if the material index is more than 1 and their share of the index is at least equal to the other materials plus the weight of the finished product. This is the situation described for Firm E above.

To apply his theory Weber envisaged a triangular situation with two sources of raw material and one market. An example of this situation is shown in Exhibit 14.3. To show how the theory is applied we will assume that the following weight situations exist. In the case of Firm 1, the raw material weight per weight unit of finished product coming from source *a* is 4 units, from source *b*, 2 units, and the weight of the finished product per unit is 0.5 unit. Then we can say that the materials index is 12, i.e. $(4+2)/0.5$. If we apply the three basic propositions then it is obvious that for this company a location at the market is not desirable, the material index being well in excess of 1. The next step is to see which raw material is capable of exerting the greater pull. The three propositions can help solve this. The third pointed out that a localised material could influence location if the index was greater than 1 and that its portion was greater than the remainder plus the weight of the product. To apply this here we calculate location weights for each source. These are simply the ratios of localised weights to finished product for each source. For material *a* it is $8(4/0.5)$ and for *b* it is $4(2/0.5)$. The location weight for the raw material will always be 1. Since 8 is greater than $4+1$ then raw material source *a* will exert the greatest influence over the choice of location.

If we examine the conditions of the second firm, a similar set of calculations

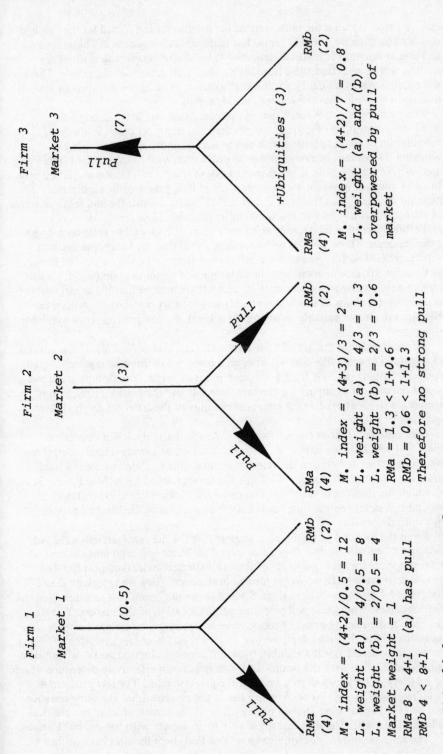

Exhibit 14.3 Weber's transfer costs

Firm 1 — Market 1

(0.5)

RMa (4)   RMb (2)

Pull

M. index = (4+2)/0.5 = 12
L. weight (a) = 4/0.5 = 8
L. weight (b) = 2/0.5 = 4
Market weight = 1
RMa 8 > 4+1 (a) has pull
RMb 4 < 8+1

Firm 2 — Market 2

(3)

RMa (4)   RMb (2)

Pull   Pull

M. index = (4+3)/3 = 2
L. weight (a) = 4/3 = 1.3
L. weight (b) = 2/3 = 0.6
RMa = 1.3 < 1+0.6
RMb = 0.6 < 1+1.3
Therefore no strong pull

Firm 3 — Market 3

(7)

Pull

RMa (4)   RMb (2)

+Ubiquities (3)

M. index = (4+2)/7 = 0.8
L. weight (a) and (b)
overpowered by pull of
market

may be made. Assume the same weights for products *a* and *b*, and let the finished product this time be 3 weight units. The materials index is now 2. Therefore a location at the market is still undesirable. If locational weight calculations are made it will be seen that there is no overbearing pull present at either side. There will be, however, a tendency for the best location to be in the direction of raw material *a* since this has the greater individual pull.

Many objections to Weber's theories can be raised, not least amongst them being the assumption of uniform weight distance transport costs. In the basic formulation of his propositions this can be accommodated quite simply by weighing the content of raw materials in proportion to the real transport rates applying. In other words, if the transport rates for one individual material are, say, twice as much as those for another, then the pulling power of this individual material increases by a factor of 2 over and above its weight; the end result in terms of attraction with regard to locational influences should be the same.

Before examining the realism of Weber's ideas, it is as well to refer back to his basic concepts. These were, it will be remembered, that the locational decision will be decided with regard to three influences: transport costs (which we have just examined), labour costs, and the economics of agglomeration (which we can look at as including area economies of scale). If we assume that the actual costs of production (in terms of fuel and material) will not vary significantly within the UK, then the major variable to be considered is that given pre-eminence by Weber – labour.

To accommodate this set of basic circumstances, Weber formulated the concept of *isotims*. These are like contour lines on a map, but in this case represent equal cost of transport per unit from a common point of origin. The isotims are drawn round the sources of supply for the raw materials and the market. Each isotim represents an identical cost for transport per unit to the areas cut by the line in question.

Given the fact that as far as transport costs for raw materials are concerned there will be a location where the different costs are at a mutual minimum, then we can select a site between the relevant isotims which would represent a minimum cost location. In Exhibit 14.4 this site is represented by A. M is the market to which the finished product must be delivered. Isotims can also be drawn around this point representing equal cost of movement of the finished product out from the market.

From the location of minimum transport cost for the raw materials a second category of equal-cost lines may be constructed. These will represent the cost of total transport for unit quantities of the raw materials concerned plus finished products to market. These Weber termed *isodapanes*. They are represented in Exhibit 14.4 by the unbroken lines. Since A is the minimum cost location then the first isodapane from there will pass through the location of the market. To take account of the already-assumed major variable (labour) then we must assume other locations within the areas depicted that can show different labour costs.

As can be seen from the Exhibit, these differing 'production costs', when taken into consideration with the isotims and isodapanes, can effectively determine which of a variety of locations should be given the greatest value. The real problem is what relevance, if any, Weber's theory has at the present time. The same question can be asked about Von Thunen or any other of the contributors to the classical school of thought. The short answer is very little, except with some modifications.

The most important contribution has been that these theories have formed a

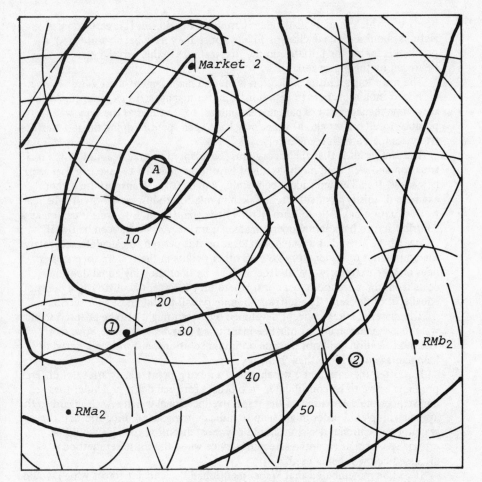

Exhibit 14.4 Weber isotims/isodapanes. Represents Firm
2; - - - isotims, ———— isodapanes. The isotim gives
equal costs of transport for raw materials from locations
RMa_2 and RMb_2 and for finished product from market 2.
A is the point of minimum transport costs. The isodapanes
give the equal costs of transport for raw materials to A
and finished products from A.

Assume two other possible production points ① and ②.
Because of regional differences the cost/unit produced at
② is 15 units less than A and at ① 22 money units less
than at A. On comparing costs:

Cost per unit at ① = 30 − 22 = 8
Cost per unit at ② = 50 − 15 = 35
Cost per unit at A = 10

Therefore ① is 27 units cheaper overall than ② and 2
units cheaper overall than A. Therefore the best location,
taking account of total transport costs and labour variations, is at ①

base from which more realistic ideas have been developed. It is easy to raise objections about and make changes to ideas once they have been formulated; the problem is taking the initiative in the first instance — this was the main benefit bestowed by these pioneers.

The most important qualification is that no management theory ever can be, or indeed should purport to be a substitute for management experience. At the same time management experience should not be regarded as the only way to produce results; after all, 40 years may have been spent in doing the job ineffectively compared with competitors.

The end result is that the theory must be adapted to take account of the real situation and well used methods might have to be changed to take cognisance of new ideas. Von Thunen's ideas concerning equal cost of transport are a good example of this type of situation. Taken in relation to his overall theory the real work situation has little to learn. With a little adaptation, however, it can make a contribution to help actual operating management. As will be seen below, if once we have arrived at a warehouse location it is desired to calculate accurately the boundaries of its territory *vis-a-vis* other depots in the system then *isocost* lines may be extremely useful. Isocost lines are lines showing equal delivered costs from the warehouse locations. Where they intercept is obviously a point of equal cost of delivery. The territory boundary will follow these intersections.

The material index concept developed by Weber might also be adapted to aid warehouse management. It must be mentioned that *aid* is the operative word. The modifications will not provide optimum solutions, but they will certainly help management more than 'hunches'.

It is often the case that a warehouse is a mixing point, i.e. a variety of different products arrive to be consolidated into orders for final delivery. Under these circumstances the calculation of the respective locational weights with regard to the average completed order might help to indicate the general direction that the warehouse locational decision should pay most attention to. This would be especially useful as an initial screening device when the finite set method discussed below is being used.

It will be remembered that Weber mentioned three major forces which would be likely to be of major importance in the location of fixed facilities: transport costs, labour costs and the economies of agglomeration. The first two have already been dealt with and we must now turn our attention to the economies of agglomeration. These are met with frequently in economic discussion and are often referred to as external economies of scale. It is a generally accepted proposition that, for the individual firm in most forms of production, one variation or another of a U-shaped long-term unit cost curve is experienced. That is to say there are economies of scale at least to a certain level of output. The idea of external economies of scale rests on the concept that a large number of individual firms locating in the same geographical area may all experience certain cost reductions. The usual examples quoted include factors like ancillary industries being set up to satisfy large consumers. If the major producers of a particular industry are located in a relatively small area then subsidiary suppliers will also tend to locate there. Witness the components supply situation for the car industry in the Midlands as opposed to say Scotland. There may also be savings in communications and flexibility can be higher. Thus if a short local trip to your supplier is all that is required, less time is spent on contact and modifications may be easier to negotiate. A pool of labour skilled in the traditional trade of the area may grow up and this in itself is a substantial benefit.

If any or all of these external economies develop then they will naturally exert an additional attraction for any firm over and above labour and transport costs. They were never treated in a rigorous manner by Weber. In the application of his theories the essential point would seem to have been that once a particular site had been chosen on a preliminary basis, then a further examination would have to be carried out to determine whether or not such economies could be achieved elsewhere and if so how significant were they likely to be. If, between the various equal cost lines, such a site existed such that it did not represent a significant increase in the major costs so represented, then a move to that location should be made forthwith. If on the other hand such a move would mean crossing an equal cost line to a higher-cost location then the problem was different. Under such circumstances the move would be made only if the external economies of scale likely to be attained outweighed the increase of costs in question.

A more basic objection than those mentioned above can be levelled against the minimum-cost school of thought. This is that they are, without exception and indeed by definition, all cost-oriented. This will be justified only when the location of the facilities has no effect on the level of demand experienced for their product. This is obviously a very exceptional circumstance. A body of economic thought grew up to counter this flaw. This tended to concentrate to a very large extent on the belief that within a specific local area firms have a degree of monopoly power. These lines of thought tend to take their inspiration from the theories of imperfect competition, i.e. where individual firms can influence market size, price and supply. As always, however, these new lines of thought tended to overconcentrate on the area that they felt had been ignored in the theories they set out to reform. This results in market-oriented approaches that almost ignore the cost aspects.

The concept behind these schools of thought can be stated as the proposition that the extent of any firms market, in terms of share of sales, will be dependant on only two factors: factory price and transport costs. They therefore assume that production costs are the same throughout the geographical area under consideration and that all companies sell on FOB terms, i.e. all customers pay the same base price and then bear the cost of transport themselves. This is a very restrictive condition, but one must remember that all of these theories have such conditions attached. This particular one is in some cases not far removed from the real world as some industries do in fact adopt a base pricing system. The EEC insists for example that such an approach be used with regard to the steel industry.

Given the basic assumption the theory goes on to develop rules for calculating the extremities of the individual markets for competing firms. From the above discussion it will be obvious that boundaries between firms will occur when the cost of transport and market price are equal. Consider two firms, A and B. Their costs to consumers is a function of the market price and the transport rate to the point of consumption. In one market the price is P_1 and in the other P_2. The transport rates for firms A and B are R_1 and R_2, respectively, per unit of distance moved. If X is the customer location, D_1 the distance from A to X and D_2 the distance from B to X, and since we have said that the cost to consumers will depend on market price and transport costs, the boundary between the two markets will be where the prices are equal, i.e. where

$$(P_1 + R_1 D_1) = (P_2 + R_2 D_2)$$

214

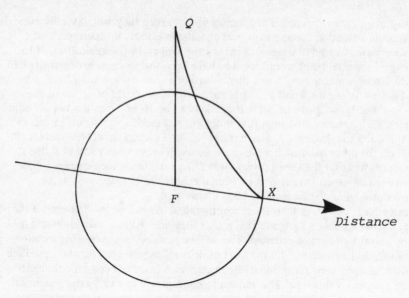

Exhibit 14.5 Losch demand cone

It will be seen that when $P_1 = P_2$ and $R_1 = R_2$ then the only variable left is the shifting distance between the plants and the point of consumption. Given that the market boundary will be found where the above conditions are satisfied, the boundary is thus at the mid-point of a straight line joining the two plants.

The influence of variations in transport rates on the market boundary can be easily illustrated from the foregoing, as can that of price movements. Suppose, for example, that firm A managed to reduce the FOB price from 50 to 40 units. Since it was assumed initially that FOB prices were the same then this would give firm A extended penetration of B's market. If transport rates were assumed to be, say, 2 money units per mile, since there has now been a drop in A's favour its products can move a further 5 miles before prices to consumer would again be equal: $40 + (5 \times 2) = 50$. In the same way the negotiation of favourable transport rates can allow greater penetration of a rival's area. (Remember we are talking about market area in terms of share of sales.)

In general terms it can be seen that the market area becomes greater with increases in the ratio Pa/Tr, where Pa is the price advantage of the firm lowering prices over the competitor and Tr is the transport rate of the competitor. Thus price advantages can be offset by more favourable transport rates on the side of the competitor. Market size will vary directly with FOB price and inversely with transport rates.

The propositions available from this school of thought can be summed up by saying that producers may extend markets by either price advantages or cheaper transport rates, and the market can be extended until price plus transport costs between competitors are equal.

The most important disciple emerging from this general background was Losch who developed his ideas in Germany and the United States. Since he was interested chiefly in the market aspects of location he removed the problems of production factors by the economist's favourite method of dealing with complicating factors – he assumed them away.

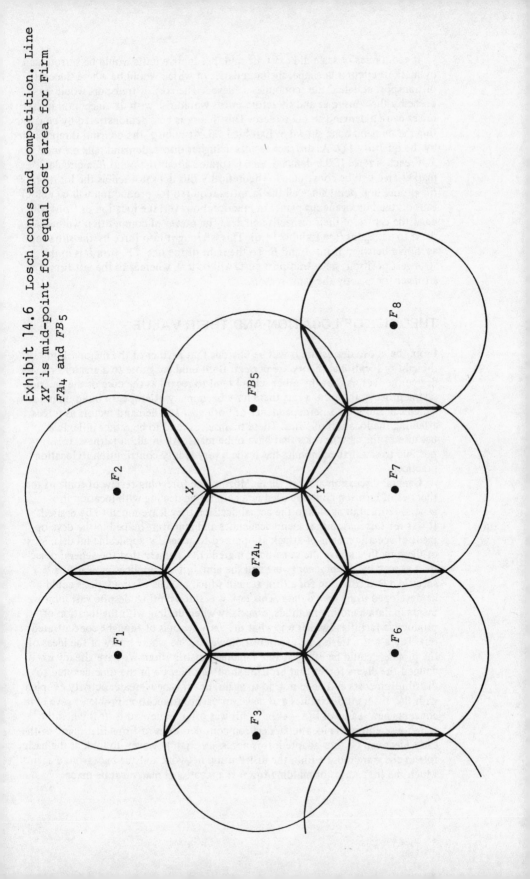

Exhibit 14.6 Losch cones and competition. Line XY is mid-point for equal cost area for Firm FA_4 and FB_5

If economies of scale did exist, he said, productive units would be surrounded by markets circular in shape, the boundaries of which would be where the cost of transport equalled the economies achieved. The cost of transport would be borne by the consumer and therefore prices would rise with distance until higher prices caused demand to fall to zero. This theory is best demonstrated by constructing the demand cone shown in Exhibit 14.5. At point F the demand is represented by the quantity FQ. As distance results in higher prices, demand tails off until at X it reaches zero. If the demand cone is rotated about the point F, a circular market area will be constructed. Theoretically this does not tell us the location of the production point since all the facilities required for production will be ubiquitous on the homogeneous plane. In practice, however, the location of firms will be at the centre of their respective circles. The power of competition will reduce these to hexagons (see Exhibit 14.6). This is brought into force by the situation as shown between firms A and B. To the right of the line XY, firm B is in the strongest position, since transport costs will be less, whereas to the left firm A is stronger for exactly the same reasons.

THEORIES OF LOCATION AND THEIR VALUE

From the above discussion it will be obvious that neither of the major schools of thought of locational theory are perfect. Both tend to ignore to a greater or lesser degree the factors that the other school tend to regard as the core of the decision-taking process. In recent years there have been many attempts to build up models which can show the interdependence of both cost and demand factors as forces affecting the location of firms. These themselves tend to be rather inflexible because of the assumptions that have to be made. All in all, in fairness, it is possible to say that economics has made a very scanty contribution to location practice.

General discussion aids are there. Most of the foregoing review of some of the theories of location could be used in a committee dealing with location in general terms, but as aids to the actual decision they leave much to be desired. It was for this reason that many academics and managers helped in the development of specific means of attack as opposed to generally applicable models. Most of these methods have the same basic ingredients, namely that the general objectives as seen by the pioneers were still the aim, but the application was to a specific micro situation for a firm around which models or simulations could be developed using actual data. This task was still daunting, despite vast improvements in data-handling methods, especially when dealing with the location of productive facilities (which was what the early schools of thought concentrated on). There was a fresh area of interest, however, one where many of the ideas of the pioneers could be easily adapted, namely distribution. We have already examined the divers forces that brought about an increase in the time devoted to distribution costs and need not do so again, but this new greater activity coupled with the different disciplines and new approaches to location problems gave old concepts new leases of life — even if this was often in new suits. It is when the warehouse enters the locational decision considerations of firms that many of the early ideas can be thus adapted. It is necessary first, however, to look at the basic role of the warehouse within the distribution network and the background against which the first stages of building towards a locational plan must be made.

15 Locating the warehouse: general background

We have already examined the proposition that the true function of inventory is to act as a buffer between fluctuations in demand and the most economic rate of production. Inventory acts as a reservoir for the product, but since demand is often geographically dispersed, we must consider location as well as quantity when deciding operating policies for inventory.

The warehouse is the means whereby inventory is enabled to carry out its major function. The warehousing system makes the product economically effective by locating supply at those points which will ensure the service standards of the company are carried out at the most efficient cost level. This contribution that the warehouse makes to the overall trading position of the firm must always be borne in mind when dealing with this subject. There is a very real temptation to regard the warehouse simply as a place to store goods. This can be disastrous to any executive who tries to attract the attention of upper management to this question.

The value of a product to a customer can, for our purpose, be regarded as dependent on two main factors: value for cost and location. A potential customer will look at the benefits (in the widest possible sense) that he will receive from the purchase of a particular product. He will match these against the cost and decide if the purchase offers a desirable return.

All of these considerations will be affected to a greater or lesser degree by the location of the product, in other words by its availability. The stress he puts on the factors mentioned can be altered by the amount of time over which the transaction will take place. The purchaser might very well accept an inferior (from his viewpoint) product because of this factor. It is the role of inventory to ensure that this situation does not occur, but there is little point in having ample inventory in hand if the location is incorrect.

Demand must be matched not only with a product to supply, but this product must be in the most effective location. It is this aspect of the firm's activities that an efficient warehousing system can bring economies to. To ensure that this function is made to contribute the maximum benefit to the firm, we must examine a variety of facets of the warehouse. These will include the number and

217

location of warehouses, service territories and other external factors, as well as internal factors such as identification of cost centres, layout and equipment.

The external factors are of most interest in the situation where the firm is either setting up a completely new network or is undertaking a full-scale revision of an already existing system. The internal factors are aimed to help in the situation where the company realises the importance of the warehouse function, but is satisfied with the existing physical layout; or alternatively is prevented by policy decisions or capital shortage or both from carrying out a complete overhaul, but nonetheless wants to increase the effectiveness of the warehouse function.

EXTERNAL FACTORS

When considering the external aspect of warehousing three broad areas will be at the basis of any attempt to produce an effective system: the nature of the product, the nature of the market and the company policies within which the network must operate. Each will be examined in turn before actual techniques are discussed.

The attitude of higher management to the warehousing problem has already been mentioned as having an important influence on the ability to perform its role effectively. This attitude will make itself most apparent when company policy to the warehouse is being reviewed and this is the first of our three factors to be examined.

The most obvious policy having a major effect on the warehouse network is service levels, but these have already been examined in the section on inventory control. The most important point to remember in this discussion is that increased sales do not necessarily contribute the profit that the marketing department will nearly always assume they do. Above a certain level, great care must be taken before committing the distribution function to any increases in inventory.

Once the service targets of the firm have been decided, however, it is the job of the distribution arm to ensure that they are provided — always assuming that these levels have been arrived at in consultation with distribution management. This is not to say marketing and production become subordinate to distribution, but the management of these areas must be fully aware of the influence of their decisions on the distribution side of the firm's activities (bearing in mind that 16 per cent total cost average). We will assume that these general points affecting the whole of the distribution function have already been decided, and concentrate here on the more detailed question.

As ever, the first of these is more likely to be financial. With respect to warehousing this is likely to be especially difficult because of the wide range of alternatives with varying cost characteristics. These are briefly, to lease or buy or a combination; to hire, not only space but also to some degree distribution activity; and to operate on a centralised or decentralised basis. Indeed the problem is nothing like as simple as this, because in the real situation one also has to decide the desirability of a combination of some or all of the methods mentioned.

The first question, that of lease or buy, will always cause a great many difficult decision problems. The difficulty might basically be reduced to one of flexibility. If a company involves itself in the capital expenditure of constructing a warehouse network, then it is, to some extent, committed to the system good or bad for some considerable time. The length of this time will depend not only on the investment sum involved, but on the willingness of the firm to accept the loss that a less than full utilisation of the system's life would involve. If the firm has inherited its warehousing system over a long period of time, it might very well find that a completely new network is called for. If this involves writing off substantial sums, a great deal of difficulty might be encountered from the management of other areas. At the same time the distribution activity is not static; its methods and requirements can and do change with stages in the firm's growth. This can happen over a fairly lengthy span if the company is in one of the fast-growth markets which are with us today. If this is the case distribution management could find that, over a given range of product movement to a particular market, one distribution method is the most efficient, say, for example, TIR road to a number of local warehouse points. As the volume of product increases this might change to air freight with a reduction in local warehouses and later still back to the original method. The key in this extreme situation is time span, but it illustrates the flexibility problem.

If the time span was short then management would have to decide which method the company is to be committed to. Investment in fixed facilities cannot be altered as quickly as might be theoretically desirable in any particular situation – possibly a complete reversal of policies in two or three years If, however, distribution management is aware that this situation is likely to occur, then flexibility might be introduced through leasing the warehouse requirement for the period with the shortest time span, while at the same time scheduling the estimated long-term requirement into future capital expenditure forecasts.

The desirability of this course of action will depend, in the last resort, on the relative profit levels that can be expected to arise from the various options open to the firm. On the other hand, it is often pointed out that the leasing alternative gives flexibility on ownership only at the cost of flexibility in design.

What is the point of introducing effective planning in facility ownership if it results in less than maximum efficiency in the operation of the facility? There is little doubt that this viewpoint is often true. The degree of difficulty here will, of course, vary from firm to firm, but nonetheless it is always wise to investigate the design of the warehouses available before entering into any internal discussion concerning the benefits and disadvantages of leasing.

This is not always as easy to accomplish as it sounds since there might very well be a great deal of travelling involved, preferably by the person who is responsible for the overall planning of the system, a practice that could mean his absence for a significant time. It is also possible to find conflict here, between desired flexibility and the financial policies of the firm. Distribution may, because of factors similar to those already mentioned, decide on leasing in a particular area. It is not at all unlikely that this decision will have to be revised under pressure from the financial function.

Although leasing can have many advantages for distribution it must always be borne in mind that the ultimate objective is to improve on the overall profitability of the firm. Leasing may thus be rejected, even though it appears to be the most suitable method of providing the required warehousing space. It is not the purpose here to give a deep discussion of the leasing problem, but an outline of the question may be of some use to distribution management which has found itself in the position mentioned above.

The concentrated streams of advertising pressure extolling the virtues of leasing equipment might possibly have been so powerful as to encourage the decision without thought. This is not against the leasing concept. Indeed, there can be little doubt that in certain conditions the leasing alternative is by far the more desirable. The key phrase is, however, 'certain conditions'. A good case can be made to support the contention that these conditions are few, and refer to rather specific circumstances, circumstances which in all probability are not very widespread.

Before dealing with a specific example, perhaps it would be of some use to look at the general beliefs normally surrounding leasing and also to glance at the implications of a leasing commitment on the existing capital structure of a firm. In all questions of finance, it is of the utmost importance to have a clear conception of the cost of capital to the firm, in order to discover the minimum rate of return which must be obtained from any project if it is to justify the cost of initiating it. Coupled to this, most firms will normally have an additional rate added to allow for the risks associated with the project in question.

This figure varies with the capital structure of the individual firm. It could conceivably range from the rate on a bank overdraft, in the case of the very small firm, to the more complex weighted average cost of capital where a firm is drawing finance from all the various sources open to a public company. This cost of capital concept is in fact an ideal point at which to commence the discussion of the financial implications of a leasing decision. In the general run of events in distribution it is normal that in the class of building hired there are few exceptional types. It is, in other words, not subject to a special type of commercial risk and runs the normal possibilities of variations in profit.

In these circumstances, it is not likely that the lessor company will find it possible to obtain capital at a cheaper price than the lessee. Moreover, an advantage will be gained in purchasing the building in question, since the capital used is obtained at a cheaper price. This is not a general rule, however. If the lessee company has had a bad profit record, if future forecasts for its particular industry are bad or if, let us say, the lessee company's share of the market was dropping, all or any of these conditions could result in the demand for the company's equity to fall and the price of capital to increase. In the same manner, if the lessor company was substantially larger than the lessee, then it is most likely that they would be able to raise capital on the open market at a cheaper price.

One of the points which is often used to sell the leasing of many types of specialised buildings is that the risk of obsolescence is removed from the lessee company and taken upon the shoulders of the lessor. From one point of view this is entirely true. The relevant factor is how much does this transference cost the lessee? Since it is obvious that even with the best will in the world the cost of this risk must be borne by someone, somewhere, the implication in saying that the lessee no longer bears the risk must surely be that it is the lessor who does so. Forecasting is a delicate and difficult science to master. But only if the lessor has developed this to a much higher level of efficiency then the lessee, thus enabling him to be sure of the degree of risk in question, will he be able to accept this risk at a smaller price. Assuming that this is not the case, what then is the conclusion regarding this claim? It is necessary first to look at the assets of the respective firms. In the case of the lessee it is doubtful if all or even a significant proportion of his capital will be tied up in the building question. On the other hand, by the very nature of his business, the building will represent a very much higher proportion of the assets of the lessor. The end result of this is that the lessor might very well require a much higher premium for the risk of obsolescence because he has a greater proportion of his capital at risk than the lessee, on the same assets. In other words, the lessee must meet, albeit indirectly, a higher payment for the risk of obsolescence than if he himself owned the building in question. On the other hand, if the lessor is prepared to accept a much lower profit margin or if he has a greater degree of skill in the appraisal of the risks to the building or if he has access to cheaper finance than for the above considerations, he has an advantage to offer the lessee.

The foregoing considerations are aimed chiefly at the popular, if this term may be used, beliefs surrounding lease finance. But, after all, the acceptance by management of a lease commitment is as concrete a proposal of future debt as any other form of debt finance. Again, as in all questions which involve such a wide range of companies, it is quite impossible to lay down any absolute rules which will apply under all circumstances.

To give a general view of the position within the UK is also difficult for the simple reason that there are no statistics covering the lease commitments of UK industries. At the moment there is no legal obligation for firms to show their lease commitments in their annual accounts. This at first glance may seem of no particular importance. But when the influence of a lease obligation is looked upon regarding the capital structure of the firm, some rather important if not possibly catastrophic problems are involved. This position depends entirely on the attitude which prevails towards the influence of lease payments. One view is that they do not really influence the firm's position.

On the other hand the more realistic method is to look upon the commitment as the equivalent of being engaged simultaneously in the purchase of the asset and the raising of capital to pay for it. Perhaps a theoretical example might be useful to exemplify this contention.

For illustration's sake, let us assume that a company has a choice of purchasing or leasing an asset with a value of £100,000. Let us also assume that the reasonable life of this asset is 20 years after which the value of the building is negligible. The alternative is to lease the building for 20 years at £8718 per annum. Assuming that the leasing alternative is adopted, then it is fairly obvious that the company would be in much the same financial position as it would be if they had bought the asset for cash and at the same time raised capital on the open market, the cash raised and interest paid (at 6 per cent) being repaid in annual instalments equal to the lease charges. Whichever alternative is taken, a company would still be committing itself to payments of £8718 per year for 20 years. In actual fact then, as opposed to that which might appear on the balance sheets, both actions commit the firm to much the same obligation. The critical factor is the position as it appears on the balance sheets of the firm, especially as to how an examination of these will influence the company's borrowing position.

It is entirely possible, by utilising leasing opportunities, for a company to introduce a degree of 'gearing' into its capital structure beyond conventional limits. In this way it could be feasible to run a high proportion of debt capital without this appearing on the balance sheet. Inevitably this leads to the question: is this of significant importance? Before answering this it is necessary to have a brief glance at the standard financial ratios. These are a quick reference help in deciding the financial position of a company. They are normally applied, among other things, to determine the creditworthiness of the company. One of the most common for this use is that known as 'long-term debt to net assets'. Utilising this ratio, it is possible to indicate the value which is available to cover long-term debts, if for any reason the firm goes into liquidation. In this ratio, however, no weight is given to the proportionate effect of lease commitments. Suppose, for example, a company has tangible assets amounting to, say, £100,000 and assume that its maximum debt level is 30 per cent or £30,000. Rather than borrowing additional capital to buy a particular asset, let us assume that the firm decides to lease the building it requires. Assume further that the building itself is worth £50,000. This sum is not included in the long-term commitments, nor is the value of the asset included in the net worth of the firm. Had this been done the effect would be to increase both these figures by £50,000 with the result that the assets would now be worth £150,000 and the long-term debt would now be £80,000. In this position, debts now represent 53.5 per cent of net assets worth.

It might be said that this is of no consequence because the actual resale value of the building being leased covers any emergency requirement to pay the commitment in full. Possibly this may be true where the building in question is highly marketable. But in the general run of events, it is usually the case that the resale value of the most common type of building does not equal the full value of the lease commitments although, if the company was faced with liquidation, the lessor would have a right by law to ownership of the building leased and to sue for any balance outstanding. This approach to the importance of lease commitments is detrimental to the correct evaluation of a company's credit worth. Although this might not appear important (indeed it might possibly be looked upon as an advantage) it must always be borne in mind that a company can outstretch its debt capital and land in trouble. Again, the true capital structure of the company is never available to intending investors. Other financial ratios, such as times covered, are also adversely affected. Taking an overall view, however, it is a fair statement to say that lease commitments impair the financial strength of the firm. Moreover, because of the various effects outlined above, it can also be said that undisclosed commitments (as most are) are a threat to the security of the potential lenders to the firm, as much as direct debt financing of the same assets. When an asset is, in fact, purchased outright, the chief annual 'costs' which can actually be laid at the door of that building are the annual depreciation charges plus, in the case of an outright purchase, the sinking fund charge, which will be set aside to provide for the purchase.

Looking at this from the lessee's point of view, it is likely that the lease charges must exceed these two figures. This is because the lease payments must cover not only the lessor's administration charges, but also his profit margin. The latter must also include a return to his equity capital. Again, it is repeated that lease commitments represent an impairment to lenders at least equal to the capitalised value of these payments discounted at the firm's normal rate for borrowing.

Surely, however, as it is apparently implied here, leasing is not always harmful to the firm? The answer to this must certainly be that it is not. There are situations where leasing is not only the most efficient method, but also the only one. The foregoing discussion is meant chiefly to emphasise the fact that leasing is not always the best method. Indeed, as has been pointed out, serious consideration must be given to the effect on the financial standing of the firm. However, there are certain considerations which tend to push the decision in the direction of leasing.

Perhaps the basic essence of leasing is the fact that an asset is secured against future fixed money payment. This concept of the future fixed payment is most important, and it is often overlooked when leasing is being considered. One of the most striking characteristics of the modern economic scene is the existence of endemic inflation. An attempt to clarify the meaning of inflation might be justified at this point. Inflation does not mean high prices, nor is it an increase in prices. It is not really a point in time, but a continuous process — rising prices, i.e. a continuous progressive reduction in the purchasing power of the monetary unit. In the UK this decrease in purchasing power has fluctuated wildly in recent years and has risen to as much as 20 per cent in a single year.

This figure has a profound effect in the calculation involved in company leasing or hiring. Perhaps a simple example might be the best method of illustrating this point. When employing one of the discounted cash flow techniques for the appraisal of the two courses of action, a close approximation to the correct discount factor can be arrived at by adding the expected rate of inflation to the firm's marginal cost of capital. Assume that a firm is faced with either leasing a building at £30,000 per year for 10 years, payable ahead, or initially purchasing the building outright for £250,000. After 10 years it has a value of £100,000. However, maintenance costs are identical, and there are tax complications. The value of the lease is simply the first year's payment, plus the next 9 years' reduced to a net present value. Assume also the marginal cost of capital at 8 per cent. The leasing alternative is then worth:

$$30{,}000 + 30{,}000_{a\,9/8}$$
$$= \text{NPV } £217{,}406$$

Purchase equals:

$$250{,}000 - 100{,}000_{v10/8}$$
$$= \text{NPV } £203{,}680$$

From these figures it is evident that the purchase of the building is the cheaper method. Suppose, however, that there is a 3 per cent annual net inflation. Then the leasing alternative rate would be:

$$30{,}000 + 30{,}000_{a10/11}$$
$$= \text{NPV } £196{,}111$$

The net present value of the purchasing alternative now becomes:

$$250{,}000 - 100{,}000_{v10/11}$$
$$= \text{NPV } £214{,}782$$

The effect of inflation has been to change the relative values in the following manner. Without inflation it was cheaper, by approximately £13,726, to purchase the building in question. However, once the effect of inflation has been taken into consideration, it is cheaper by £18,671 to accept the leasing alternative. It is possible, rather than be involved in these calculations, to devise a formula where the break in the rate of inflation can be arrived at. By substitution, given the required figures, it is possible to determine whether a given rate of inflation will swing the decision one way or the other. In the above example, however, it was not assumed that capital was not raised on the debenture market. This is obviously too much of a simplification for the illustration above. If a proportion of the purchase price were financed by debt capital, the calculation would then be as follows (the proportion raised for simplicity is then assumed to be half at 8 per cent the loan being repaid at the end of 10 years):

$$125,000 + 10,000_{a10/8} + 125,000_{v10/8} - 100,000_{v10/8}$$
$$= \text{NPV } £203,677$$

It can be seen from this that the introduction of debt capital (even without allowing for the effect of inflation) results in substantial saving in the purchase price, which in the first example was raised solely from equity capital. In other words where there is a degree of debt capital involved, this tends to upset the gains which inflation may give to the leasing alternative.

In other words, regarding the question of assets, outright purchases by debt capital may be more attractive than leasing. This, of course, depends entirely on the capital structure of the company in question. Its financial policy can affect the amount of its debt capital. For example, by taking advantage of the net rate of inflation, it would be possible to periodically revalue the firm's assets, and in this manner increase the permissible ratio of long-term debt to net assets. Again, this depends entirely on the structure of the company in question.

Inflation then, in some circumstances, can swing the balance in favour of the leasing alternative. Many companies may find that their need — and this might be specially true in the case of certain distribution buildings — is purely seasonal, or that the useful life of the building is longer than the period in which they would require its services. In these circumstances there is little doubt that leasing is not only the more attractive but also the only viable decision. A special application may also justify the leasing move.

Leasing then should be examined most carefully, not only within the context of the company, but also with relation to the general economic situation. As in all questions of investment appraisal, discounted cash flow techniques should be used. But the effect of a large leasing commitment on the financial standing of the firm should receive the utmost attention. Alternative sources of capital also deserve examination regarding relative cost. Special conditions, either financial or technical, whereby the balance might be swung in favour of leasing should also be considered.

The leasing question is one which causes a great deal of controversy both within the financial area and distribution itself. The ultimate decision will depend on the particular combination of factors which faces the individual firm. The most important point to make here is that there should be adequate consultation between management involved so that all relevant arguments can receive a full review.

THE PUBLIC WAREHOUSEMAN

These are firms who will not only provide warehousing space, but a very wide range of services as well. These might include collection from the point of origin, provision of special storage conditions (temperature, etc.), inventory control information and the final delivery to the customers, or in some cases delivery over a wide territory. To look at it from another angle the public warehouseman

will take over the complete distribution function from the production line to the
final customer.

When considering this point, the same general considerations as before hold true: it is impossible to give a general answer as to whether the service is 'economical' or not. The answer as always will depend on the position of the individual firm. There are, however, some factors that may help to point the way to the solution.

The first of these concerns the importance of the market served. This type of service is at its best when the company has a market which, although its total value is significant, is located in such a way as to cause a higher distribution bill than is desired. Such a market is most common in the consumer goods field, where geographical distance from the major markets is great, and the secondary market demand tends to be in a wide area but in small individual lots.

Very often distribution management is in a dilemma. The total market is great enough to justify it being brought within the firm's target, but is not large enough to allow a regional depot, and yet is expensive to supply from the main market depot areas. In this situation it is highly likely that the answer is the public warehouseman located in this area. He will normally be happy to provide a complete distribution service at a price that the selling company could not possibly match. In this way not only is the market served but the effectiveness of distribution in that area increased.

The example above is in the consumer goods field, but the service is not limited to this. Industrial products will normally also be handled provided that they do not come within certain handling areas, i.e. the one-off job, or the very heavy category. Where the product in question has no special handling requirements and a reasonably steady demand pattern it too will normally be accepted by the public warehouseman. Indeed even those products which do not have the demand characteristics outlined above will often be taken on under special arrangements and prices.

The question that now arises is how do these operators provide such services more efficiently than the selling firm? The most obvious reasons are location, consolidation and specialisation. The warehouseman can be found in most population centres and he is prepared to serve within that area, some to a greater radius than others. There is a very definite advantage because the selling firm can engage a variety of warehousemen over much wider areas than he could possibly justify for the construction of depots. In this way the market effectiveness of the firm can be increased through penetration in markets that would otherwise not prove profitable.

Although the selling firm may be faced with a large number of small drops, consolidation can remove this problem for the public warehouseman. This is especially true in the consumer products field where each drop may be served by a large number of different firms. When the public warehouseman takes over these are consolidated into composite loads as he is not limited to carrying one firm's products. The effect of his activities is illustrated in Exhibit 15.1.

Specialisation in the distribution function within his areas and conditions also allow operating economies. The original selling firm must make allowances for all his markets when deciding on the types of distribution equipment which he will purchase. The public warehouseman knows exactly what the demands on the equipment are going to be and because of consolidation can often buy vehicles that the normal operator would have to compromise on. He may, for example,

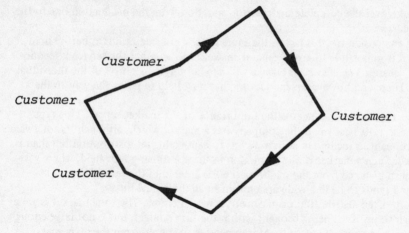

Consolidation by independent warehouseman

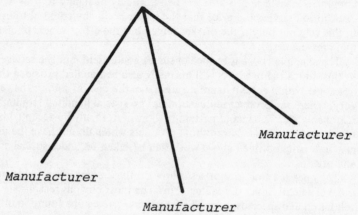

Exhibit 15.1

have such a range of products with individual handling characteristics that custom designed vehicles can be justified. Flexibility of service is another important advantage that can be had by the employment of the public warehouseman.

For products having a marked seasonal fluctuation, the use of his services coupled with the firm's internal warehousing system can, in some cases, greatly reduce the total distribution costs. If a firm's main production points and distribution services are concentrated close to the major markets then seasonal fluctuations in minor markets may prove expensive. The application of the specialised warehouseman in these situations is obvious.

On the other hand, minimal stocks can be located in a wide range of markets at peak times at very low costs. In this way high service levels can be kept for year-round customers at a level of effectiveness impossible without the public warehouseman. Costs of storage in these cases are known in advance and the requisite information and planning can be made more effective. As a final word on the public warehouseman, it will be remembered that he will provide inventory

information to the selling firm and if desired act independently regarding restock-
ing and so on. The more progressive organisations are prepared to bring their own
data processing equipment 'on line' with their customers, so that there is a complete exchange of relevant information between all concerned.

The point is, of course, to remember that this is a specialist service and is not
usually generally applicable over the entire range of a firm's distribution problems.
But where he can be used efficient economical service is the norm.

CENTRALISED AND DECENTRALISED WAREHOUSES

The problem of the centralised system versus the decentralised system will never
be finally solved. Distribution patterns are dynamic and a solution for one set of
conditions is appropriate only as long as those conditions are in existence. It is
possible for the same firm to favour both centralised and decentralised warehousing systems at various stages of development. Changes in marketing strategy and
product strategy will pull distribution from one policy to the other. As with all
external factors considered so far, only very general guidelines can be laid down
and the best answer will depend on the individual situation.

There are certain product/market characteristics which work in favour of decentralisation. Those products dependent on rapid service for sales, either because of inherent nature (food products) or intensive competition, will tend towards a well spread network of depots/warehouses. Where the product is in a very
competitive field but has a low value/volume relationship, storage closer to the
demand points may be the most effective strategy. Those products which are not
normally purchased in large quantities will normally be held in warehouses, otherwise transport and other costs could become prohibitive through small order
quantities. The cost and availability of warehousing facilities (perhaps the public
warehouse) and the effectiveness of reordering procedures will also have an influence here.

Obviously where the situation does not contain considerations such as those
above the trend is to centralised warehousing methods. This trend will be reinforced by a few other common conditions such as the case where the distribution network is designed for intercompany transfer of known quantities of replacement goods, or where a broad range of high value/volume products are
required over a wide geographical area, but at concentrated demand points and
so on.

From the foregoing discussion it should be obvious that our other two factors
(nature of product and market) are not considered in isolation, but are constantly
referred to as policy decisions are reviewed. Perishability, for example, will be
considered under both decentralisation and the leasing decisions; it will also be
encountered when reviewing the role of the public warehouseman.

The nature of the order pattern will be considered chiefly in relation with the
warehousing specialist. If it is small and frequent then the greater the advantage
of movement in bulk whenever possible, from the production point to the warehouseman's depot for example. If the market is such as to result in severe demand
fluctuations then this must be examined against the policy alternatives available.

It is of the utmost importance that none of the factors which have been discussed are examined in isolation. The most desirable method is to advance on all
three fronts simultaneously so that cross-reference and liaison are accurate and

timely; examples have already been noted of the problems which can arise if this is not done. Many decisions can be made considering only product and market factors, but irrespective of how efficient they are, they become ineffective if made without consultations in the policy area. It is for this reason that the greatest weight has been given to the policies in this section.

Now that the broad general areas have been dealt with it is time to be more specific. The firm has decided that its preference is for a particular pattern of warehousing development, all the broad considerations discussed have been reviewed and the general operating policies been agreed upon.

16 Locational methods

NUMBER AND LOCATION

The most important external factor now to be examined is the question of number
and location. In the past there has been a very strong tendency to formulate
specific methods to deal with this problem. While the techniques developed were
and are of undoubted value in the theoretical situation, they very often fall short
in their practical application. Far too many assumptions are made about the conditions under which they are to be applied. For example, they often assume that
one warehouse problem is to be solved or that there are no factors at work other
than the pure market forces involved.

In the real work environment the situation usually is that there are forces outside the distribution man's control that must be taken into consideration just as
much as statistical information. He may desire a particular geographical management control structure which although ideal for distribution is in conflict with
divisional territories; or he will often find that service level policy will determine
to a great extent the number of warehousing points, rather than operating costs
alone. These purely theoretical studies are of use as a starting point from which
the company policy, market and product considerations are taken into account
and their influence allowed to develop the initial answer to a practical solution.

The question 'How many?' is likely to be the first to require an answer. This
problem will depend for its solution to a great extent on the type of market that
is to be served (we are assuming service levels and so on have already been decided), its location and distribution. We have already pointed out that the theoretical approach to this problem can leave a great deal to be desired. The answer
then must lie in the examination of information gathered in the real work
situation.

We must gather the relevant market information and use exhaustive search
methods to come up with the best answer to the question of number and location. Obviously we cannot formulate a general solution that can be used by all
firms for their individual set of conditions; all we can do is to keep the method
as general as possible so that the firm can adapt it to its own needs.

We will assume that the need is for the national distribution of a product, and that the market spread is indicated by one or all of the following factors: population, working population (manufacturing), share of national income, or share of national retail turnover and/or retail expenditure per head. These will cover a great many firms' requirements.

Population will be coupled with a wide range of consumer products, working population reflects the pattern of industrial distribution, share of national income will be linked to all of the considerations already mentioned, whilst the share of the retail turnover and per capita expenditure will be of the most interest to those firms whose distribution requirements are dictated by the retail markets. This information is laid out in Exhibits 16.1 and 16.2 for selected regions of the UK and the largest 20 towns. With regard to the regions, these are the standard planning divisions of the country. There is, of course, no need that they be followed, since any delineation can be adopted to suit the needs of the firm making the survey. Indeed the information given in these tables can easily be used to give a wide variety of territorial divisions. It can be seen that the location of a great many types of distribution points will be decided to a great extent by the pattern of the industrial and commercial patterns that have grown up in the UK over the years. An examination of Exhibit 16.3 will indicate that certain broad geographical areas of the country demand the situation of a distribution point somewhere in their area.

Our procedure is to estimate the costs involved with a variety of warehousing giving a wide range of coverage and availability. Subsequent decisions can be made on this basis. If we plot the location of the 20 largest towns on our map we have a starting point. It will be seen from Exhibit 16.4 that there is not a single planning region that does not have at least one of these towns in their area. In fact, for the greatest areas there is generally more than one of the largest towns. This is hardly surprising, but it should lead us to inquire what the result would be of a 20 point distribution network, warehouses being located at each of the 20 largest towns in the county.

Exhibit 16.1   Share of national cake in regions

Region	UK pop. %	UK industrial pop. %	UK income %	Retail turnover %
South East	31	30	36	35
South West	7	5	5	7
Wales	5	4	3	5
W.Midlands	9	12	10	8
E.Midlands	6	7	9	6
E.Anglia	3	2	3	2
North West	12	15	12	12
Yorks Humber	9	10	9	9
Northern	6	5	5	5
Scotland	10	10	10	10

Exhibit 16.2   Share of national cake in large towns   *231*

Town and immediate area	UK population %	UK industrial population %	Retail turnover %
Birmingham	2.0	4.0	2.4
Bradford	0.5	0.8	0.6
Bristol	1.9	2.0	2.0
Cardiff	2.2	1.8	2.1
Coventry	1.7	2.0	1.5
Edinburgh	0.8	1.4	1.3
Glasgow	2.8	3.1	3.1
Hull	0.9	0.7	0.9
Leeds	1.0	1.3	1.1
Leicester	1.3	1.7	1.2
Liverpool	1.3	2.0	1.6
Manchester	8.0	11.0	8.0
Newcastle	1.4	1.2	1.8
Nottingham	1.6	1.6	1.6
Plymouth	1.4	0.7	1.6
Portsmouth	0.4	0.3	0.5
Sheffield	5.5	5.9	4.8
Southampton	2.1	1.3	2.5
Stoke	3.3	4.6	3.0
Greater London	18.0	17.7	19.8

It can be seen that this would bring within our orbit 57 per cent of the total population of the country, approximately 65 per cent of the population engaged in manufacturing (and presumably a similar proportion of the country's industry) and 62 per cent of the total retail turnover. This share of the national totals of these factors we are assuming can be easily satisfied within 24 hours by depots located at these points. In practice, of course, this share of the total amounts would be larger, as with larger distribution fleets there is little doubt that at least 90 per cent of the working population and so on could be serviced in 1 day from a network located in or near these 20 towns. The remaining 10 per cent could, in theory at least, be covered in the next or third day. It is likely that 97 per cent could be covered in 2 days and the full 100 per cent in 3 days. Indeed, many would maintain that the 3 day 100 per cent service is a little on the generous side, preferring 2 days 100 per cent.

What this means is laid out in Exhibit 16.5. The main problem for the distribution man is to decide the costs which would be associated with this system and also at this stage to introduce any changes which he may feel are required. He may, for example, feel that some of the locations mentioned are too large to be serviced in the time involved by one depot, and increase the number involved for this reason. London perhaps will receive 2 or more depots depending on the product

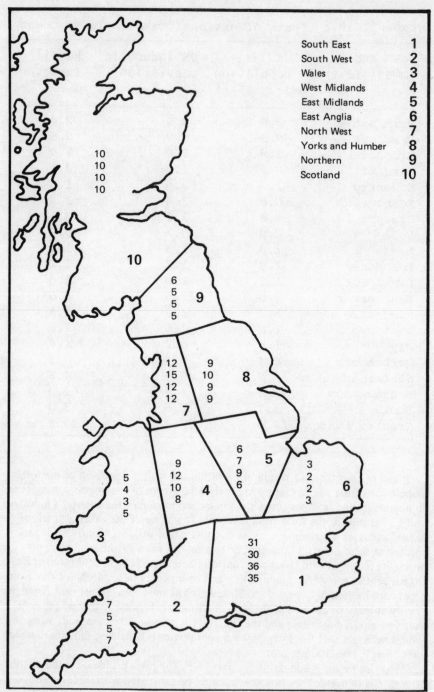

Exhibit 16.3 UK regions: the figures in each region, reading from top to bottom, give the share of the UK population, the share of the UK population in industry, the share of UK income and the share of UK retail turnover

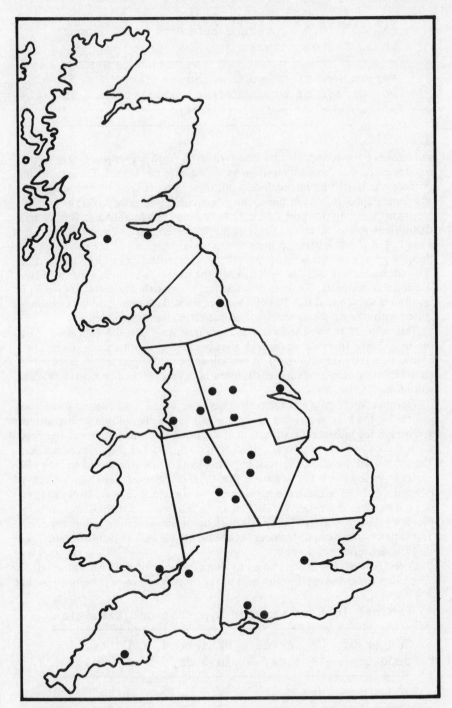

Exhibit 16.4 UK regions as in Exhibit 16.3. Each dot
represents one town with a population of more than
200,000. Note that there is at least one such town in
each region

Exhibit 16.5 Coverage achieved with depots in 20 largest towns

Percentage of UK population	57
Percentage of UK industrial population	65
Percentage of retail turnover	62

and market to be served. He may also feel that a much higher percentage of the country could be covered than those which we have mentioned. The market and product which he is dealing with may not need to cover the entire geographical and demographic regions of the country, and could well satisfy 100 per cent of his market in 1 day from the 20 locations or even considerably less. But we are dealing here in general terms. Yet it might be worth mentioning at this point that areas 1, 4, 5, 7 and 8 between them encompass 67 per cent of the total population, 74 per cent of the working population in manufactures and 76 per cent of the national income and thus will demand the special attention of the majority of distribution managers. We must now attempt to estimate the costs that would be involved if we adopted this 20-point system; we will also estimate the costs involved with other systems which utilise decreasing numbers of depots.

The methods involved will as always be a mixture of the theoretical and what can be gathered from search through already existing information sources. The costs incurred by the different systems will all be made up from the same basic considerations: transportation costs, inventory costs, warehouse operating costs and administration costs.

Transportation costs will themselves have two broad components: those costs incurred in the bulk movement of the product to the distribution points and those involved in the individual distribution of the product to the customer. The first of these should be easy to quantify either from internal sources or outside hauliers. The second will have to be estimated on the basis of the area served and the likely routes to be followed. Let us assume that these calculations have been completed (see Exhibit 16.6). Experience has shown that combined they are likely to have one outstanding characteristic, i.e. that as the number of distribution points decreases the proportion of the costs of transportation services will increase. This is due to the basic differences between costs for bulk movements and those for local deliveries.

Coverage times have been chosen to allow some time for delays and so on. The conclusion to be drawn from this part of the investigation would seem to be that

Exhibit 16.6 Costs for hypothetical situation

Number of depots	UK served in 1 day %	UK served in 3 days %	Costs, £'000s
20	98	2	1100
15	95	5	1700
10	90	10	2000
5	65	35	2800

the greater number of depots the higher the coverage and the lower the costs.
Needless to say transport costs are not the only ones to be taken into consideration. On estimating the inventory costs for the various systems we can expect
that the main characteristics of the data will be that the greater the number of
distribution points then the more expensive will be the inventory levels required
to maintain our service coverages.

Exhibit 16.7 shows the assumed figures. The main factor to be remembered
here is that the higher numbers of depots will most likely have to carry more inventory because of the longer replenishment times that will probably be required,
when compared to the lower number systems.

With warehouse handling costs, the same broad qualities can be expected as
were found with inventory costs, namely that as the number of depots in the

Exhibit 16.7 Inventory costs and
number of depots

Number of depots	Inventory investment, £'000s	Inventory costs at 25%
20	16,000	4,000
15	12,000	3,000
10	8,000	2,000
5	6,000	1,500

Exhibit 16.8 Handling costs and
number of depots

Number of depots	Handling costs, £'000s
20	500
15	380
10	250
5	150

Exhibit 16.9 Summary of various choices
open to management

Number of depots	UK served in 1 day %	UK served in 3 days %	Costs
20	98	2	5,600,000
15	95	5	5,080,000
10	90	10	4,250,000
5	65	35	4,450,000

system increases costs also go higher. The hypothetical values for these costs in our assumed system are shown in Exhibit 16.8. The same considerations are likely to arise with data processing costs as well; we can expect these to decrease as the number of distribution points decreases.

Here we are using purely hypothetical values. The direction which we have expected costs to move in are only average and in the real work situation differences may occur. The costs for any particular system will be peculiar to that individual's procedures and conditions. The crux is that the distribution department should draw up a summary of the various costs centres such as is shown in Exhibit 16.9. The final decision will be taken on these figures plus an additional factor to include the cost of the final service levels decided upon by the firm.

When the data is drawn up in this form the decision as to which system the firm wants can be taken. This will be made against the background of general policies and attitudes that has already been discussed. Once this initial decision is taken it will of itself narrow the areas under consideration. The next step is to locate the warehouses selected within their areas at the most desirable locations. There is a wide variety of methods available for this purpose. Again the purely theoretical ones can have objections raised to their use as the only method of attempting to reach a solution. But they will undoubtedly reduce the time and effort involved if they are used to obtain an initial solution which is then altered to fit the company structure.

Even within the choice of mathematical techniques though a further decision must be made. The more accurate the method, then the more complex and expensive it is to employ. Very often the more simple methods can be used, and a nearly best solution obtained at a much lower cost. The decision is up to the management.

One of the simplest methods is to take the area within which the warehouse falls and to calculate the ton-mile centre for that area. That is we decide where there is likely to be a depot by following the search method already dealt with and, having selected an area, we find within it the location which will minimise costs, this being the appropriate location for our distribution depot.

Before going on to discuss the ton-mile centre approach it is important to remember that this is a simple method. Assumptions are made that will ensure that the answer developed is unlikely to be the best possible realistic one. But bearing its limitations in mind and altering the theoretical answer to take account of as many practical considerations as possible, there is little doubt that a good approximation to the optimum answer can be obtained at comparatively small cost and in a short time.

We will assume that the search method is duly completed and that the firm has decided on the number and general locations of its warehouse points. Before the ton-mile centre is calculated it is necessary to make some estimate of the firm's transport costs within the area concerned. There are various approaches to this problem ranging from the use of simple transport rates averaged out to a per mile basis, or to calculate a weighted rate that will reflect the total costs of the movements involved within the area under review. We must also accurately plot within the region the location of our demand (customer) points and source of supply of product if this, in fact, is in reasonable proximity.

Assume that the market layout is as in Exhibit 16.10. The number of demand points, T, have been kept at a minimum for the purpose of illustration and for the same reason it has been decided to show only one product being moved.

In the real situation, however, there will be greater complexity in both of these

areas. However, in the case of higher numbers of demand points the calculations
are the same only more involved, whilst for the greatest number of products the
rates in question are dealt with in an identical manner as that to be shown, differentiation being introduced by the use of subscripts.

The information is then transferred to a simple grid arrangement such as is
shown. It is important to maintain the special relationships between the various
points, and if it is preferred the data can be plotted on a map of suitable scale.
The important feature is the construction of the grid itself. For ease of calculation the origin of the grid should always be located in the south-west corner of
the layout. The scale which is decided upon depends entirely on the individual
situation, and the extent of the market and the number of demand points to be
included will be the most important influences to be borne in mind when this is
being decided.

Conventionally the rows are given letter designations, R1, R2 and so on, the
same procedure being followed for the columns, K1, K2, etc. By this means any
particular grid square can be referred to easily. Demand point K2R5 would refer
to the grid square in the top left-hand corner having the value 150 units of
demand.

In this example we have decided that the value 10 monetary units will be allocated to the demand points, and our source of supply points, t, have been given
the value 5, i.e. we assume that the cost of movement from the supply points to

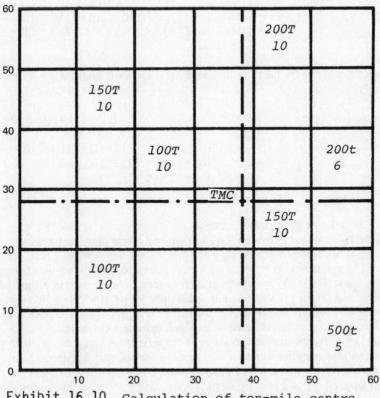

Exhibit 16.10   Calculation of ton-mile centre

the demand centres is 5 units whereas the costs associated with the local distribution of the product amount to 10 monetary units per unit of local movement.

It is assumed for the purpose of this calculation that the demand in any particular grid square is evenly distributed over that square. Thus the distances from
the origin of each of the grid square demand locations is taken as the midpoint
distance of that square. In this manner, supply source at location K6R4 is
reckoned to be 35 miles to the northward from the origin and 55 miles to the
eastward.

To find the northward coordinate for our ton-mile centre we complete the
calculation as follows:

$$\text{Northward coordinate} = \frac{\Sigma(CDT) + \Sigma(CDt)}{\Sigma(CT) + \Sigma(Ct)}$$

where C are costs allocated to demand points, T or supply points t, D are distances
from origin to demand or supply points to the northward and T or t are loads in
weight units allocated during study. This will give us the northwards coordinate
of our ton-mile centre. The eastwards coordinate is calculated by a similar process except that the distances eastward for each point are taken, by rows, rather
than northwards by column. Thus:

Northward coordinate $= [(100 \times 10 \times 15) + (150 \times 10 \times 45) + (100 \times 10 \times 35)$
$+ (150 \times 10 \times 25) + (200 \times 10 \times 55) + (200 \times 6 \times 35)$
$+ (500 \times 5 \times 55)] \div [(100 \times 10) + (150 \times 10)$
$+ (150 \times 10) + (200 \times 10) + (200 \times 6) + (500 \times 5)$
$= 28.8$ miles

or, say, 28 miles to the north of the origin. The eastward coordinate is determined
similarly:

Eastward coordinate $= [(500 \times 5 \times 55) + (100 \times 10 \times 15) + (150 \times 10 \times 45)$
$+ (100 \times 10 \times 25) + (200 \times 6 \times 55) + (150 \times 10 \times 15)$
$+ (200 \times 10 \times 45)] \div [(500 \times 5) + (100 \times 10)$
$+ (150 \times 10) + (100 \times 10) + (200 \times 6)$
$+ (250 \times 10) + (200 \times 10)]$
$= 39.4$ miles

or, say 39 miles to the east of the origin.

These two axes are drawn on the grid map and where they intersect is the
location of our ton-mile centre. By using this site for our depot our costs are
reduced to the minimum in that area. These, remember, will be simple transport
rates or some weighted variation such as, for example, to include an estimated
handling cost, at each of our demand and supply points. It will be noted that in
the example shown the result is placed outside every one of the locations from
which supplies are to be collected or to which deliveries are made.

The key to success is, then, to arrive at the theoretical best location, then to
examine all the conditions in that area to see if any substantial improvements can
be made on the original ton-mile centre always assuming, of course, that the required land, labour and primary services are available at the calculated ton-mile
centre in the first place. It is frequently the case that a firm calculates its ton-mile

centre only to find that the centre and the entire surrounding area is either unsuitable for physical reasons or is already built upon anyway. If this situation
occurs then the only course of action open is to locate as closely as possible to
the ton-mile centre.

The problem is not solved at this stage though. What we have done so far is to
locate a single warehouse within one sales territory. There will remain the problem
of accurate delineation of sales areas. There will always be overlapping areas where
it is difficult to decide which warehouse in the overall system will satisfy customers
located there.

This decision is aided by the construction of isocost lines. These are lines re-
sembling contour lines, which take account of the relative handling and transport
costs for each of the depots under consideration. These are calculated and drawn
on the map and where there is an intersection of equal cost lines this is the boundary between the relevant warehouses. In Exhibit 16.11 an example of this isocost
approach is shown.

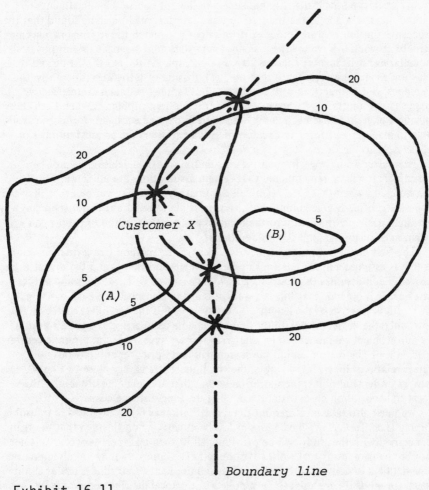

Exhibit 16.11

Each of the isocost lines represents the area where a delivery can be made at the cost shown from the respective warehouses. The boundary will follow the path made by the intersection of same cost curves. The pattern of these intersections will often allow adjustments to be made on the ground to try and accommodate the actual breakdown by sales management. Let us look for example at the customer represented by X. It can be seen that he falls between the 10 units isocost lines of the two depots. At this point the dividing line could follow either the 10 curve of A or B. In either case the cost of delivery would be under 10 units but more than 5. The only difference would be within which territory X fell. If the isocost curves of one of the depots tend to be very close together in the particular direction and the other far apart, this would tend to favour including the customer in question in the sales area of the depot with the wider cost curves as this suggests that costs are rising less steeply there, and inclusion might afford a marginal advantage. The important point is that flexibility is possible.

As always this theoretical answer must be examined in the light of practical considerations. It may be desirable that a particular area or customer be supplied from a special point; if the firm has such a policy, of course the adjustments required must be made to the theoretical boundaries. It might also be found that the isocost definition of warehouse territories does not match the regional management structure; when this occurs then, again, alterations must be made. Major physical boundaries might involve changes also. For example, in the North of England it may appear from isocost maps that the best division of territories runs across the Pennines. But in practice north-south distribution may be much more effective than east-west in this area, because of communications problems. When both these planning exercises have been completed there should be enough information available to management for it to decide which system offers the greatest number of advantages to the firm.

Even after we have performed the calculation our final decision cannot be taken yet. It will be remembered that certain assumptions are inherent in this method, and when these are examined the final location may yet be other than the ton-mile centre, even assuming that it was possible to build our depot there anyway (it might easily be the centre of the local lake, since the method of itself takes no cognisance of topographical considerations).

The first major limitation of the usefulness of the method (for a final answer) is that it assumes a linear relationship between transport costs and the distance moved, i.e. it assumes that each successive mile moved will cost the same as the last one. It is obvious that this is a weakness as the transport rate system normally met with is tapered; as the length of journey increases the last miles cost less. To introduce the degree of flexibility that will enable us to arrive at a good solution to our problem we must examine the grid after we have made the ton-mile centre calculation. The reason behind the search will be to discover any obvious non-linear relationship. If, for example, the ton-mile centre is very close to a large supply or demand point, then location within that area may greatly reduce the local transportation costs without affecting the long-distance costs.

We must also take into account the real situation as far as any outside transport supply is concerned. We have more or less been working on the idea that the firm concerned with the study will be providing all its own transport services. This need not be the case in the real work environment. The company may be relying on outside hauliers to deliver a proportion of its requirements. Indeed it is not at all unusual for all of the material to be supplied to the local distribution points by another firm. If this is the case, then any zoning arrangements must be examined. *241*

Zoning rates are used by firms such that the entire country is divided into broad zones or areas, and the same charges are made for delivery anywhere within these zones. It might be found that a short move of the ton-mile centre can result in substantial overall savings. Many firms in the UK adopt this zoning practice.

It will be realised of course, that the isocost line approach is nothing more complex than an elementary adaption of Losch's lines of equal delivered cost. The main alteration is the realisation that traffic conditions, topography and driver performance can change the theoretical concentric line of equal delivered cost to a variety of shapes. The very simple method (but sometimes very effective) described above for the determination of location can be improved on without too much effort — although a slight increase in time required and hence costs is unavoidable.

The method is a mathematical refinement of the ton-mile cost-centre approach discussed above. This results in the following formulae for the solution of the x and y coordinates:

$$ x = \sum_{j=1}^{n} (cdx\alpha/m) \Bigg/ \sum_{j=1}^{n} (cd\alpha/m) $$

$$ y = \sum_{j=1}^{n} (cdy\alpha/m) \Bigg/ \sum_{j=1}^{n} (cd\alpha/m) $$

where c is the cost of movement to customer per unit weight per mile, d the demand, x and y the coordinates of the customer, m the distance from the depot to customers, $j = 1, 2, 3, \ldots, n$ and $\alpha = 1$ if the depot under consideration serves the customer, otherwise $\alpha = 0$.

When applying this formula an improvement method is adopted. Once the new location has been calculated, customers are allocated to those depots which can serve them most effectively. This could be done on the basis of a VAM allocation. This method then can be seen to have the following stages. First, original calculations give locations for the depots (this could be done by a simple ton-mile cost-centre technique). Secondly, these locations are used as a basis for improved calculations. Thirdly, new allocations of customer to depot are completed by the use of VAM. The procedure is carried out until no improvement on costs is possible. This will be recognised when an allocation schedule repeats itself.

Mossman and Morton developed yet another method for determining the co-ordinates for a warehouse within a known servicing area. Their method is quite sophisticated and the final equations are not suitable for solution by hand. Some form of electronic data processing equipment should be used. At the basis of their approach is the idea that service times will be looked upon by the customers of the firm in more or less the same way as price benefits. This is because it is maintained that a reduction in service times will in effect be the same to the customer as a price reduction. If the consumer finds that he can now obtain his requirements in a shorter period then he needs to carry a lower amount of inventory to achieve the same service level coverage as before. There will also be advantages to his stock control systems in as much as he will be able to achieve greater rates of stock turnover, which will encourage higher liquidity and greater profitability.

If through improved service the customer can reduce his service inventory by say £10,000 and his carrying costs are 25 per cent then he has reduced his commitment by £2500. There is the chance of other benefits such as reductions in insurance costs, less risk of loss through price changes and, in certain circumstances, he may be able to utilise more space for selling.

Disadvantages do arise, however, at the limits of increase in the rate of stock turnover, especially increased clerical and managerial costs, but by and large those industries where competition is strong can usually find benefit from this area.

Mossman and Morton take the view that the savings potential is such that any improvements in service times as a result of location of the warehouse will improve the market penetration of the firm operating the distribution system. They term this concept 'elasticity of demand for service' or 'service elasticity'. Since variations in service would be looked upon by customers in much the same way as price movements they developed a measure for service elasticity very similar to the economists' concept of price elasticity.

It is of interest to note that empirical studies carried out in the USA tend to support the idea that customers will often regard service improvements in the way suggested above.

Applying these ideas it is possible to calculate the likely response of customers to improvements in service. This is done by market reseatch. Customers are questioned to find out what their actual reactions would be to alterations in service times and the following function developed

$$q = q_1^{-pt/t_1}$$

where q is quantity ordered with delivery time t, q_1 the quantity ordered with delivery time t_1, t_1 the competitors' delivery time, t the delivery time from new location and p a proportionality factor for the market under consideration.

Mossman and Morton proceed as follows. The cost of movement to any one centre will be given by the product of quantity moved (q), cost per unit moved (r) and the distance from the warehouse to the demand location (d), i.e. cost per unit moved *(r)* and the distance *(d)* from the warehouse to the demand location, i.e.

Cost = qrd

But the quantity likely to be ordered from a new location has already been calculated above. Therefore, in substituting, we obtain:

Cost = $q_1^{-pt/t_1} rd$

But the warehouse must be within a delivery system itself and, for the total cost of operations, these movements must be included in the expression:

Cost to warehouse = RDq

where R is the transport rate to the warehouse, D the distance to the warehouse and q the quantity demanded in the system. Taking these two expressions together, we obtain the total cost of the system.

Since we will be dealing with more than customer and location, the modified cost
is given by:

$$\text{Total cost} = \sum_{i=1}^{i=n} q_{1i}^{-p_i t_i / t_{1i}} \, (r_i d_i + R_i D_i)$$

By applying normal mathematical manipulations, the x and y coordinates
can be derived from the following equations:

$$\frac{dTC}{dx} = \sum_{i=1}^{i=n} q_1^{-p_i t_i / t_{1i}} \, [\frac{p_i}{t_{1i}} \frac{(X - x_1)}{d_1 v_1} - r \frac{(X - x_1)}{d_1} - \frac{RX}{D}] \log q_{1i} = 0$$

$$\frac{dTC}{dy} = \sum_{i=1}^{i=n} q_1^{-p_i t_i / t_{1i}} \, [\frac{p_i}{t_{1i}} \frac{(Y - y_1)}{d_1 v_1} - r \frac{(Y - y_1)}{d_1} - \frac{RY}{D}] \log q_{1i} = 0$$

where t, the delivery time, is a function of distance d and average speed v.

There are many such methods available and the choice of the most suitable for
an individual company must be left to that management. The final decision will
be made bearing in mind the all important proviso made earlier, namely that increasing accuracy involves increasing cost.

In the many approaches to solving the location problem that will be found in
the literature one basic difficulty will be seen. This is the dynamic nature of the
business environment. In all of the models and formulae available the basic viewpoint is that the firm's activities are stopped, essential information is extracted,
and this data used to come to a conclusion. This indeed is the method of most
approaches to business problems from accounts to production. The drawback is,
of course, that a business is not static, environmental factors change, costs may
vary, sites may become accessible or be withdrawn from the market, costs can
change up or down, markets can expand and contract, or competitors may come
into the field or the company may go into liquidation.

It is not possible to cater fully for all the possible variations that a firm may
face, but it is desirable to try and accommodate at least the most likely major
changes. This is done by conducting a sensitivity analysis, i.e. we alter the variables
in the model to reflect likely changes in the operating conditions. We might, for
example, like to see what effect increasing fuel costs might have on location, or,
indeed, the effect of any other factor which might increase transport costs. We
might also want to take account of variations in demand, or changes in the
strategy of our competitors and so on.

These aims can be met by altering the relevant factor in the basic calculation.
In Exhibit 16.12 it has been assumed that there has been a request to show the
likely effect on total costs for various systems of the introduction of some form
of increased road taxation and hence an increase in transport costs.

Yet another approach to try and accommodate the dynamicism of the business
environment was developed by R.H. Ballou. This method adopts the view that in

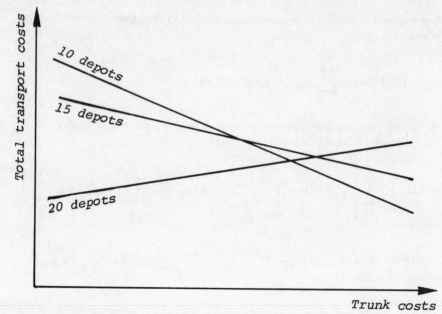

Exhibit 16.12 Sensitivity graph

the long run profit will be the most important factor influencing the location of a warehouse and it is any changes in this that should be paramount in decision-taking. The viewpoint assumes that such changes will not alter only operating costs but the best location for the warehouse over a given time period. This is naturally taking flexibility to its limit, and it is a fair comment to point out that such radical changes in conditions, whilst not unknown, are rare.

The situation envisaged is such that after a warehouse location has been decided upon, it is known that over the firm planning time scale there are likely to be such basic alterations in conditions that from time to time the 'best' location will vary. The method tries to develop a solution which will enable the management of the company to achieve maximum profits under these circumstances.

An example of this kind of problem might be where a firm is in a growth situation and expects to move into different market areas as those closest become satisfied. Or, it might be expected that the relevant importance of a firm's markets will change drastically over the next few years. This might be due to a heavy reliance in the past by an area on an industry (hence income and expenditure) now in severe decline, or through a particular area experiencing an upsurge in income as might be the case in certain areas in, say, Scotland.

Nevertheless it can be seen that the nature of the kind of changes mentioned is fundamental. It is not a shift in a variable that is being examined, but a total variation in conditions. This being said there will no doubt be areas of activity where the method is of use.

There are basically two stages in the formulation. First, the likely changes are
forecast and the best locations consistant with the variations are calculated for
each of the planning periods in question. This can be done using any of the
methods discussed previously. Secondly, profits for the chosen locations are calculated as below and reduced to a net present value. At the same time an estimate
is made of the cost of movement between the various sites and this is also reduced
to a net present value.

It will be obvious that the profit to be expected at the locations will depend on
the selling price of the products handled and the costs of transporting them to the
warehouses and thence to the customer. From what has already been developed, it
is a simple step to calculate profit:

$$\text{Profit} = \sum_{i=1}^{i=n} \left(S(q_1^{-p_i t_i/t} 1i) \, [q_1^{-p_i t_i \, t} 1i \, (r_1 d_1 + RD)] \right)$$

Where S is the selling price from each warehouse. This is simply the starting equation for our location formula except for the inclusion of price considerations.
Exhibit 16.13 gives the end results for a hypothetical situation.

To apply the technique a further assumption must be made, namely that it is
possible to close down a location and reopen another within one planning period
and that all such moves will take place within one period.

The method is a simple reiterative one which can be split into the following
steps. Starting at period 5 we assume location at a specific site, let us say A. From
Exhibit 16.13 we can see that the profit accruing if we stayed at this site would
be £2.6 million. There is however the possibility that this may not be the best
location. If there is a better location, i.e. one with higher profit, then it must be
at the other possible sites. We have nonetheless located at A. Therefore, if there is
to be an improvement through moving, the profit available must be such as to be
greater than that at A even after the cost of movement has been deducted. The
next step then is to examine the forecast profits at the other sites and see if any
are more attractive after movement costs (see Exhibit 16.14). As can be seen if we
were to locate at A, then there would be a better site available at E. This,
even allowing for the cost of movement, would increase profit by some £510,000.
Therefore the decision would be taken to move to E is we were located at A. (To
show this in Exhibit 16.15 below, MA is added in parenthesis after A.) Note what
was done. We assumed location at A, calculated the available profit, then said that
perhaps A was not the best site, and if there were a better one that it must be at
one of the other possible choices. To test this we assumed that we would move to
each in turn and if there were a greater profit available at any of them (net of
movement) then we would choose that site. From the exhibit it can be seen that
the decision path that would provide the greatest profit is to move to E.

There is no particular reason why we should locate at A in period 5. Therefore
the same procedure would have to be carried out making the initial assumption
that we were located in each of the sites in turn. The final decisions as indicated
by letters in parenthesis would then be transferred to a final decision path table
for that period and the next planning time span dealt with in a similar fashion.
This is a tiresome and time consuming procedure and a short cut is possible.
Exhibit 16.15 shows this method for the entire period 5. Construction is carried
out in the same manner as before. In the original first step where each site was

Exhibit 16.13 Forecast profits at net present value for sites in dynamic location problem

Site	Period 1 forecast profits	Period 2 forecast profits	Period 3 forecast profits	Period 4 forecast profits	Period 5 forecast profits
A	380,000	700,000	1,200,000	1,240,000	2,600,000
B	340,000	720,000	1,400,000	1,500,000	2,800,000
C	330,000	680,000	1,640,000	1,720,000	3,000,000
D	320,000	640,000	1,500,000	1,800,000	3,160,000
E	300,000	600,000	1,440,000	1,780,000	3,200,000
	Cost of move	Cost of move	Cost of move	Cost of move	Cost of move
	200,000	190,000	140,000	110,000	90,000

Exhibit 16.14

Site	Profit available	Cost of move	Net profit
B	2,800,000	90,000	2,710,000
C	3,000,000	90,000	2,910,000
D	3,160,000	90,000	3,070,000
E	3,200,000	90,000	3,110,000

Exhibit 16.15

Site	Profit available	Cost of move	Net profit
A (ME)	2,600,000	90,000	2,510,000
B (ME)	2,800,000	90,000	2,710,000
C (ME)	3,000,000	90,000	2,910,000
D (SD)	3,160,000	90,000	3,070,000
E (ME)	3,200,000	90,000	3,110,000

Exhibit 16.16

Site	Forecast	Best decision	Profit	Move	Res
A(ME)	1,240,000	+ 3,110,000	= 4,350,000	- 110,000	= 4,240,000
B(ME)	1,500,000	+ 3,110,000	= 4,610,000	- 110,000	= 4,500,000
C(ME)	1,720,000	+ 3,110,000	= 4,830,000	- 110,000	= 4,720,000
D(SD)	1,800,000	+ 3,160,000	= 4,960,000	- 110,000	= 4,850,000
E(SE)	1,780,000	+ 3,200,000	= 4,980,000	- 110,000	= 4,870,000

Exhibit 16.17

Site	Period 1	Period 2	Period 3	Period 4	Period 5
A	7,450,000(SA)	7,070,000(SA)	6,370,000(MC)	4,870,000(ME)	3,110,000(ME)
B	7,430,000(SB)	7,090,000(SB)	6,370,000(MC)	4,870,000(ME)	3,110,000(ME)
C	7,520,000(SC)	7,190,000(SC)	6,510,000(SC)	4,870,000(ME)	3,110,000(ME)
D	7,420,000(SD)	7,100,000(SD)	6,460,000(SD)	4,960,000(SD)	3,160,000(SD)
E	7,320,000(SE)	7,020,000(SE)	6,420,000(SE)	4,980,000(SE)	3,200,000(SE)

taken as the original location and a move then assumed it will be noticed that most of the calculations are repetitive. After one location has been dealt with the only variable in succeeding sites was the chosen location where no move is required, all other movements having been calculated previously. This is taken account of in the shorter table.

When we have all the discounted profits and all the net profits all that is required is to examine the table and decide the relevant moves. For site A the available profit is £2.6 million without a move. Net profits of £3.11 million are available at site E, so move to E. The available profit at site B is again £2.8 million without a move so again a move to E is the best. The same applies to site C. The situation changes slightly at site D. By staying at site D profits of £3.16 million can be made. From the table it can be seen that after the cost of movement has been covered the best available alternative is site E with £3.11 million. Since this is £50,000 below those possible at D then the best decision is to stay at D, hence the (SD) annotation. The same applies to site E.

Exhibit 16.15 then is a decision plan for the planning period 5. By following the annotations we ensure that the greatest profit is achieved. We then move to planning period 4 and so on backwards from the final planning period to the first because we are trying to build up a decision path for the five periods. By the time we reach the first period we will have calculated the maximum NPV profits available over the entire time span, thus allowing us to pick the path which is likely to bring greatest profits.

Having just calculated the maximum profit in period 5 we then must carry this into our calculation for period 4. Thus for period 4 we construct a table very similar to Exhibit 16.15 except that we must now include the best period 5 decision. Thus for site A we not only have the forecasted profit for period 4 but we add to this the result of the best decision in period 5 and from this we subtract the total cost of movement in period 4. It should be remembered that this cost of movement allows for closing-down and starting-up expenses. On completion of this table (see Exhibit 16.16) we proceed as before and choose that location decision which would provide the greatest profit. Assume we are at location A; the profit available is £4.35 million. If this is not the best location then that must be at one of the other sites and since we are at A then profit available at the improved site must be such as to produce a greater surplus even after the cost of movement has been allowed for. On examining our table it can be seen that site E has a profit of £4.87 million, a much more attractive proposition — even after movement costs there is an increase of some £520,000.

The same procedure is applied to all locations. Note that if we were located at site D no move would be undertaken.

Periods 3, 2 and 1 are treated in the same way and we end up with our final table (see Exhibit 16.17). This final table consists of the best results and their decisions for the total number of periods under consideration. Since the aim of the exercise is to enable a tool to be constructed which would help in the long-term planning the method of use is obvious. It can be seen that the most profitable course of action would be to locate at site C for periods 1, 2 and 3 and then move to E for the remaining two periods. This plan offers the maximum profit available within the parameters of the problem, namely £7.52 million. It also illustrates the foregone profits if the firm happens to be located at a different site.

Care must be exercised when looking at this particular situation. The long-term plan is a difficult area which must, nonetheless be tackled, but it must always

be borne in mind that techniques are subject to limitations as already discussed.
Such methods are management aids not management substitutes.

Let us now summarise our findings. There is no really useful theoretical method
available for making a location decision when dealing with more than one location.
The answer is to carry out an appraisal of the firm's distribution needs and to
come to a conclusion as to total numbers of distribution points likely to be suitable for the firm's capital and service requirements. Decide on the broad geographical markets that this number of depots have to serve. Using the ton-mile centre,
calculate the location of the individual warehouses within their respective areas,
and finally decide upon the detailed boundaries between each of the depot's
territories.

It may be worth repeating that the type of procedure outlined above will not
result in the best possible distribution pattern. It should however allow the firm
to determine a good pattern without it being involved in very high costs. Furthermore, if management remembers to reconcile the theoretical answers with the real
situation, the above procedure, simple though it is, will provide a compromise and
near optimum solution after the data has been collected.

There are a great many other methods of dealing with this problem of number
and location. Most of these are outside the scope of this book, but some will be
briefly described. All are faced with the same problem namely, there is no really
satisfactory method of dealing with the multi-locational problem other than
search. Consequently the more useful of them rely on the building up of a best
model, and then comparing this to the already existing pattern to make relevant
alterations. Bowman and Stewart developed such a method at the Massachusetts
Institute of Technology.

Briefly the method operates thus. It is assumed that as long as the concentration of demand for a warehouse territory remains constant, then if it is decided to
increase the extent of the area covered, the warehouse cost per unit will decrease
and the delivery cost per unit will increase, assuming that labour costs, etc., were
the same at other locations. It is also assumed that there is a class of costs that will
vary inversely with volume; i.e. as the volume of throughput increases, they will
decrease. Such costs would be associated with administration and other overhead
costs, increasing utilisation of labour, procurement costs and so on. It was also
decided that there is a further division of costs so that a class which varies with
the square root of the area served was isolated. This depends on the principle that
the radius and diameter vary with the square root of the area of a circle. If warehouse territories are drawn on a circular basis these costs would be those arising
from delivery. Finally there are other costs that remain more or less fixed, irrespective of changes in those costs already mentioned. Bowman and Stewart then
constructed an expression for the total costs incurred in serving an area from a
depot. This was

$$C = a + (b/v) + c(A)^{1/2}$$

where C is the cost within the warehouse territory per £ of goods distributed, v
the volume value of goods handled at each time interval, A the area in square miles
served by the warehouse, a fixed costs per £ of distributed goods independent of
area or volume and b fixed costs per time unit for the warehouse. When divided
by volume this will give cost per £ distributed and c costs that vary with the square
root of the area served.

Those costs that vary with delivery miles covered: the real data for $C(V)$ and A are introduced into the equation. From past operating experience and using least squares multiple regression techniques, values for a, b and c can be determined. Next the density of sales per area (K) was determined as $K = v/A$. Therefore $v = KA$. This quantity was substituted in the original equation giving:

$$C = a + (b/KA) + c(A)^{1/2}$$

By differentiation Bowman and Stewart then arrived at a general expression which could determine the best area to be served for any value of b or K:

$$A = (2b/cK)^{2/3}$$

Once the optimum area A is determined, it is a simple process to determine the location of the warehouse within its area by solving for the radius of a circle:

$$r = (A/\pi)^{1/2} = (A/3.14)^{1/2} \text{ approximately}$$

It will be noticed that although the approach outlined above is more complex than the original ton-mile centre procedure already discussed, the first step is the same, namely that management must decide by a search method the approximate overall area to be served by each depot in its distribution network. Once this has been decided the internal location can then proceed. While the Bowman Stewart method will undoubtedly give a more accurate answer than the simple ton-mile centre, the costs and time involved will also be much greater. Besides, it is likely that in most cases the end differences (once real limitations have been applied to the theoretical answer) will be small.

The above method is static in its approach. In the seventies there has been a move towards introducing dynamic elements into the solution of the locational problems. These methods rely on the solving of expected profits at a variety of locations and then discounting expected or calculated profits over the next planning period, say 7 years. The costs involved in moving between various locations under review are estimated and deducted from the expected profits. In this manner, for each of the years and between each of the locations the best course of action can be decided upon for any particular location and year bearing in mind that it is assumed that profit maximisation is desired. [See *Freight Management* (August 1971).]

On the other hand we might determine a general equation expressing all the costs that have to be minimised to obtain the optimum location of our depots. Such an equation might be:

$$TC_x = Cx_1 + Cx_2 + Cx_3 + Cx_4$$

where TC_x is unknown total costs under consideration, Cx_1 the customer service costs — cost of lost sales through absence of a depot within a particular area, Cx_2 the operating costs of depots (calculated from Bowman-Stewart formulation), Cx_3 the transportation costs (trunk) and Cx_4 the transportation costs (local distribution).

We would then evaluate the formulation for the various cost factors involved bearing in mind that the object of the exercise is to determine the lowest total

costs consistent with the predetermined service policy of the company. The procedure would once more be first to determine the location of all likely depots
within the total area covered by the firm, then by the use of minimisation
methods the best locations for the warehouses.

It can now be seen that all of the available methods follow the same broad
procedure, namely a geographical area is decided upon using the overall requirements of the company as a guideline. Then the costs involved in the
operation of a distribution depot within that area are determined, and a least-
cost location calculated. The method that is finally decided upon by the firm
will depend on the individual situation, the scope of the problem and the resources that are available to the distribution management. The more simple the
method the less expensive it is, the greater reliance placed on outside factors
and also the greater flexibility there is.

Obviously the final point to be made on these external factors affecting the
warehouse decision is that the more complex and expensive the problem then
the more complex and expensive will be the method chosen to attack it. At the
same time it must always be remembered that penny-pinching can have the
opposite result from that intended.

17 Internal operations

It will be remembered that the second broad area where the warehouse is brought to the attention of management is in the question of the operating efficiency, i.e. the internal operating effectiveness within an already existing network. The same broad area must, of course, also be considered when an entirely new system is being completed.

Our problem here can be reduced to a small number of basic considerations or cost centres within which costs must be reduced to the minimum while at the same time operating effectiveness is pushed to the maximum. These are, first, the choice of layout of the materials to be handled, secondly the choice of the handling equipment within the warehouse facility and, thirdly, the choice of the methods whereby the orders are assembled for despatch to the final customer, i.e. order picking schemes

These steps are designed for the situation where the management of a firm is setting up an entirely new distribution network, thus allowing a wide choice in matters of warehouse design and so on. In the actual work situation, however, it is more likely that the major share problem will be one of simple identification of the cost centres involved in the operation.

LOCATION AND LAYOUT

A great deal of attention has lately been paid to the most suitable type of building for the warehousing operation. The general consensus of opinion would appear to be that the single-storey warehouse has a number of advantages over the multi-storey alternative. These would seem to be centred around flexibility in internal layout and utilisation of enclosed space.

We are not concerned here with the general characteristics of the warehouse building, but with the positioning of the facilities to be employed therein. This fact tends to mean that there are some areas of conflict in layout beliefs. Here we will examine only those that have the widest application and can be utilised in multi- or single-storey buildings. The more specialised methods and ideals can be found elsewhere.

Basically the internal organisation of the average distribution warehouse is
extremely simple, consisting of a storage location surrounded by access aisles. The
storage methods employed will obviously vary to some extent but, except in
highly specialised facilities, will normally consist of one of the great variety of rack
layouts available.

Deciding the extent of these aisle widths and the method of pallet placement
are probably the two most important decisions made in this area. Exhibit 17.1
shows the two chief methods of pallet placement. Each of these methods has its
advocates. The major factors to be reconciled are the amount of space required
for pallet placement and the space taken up by the aisles. Opinion would seem
to favour angular placement under conditions of longer aisle lengths. The wastage
of storage space in the angular methods decreases in proportion to the total space
occupied by the storage area. Against this it must be remembered that the square-
on choice uses greater aisle widths. All of these factors must be examined and
appraised before any decision is made.

The next consideration is of considerable importance, but seems to receive
very little attention, this being the question of aisle widths. A significant amount
of the total space of the warehouse is absorbed by these and, when the cost of
warehouse space is remembered, it will be obvious that excess space in the aisles
can be an important loss centre.

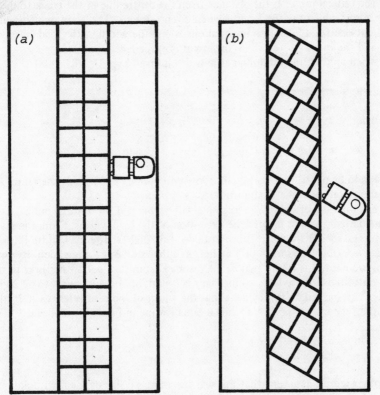

Exhibit 17.1 Methods of pallet placement:
(a) square; (b) diagonal

In any warehousing operation the two most important factors to be considered are cost of space and efficiency of materials movement; it often happens that these too are regarded as related but separate areas. This can result in the materials side being pushed to maximum efficiency without sufficient examination of any cost factors that might have been pushed on to the space factor. In this situation obviously the total approach has been ignored.

The two major types of lift truck in general use each have their own formula. Information concerning their use can be easily obtained. It is normally found in the manufacturers' specifications or from simple on-the-spot measurements.

It is intended, in the first instance, to deal with the rider type of truck, which has a seat for the operative in the normal driving position. The projecting platform or outrider type of truck will be considered secondly. Both the formulae used were first developed during the Second World War by the United States' Army Air Corps.

The symbols used for the calculation of minimum aisle widths for the rider type of lift truck are as follows: w is the minimum width of aisle, f the distance from the centre line of the truck to the centre line of the point around which the truck turns on full lock, r the running radius, l the length of load, b the breadth of load, h the safety clearance either side and d the distance from the centre line of the drive axle to the truck's face.

The critical factor is the distance from the centre line of the truck to the centre line about which the truck turns when given full lock. There are two formulae required: one for application in situations where the width of the load is less than $2f$, and the other for use when this point is exceeded.

When $w < 2f$, the minimum aisle width is given by:

$$w = r + d + l + h \tag{1}$$

When $w > 2f$:

$$w = r + [(d + l)^2 + (\tfrac{1}{2}b - f)^2]^{\tfrac{1}{2}} + h \tag{2}$$

It should be noted that the square root symbol does not include the factor h — the clearance on each side of the truck.

For the sake of clarity, an example will be worked for both formulae, using the same basic information with the exception of the load widths. From the manufacturers' specifications, it is found that $r = 62$ inches. The load width is 36 inches and a working clearance h of 4 inches on either side is recommended. By actual measurement, it is found that d, the distance from the heel of the forks to the centre of the front axle, is 16 inches; f is found, on measurement, to be 24 inches. From this basic data it is evident that the width of the load is less than $2f$, this indicating the use of the first formula. Substituting in Eq. (1), we obtain

$$w = 62 + 16 + 36 + 8$$
$$= 122 \text{ inches}$$

In other words, assuming that this was the standard size of the lift truck in use in the warehouse and that this was the maximum load length, then any aisles with a width greater than 122 inches are creating a cost centre for the business.

To illustrate the second formula, the same basic dimensions are used, except that the load width is increased to 55 inches. When using the formula to calculate aisle widths, obviously the greatest load width likely to be met is used in the basic data. Substituting in Eq. (2):

$$w = 62 + [(16 + 55)^2 + (27.5 - 24)^2]^{1/2} + 8$$
$$= 62 + 73 + 8$$
$$= 143 \text{ inches (rounded up)}$$

In other words, if this were the standard lift truck in use in the warehouse and the greatest load it would ever have to carry was 55 inches, then an aisle width of 143 inches would be the minimum. Anything above this figure is merely adding to the cost of the operation.

There are, of course, many situations in which the rider type of lift truck is not used and preference is given to the outrigger model. The most usual reason for the selection of the outrigger is the fact that this type of lift truck can often work in a smaller aisle width, and it also tends to have higher manoeuvrability than the rider type.

Under certain circumstances, therefore, the platform vehicle is more adaptable. This form of truck will obviously require an alternative formula to that already used, and the US Army Air Corps also developed such a formula allowing not only for the calculation of aisle widths but also for the minimum opening needed for loading. This latter would be of importance where, for example, the most economical distance between storage units is to be calculated.

Since this model is selected for narrow aisle widths, it is assumed that trucks are used where the width of the loads moved does not much exceed the width of the trucks. The dimensions used in this formula are much the same as those used previously, with a few additions. The former symbols will be used to denote the measurements already detailed. To enable the calculation to be made, the load overreach o, must be found. This is the distance from the face of the load to the centre of the front dollies of the truck. Only two more new dimentions are needed: e the turning radius of the rear end, and t, the distance from the centre of the turn to the outer edge of the load. These new measurements are determined by simple, on-the-spot measurement. Finally, x, which is equal to half the width of the truck, makes up the total of the new dimensions.

While it is easy to find t by measurement, it is also possible to calculate this requirement as follows:

$$t = [(x + \tfrac{1}{2}l)^2 + o^2]^{1/2}$$

When this is less than the rear-end turning radius e, the truck load does not exceed the width of the lift truck. In this case, the minimum aisle width is calculated as follows:

$$w = t + c_a$$
$$w_1 = e + c_b$$

where w_1 is the delivery berth width, and c_a and c_b are the working clearances for the moving and delivery aisles respectively. Normally the latter clearance will be slightly less than that of the working aisle. Relative sizes can be obtained from the manufacturers' specifications.

If the t is equal to or greater than e, the following method is adopted:

$$w = r + c_a$$
$$w_1 = t + c_b$$

While the use of these formulae will result in the minimum possible working aisle, a little adaptation will be necessary to suit them for everyday operation.

The first, most obvious use of the aisle is to act as a measure of efficiency. If the calculated aisle widths in a particular warehouse are significantly smaller than those in existence, then the indication is that there is a high hidden cost factor operating against the efficiency of that warehouse.

In real situations, one of the main parameters affecting the size of these aisles will be the skill and efficiency of the truck operatives. In this connection, a great deal can be achieved which will not only result in a better performance of the warehouse in strict monetary terms on the operating balance sheet, but will also bring about other benefits. These accrue through the lower damage rate, fewer stoppages and an increase in the speed of the handling cycle.

It is, therefore, a good idea to introduce a controlled instruction course with a factory certificate at the end. This will not only achieve a slightly higher job status, but should also, to some extent, remove the great variation in competence that is evident in lift truck operatives. This idea is already in use in many factories in this country, but there is an equally large number in which the progression to lift truck operative has no real set course of instruction. Help in increasing lift truck efficiency in this way could be sought from any of the major manufacturers.

By using these simple methods a great deal of expense might be saved. To illustrate just how this may come about let us continue to examine the situation mentioned above for which the aisle widths have been correctly calculated. What would happen if no total approach existed in this firm and the space and handling factors had been considered separately?

One of the basic laws of materials movement is that the greater the unit load moved then the cheaper will be the individual cost. This, like all basic laws, is valid over an impressive range of situations but not over all. Generally speaking, the efficiency of the lift truck on a given work task will increase as the lifting capacity increases. This can be seen from Exhibit 17.2 where the unit cost can be seen to be decreasing as the capacity or size of unit load moved increases. But it must be remembered that in the situation we are considering other factors have to be considered besides the materials movement efficiency.

It will be remembered that the size of the lift truck and the dimensions of its load both act to determine the minimum aisle width required for efficient operation. Obviously as the capacity of the lift truck goes up so also does the minimum size of the aisle required. In other words, increasing efficiency in the materials movement factor is offset by increasing costs in the space factor due to increase in aisle widths. This is most important in high cost locations. The critical fact is to see if one can cancel the other out. This is done as illustrated below. All data required is readily available and should in fact be ready for instant call. The key considerations are the price of the floor space, the increase in space required for each increase in truck capacity and the cost for lift truck and operative. A careful examination of these facts will result in the optimum choice of lift truck capacity, with regard to the savings made and the extra costs incurred.

The typical situation can be seen in Exhibit 17.3 where by increasing the lift

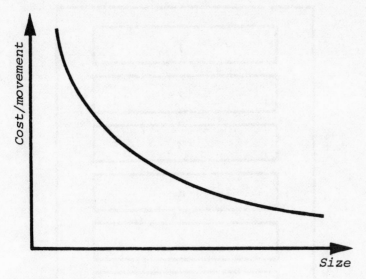

Exhibit 17.2

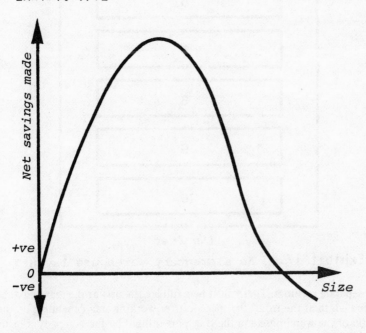

Exhibit 17.3

truck capacity there are substantial savings made in the first instance. After the point of maximum savings is reached it will be seen that the more the capacity is increased then the smaller the difference between savings and extra costs becomes.

As an example of the method assume that a situation having the following characteristics exists. As shown in Exhibit 17.4, the total length of the warehouse is 400 ft, the breadth is 150 ft and the internal layout is of the simplest, consisting

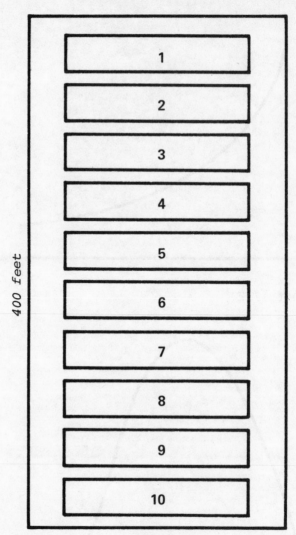

Exhibit 17.4 An elementary warehouse layout

of ten separate rackings. There must be a full-length aisle at the rear and at least the same width at the front, the space left for working area depending on the function of the warehouse and the transport utilised by the company. For the sake of the illustration we will also assume the following facts: that the cost of the lift truck plus driver worked out at £2.50 per hour and that the cost of the warehouse space works out at approximately 10p per month per square foot. Obviously the number of lift trucks required will vary with the capacity, but this does not directly affect the initial calculation since the space requirements for each truck capacity will be the same no matter if one or five trucks are in operation. The aisle will have to be the same basic width.

Using the formula already dealt with above it was found that the minimum

2500 lb	9 ft
4000 lb	10 ft
6000 lb	12 ft

Working from the dimensions already decided it will be seen that the total space requirements involved in the provision of working aisle with the above dimensions are:

2500 lb	20,268 ft^2
4000 lb	22,300 ft^2
6000 lb	26,232 ft^2

It has already been established that the total time required to complete a total work cycle is 10 min. For the final comparison it is first necessary to establish the savings due to increasing the capacities and to compare these with the extra costs incurred through the increase in space.

SAVINGS DUE TO INCREASING CAPACITY

Time   Number of trips required to move 150,000 lb of material with the 2500-lb trucks equals 150,000/2500 = 60 trips. Number of trips required with the 4000-lb truck equals 150,000/4000 = 37, therefore the savings due to using the 4000-lb truck = 60 − 37 = 23. Since each cycle takes 10 minutes the total saving is 230 minutes or 4 hours per day, which equals 100 hours per 25-working-day month Thus the savings due to the faster movement equals £250 per month, but by moving from the 2500-lb model to the 4000-lb model the space required increases from 20,268 to 22,300 ft^2 or an increase of 2032 ft^2. This is, of course, equivalent to a cost of £203. Therefore, the net gain due to the use of the larger capacity truck is £47 per month or £564 per annum. By moving further, from the 4000 to the 6000-lb model the situation changes. Time saving equals 37 − 25 = 12 trips or 120 mins, which is equivalent to 2 hr per day or 50 hr per month. The monetary savings achieved by the switch therefore amount to £125 per month. The additional costs are calculated as before.

The space requirement for the 6000-lb truck less that for the 4000-lb truck is 26,232 − 22,300 = 3932, equivalent to additional costs of £393.20. Therefore the end result in changing to the 6000-lb model is a loss of £268.20 per month, or approximately £3218 per year.

It will be noticed, no doubt, that we have been dealing with the situation where only one lift truck is under consideration. The lift truck is one of the most important pieces of equipment in the warehouse, very few operations use only one. The question we must now ask is will the same general line of reasoning hold true when more than one lift truck of the various capacities is being considered?

Some doubt may arise here. It is very often the case that the warehouse manager will agree with what has gone before and point out that this is all very well, but in his operation these considerations do not count because he substitutes a smaller number of large trucks and saves on the capital differences. He is saying that if he stuck to the smaller models he would need more of them to perform a good job in a large volume warehouse, the costs incurred by the larger capacity models being recouped from lower capital costs.

We must be careful here, however. The saving in capital cost (if it exists) is a one and for all saving, but the loss which we incur through greater space requirements will be with us as long as that given size of lift truck is utilised in the warehousing. If, for example, in the problem above we decided that substitution would be the better method and budgeted for five 6000-lb trucks rather than, say, seven 4000-lb ones, then the cost savings on the two trucks would have to be more than the annual loss of £3218 over the life of the trucks, in say 5 years. Taking the cost of this firm's capital as 10 per cent and allowing, say, 2 per cent for inflation this would have a present value of approximately £11,584. This sum is, of course, constant irrespective of the number of lift trucks being used. It is used as a base cost, i.e. the increasing efficiency brought about by larger numbers of trucks must always exceed this amount. Naturally different conditions will produce different values at this point, but the lesson should nonetheless be clear. Whilst on this subject of fork lift trucks and their numbers, many firms lose money by having incorrect numbers of trucks in their fleets, erring either by purchasing too many for the job on hand or (equally expensive) too few.

To overcome both these problems it is only necessary to apply simple methods which can save the warehousing manager a great deal of money in comparison to the amount of time that is required to carry out the procedure. There are some sectors about which management believes in equipment for its own sake. If the correct machine for the job is purchased, the feeling is that there should be an increase immediately in productivity and a decrease in costs. This can be the case, especially with the introduction of a correct number of lift trucks: but the trucks themselves cannot decide the optimum number to be purchased. This is a job for management, and a great deal of effort and money can be saved by the use of simple-to-apply methods. The introduction of the most efficient capacity by these methods can be the key to the profitability of the entire scheme.

SCIENTIFIC APPRAISAL

There are two ways in which savings can accrue to the firm in question. In the first instance, the number of lift trucks that are required may show a decrease over the figure decided by rule of thumb ideas. Not only will the initial investment be less, but the trucks purchased will be subject to a high degree of utilisation. In the long run, this means a greater return on the capital invested.

It is not only in reducing the number of lift trucks required that savings can be made. Indeed, this is probably the least important of the economies that will appear. By a scientific appraisal of the problem it is quite likely that, far from overestimating the number of lift trucks, 'rule of thumb' methods may under estimate the required capacity. If this happens, then, in the long run the real cost to the company will be a great deal more damaging than the saving in initial investment. If materials movement within the firm is slowed down because of a lack of lifting capacity, then additional cost burdens will be generated in the form of higher operating costs, increased process times involving financial losses due to capital 'tie up' and, eventually, a loss of customers. They will move their business to a firm that can deliver in a shorter period, allowing them a correspondingly longer earning life for the assets in question.

Obviously, the industrial and commercial uses to which the unit load system lends itself are far too numerous for a general formulation, applicable to all situations, to be made. In most lift truck work environments, however, there are a large enough number of common factors to allow standard formulae to be easily adapted. The final information required will in all cases be the same. What will vary will be the techniques of its collection and reduction to the final form.

The basic information required should be easily and quickly available to the executive who cares to search for it. A high proportion of the data is found in the information which lift truck manufacturers include in their publicity material. The additional material can be easily assembled by work or inspection, this task being carried out by the simple timing of operations by a stop watch. There is every possibility that the information desired has a place in a previous time and motion study. If such a study has not been carried out, then a short work sampling programme on the work cycle may be desirable. This will reveal the essential elements of the job and may suggest areas for economies which may themselves act towards the benefit of the scheme to introduce a fleet of lift trucks.

Two factors are always present which have an influence on the choice of a truck. These are the dimensions and weight of the unit load. These will determine the speed and carrying capacity of the lift truck and the distance over which the load has to be moved, which will have a direct influence on the total number required. The performance of the truck selected at the unit load weight present will also be needed and this is obtained from the manufacturer's specification. The collection of data is applied to the total workload and the outcome weighted by the coefficient of delay.

The coefficient of delay is the key to the whole situation and removes the calculation from the realms of a theoretical exercise to a valuable aid to all materials movement managers. The coefficient of delay is a ratio linking the theoretical time required for the positioning of the lift truck, acceleration and any other event which results in an increase in the time taken to complete the work cycle.

For the sake of example, the problem now considered is reduced to its simplest requirements. It is not a far step to apply the method to the problems of the shop floor and/or warehouse. It will be seen that the only difference between the theory and practice is the collection of data required for the calculation of the delay coefficient.

CYCLE TIME

In the first instance, consider that the work cycle under review consists of the movement of unit loads from a storage bay to a warehouse. The loads are collected overnight from a production line and they must be removed (minus meal times) from the warehouse over an 8-hour shift. The total load consists of 700 units, each weighing 2300 lb. The truck type has already been selected and has a lifting capacity of 2 ton. Operating speeds are 420 ft/min loaded, and 600 ft/min when light. The distance to be covered is 350 ft, pick up time 4 sec and release 3 sec. The first step is to calculate, using only the performance and work requirement figures, the time required for one cycle. This is weighted and the optimum number of lift trucks desired reached. From the performance data:

Pick up load	=	4 sec
Move to release point	=	50 sec
Return load	=	3 sec
Return light	=	35 sec
Total	=	92 sec

Thus from the data at hand and with a cycle time of 92 sec, 3 left trucks would be required.

DELAY COEFFICIENT

However, at this point, we have not yet introduced the coefficient of delay. This is calculated as the ratio of the total elapsed time to running time. In this example, suppose that the total elapsed time is equal to 6 min and the running time is 3 min. This would give 6/3 = 2. In other words, the delay coefficient for this operation is a weighting of 2. It might be mentioned at this point that experiences have shown that, as the distance to be travelled increases, the coefficient of delay decreases.

The theoretical time is weighted by 2 to give a real cycle time of 184 sec. This means that the work is completed in a time of approximately 3 min. Thus, in 1 hr, a lift truck can be expected to complete a total of 20 trips or 160 per 8-hr shift. Therefore, if the job specification is to be met in an efficient manner, there will have to be an increase up to 5 trucks (strictly 4.3).

SHORT-TERM HIRE

It can be seen that the use of the simple delay coefficient has resulted in the avoidance of installing a lift truck fleet of far less capacity than the job requires. In the above example, it is obvious that there has been a great deal of simplification; the most obvious lack is of provision for breaks for the operatives of the lift trucks. In practice there is no great problem. The carrying out of the work sampling study already mentioned will remove the unrealistic factors from the assessment of the delay coefficient taken over a period of time which the lift trucks spend in the various factors of the work cycle. Alternatively, the most straightforward solution is to construct a simple average for daily running times and total elapsed times from data obtained from work observation or, finally, simply deduct the breaks from the length of the shift.

The latter approach is better combined with the simple daily average. If the scheme is entirely new and the firm does not have a lift truck on hand for the calculation, it is easy either to hire a truck for a short period or to request the manufacturer for a trial. Whichever course is adopted, the use of this simple method will result in savings, either in the initial investment or in the more complex area of losses which would have occurred through lack of lift truck capacity.

We have spent a great deal of time on the question of fork lift trucks; this is simply because these pieces of equipment are probably one of the most common handling aids in the warehouse. They are also aids which can greatly increase the profitability of any warehousing operation provided that they are used to the best of their capabilities. What we have said about their use can be applied to all mater-

ials handling aids in the warehouse, namely that the total approach must always be
employed, great care being exercised to ensure that what may appear as economies
are not achieved by the transfer of costs to some other part of the operation.

INVENTORY LOCATION AND ORDER PICKING

When we have decided on the pallet placement method, aisle widths and types of
fork lift truck to be used our next important decision is the actual pattern of inventory location in the warehouse. The most common method is to divide warehouse capacity into a number of zones which form the basis of the order picking
system and also allow management to decide which of its products will be located
in the various zone areas, bearing in mind what has already been said on the ABC
approach to inventory management.

There are three techniques in common use for deciding the pattern of inventory
layout. Each of these must, of course, be examined bearing the specific conditions
in mind and a decision between them taken on this basis.

Exhibit 17.5 gives the characteristics of the four products. It will be noted that
the chief points which we are interested in are the volume of each unit, the number
of units normally expected to be in each order, frequency of orders and the amount
of inventory of each item which is held in the warehouse. Using these basic facts

Exhibit 17.5 Demand on hand

Item	Cube per item	Average order size	Orders per day	Capacity required, ft^3
1	3	10	200	12,000
2	5	4	400	8,000
3	2	5	250	10,000
4	10	2	500	30,000

we can form a very clear picture of the demand patterns of the various merchan-
dising groups under consideration. We will assume that the warehouse is divided
into three zones having capacities of 10,000, 20,000 and 30,000 ft^3, respectively.

Before we can actually apply location ideas we have one other factor which we
must calculate which is the cost of order selection. The best method of dealing
with this is by the application of work sampling to the warehouse operations, but
since the technique has wider implications than calculating order selection costs, a
full discussion of the method is left to the end of this section. We will assume at
this point that work sampling can be applied to determine the order selection
costs within the warehouse zones.

One of the most often encountered location methods is by popularity. The
ordering pattern of the groups held in the warehouse is examined and the most
popular items placed in the zones closest to the assembly and shipping area. This
is based on the assumption that the most common variable in order picking is the
distances that have to be travelled and time taken. This is, of course, a wide gener-

alisation, but in those operations where it does not hold, investigation through work sampling will throw up the most important, and the location of the zones be altered accordingly.

Exhibit 17.6 shows the layout that would be applied under the assumed conditions. We have rearranged the items handled in order of popularity. It will be noted that since item 4 is both the most popular and requires the greatest storage

Exhibit 17.6 Location by popularity

Item	Orders per day	Capacity required, ft^3	Zone	Order pick cost	Total cost
4	500	30,000	1-2	$7\frac{1}{2}p$	£37.50
2	400	8,000	3	15p	£60.00
3	250	10,000	3	15p	£37.50
1	200	12,000	3	15p	£30.00
				TOTAL PICK COST	£160.00

Exhibit 17.7 Location by unit size

Item	Cube per item	Orders per day	Capacity required, ft^3	Zone	Order pick cost	Total cost
3	2	250	10,000	1	5p	£12.50
1	3	200	12,000	2	10p	£20.00
2	5	400	8,000	2	10p	£40.00
4	10	500	30,000	3	15p	£75.00
					TOTAL PICK COST	£147.50

Exhibit 17.8 Location by total requirements

Item	Total space required, ft^3	Zone	Order pick cost	Number of orders	Total pick cost
2	8,000	1	5p	400	£20.00
3	10,000	1-2	$7\frac{1}{2}p$	250	£18.25
1	12,000	2	10p	200	£20.00
4	30,000	3	15p	500	£75.00
				TOTAL ORDER PICK COST	£133.25

space it must be located in zones 1 and 2, thus affecting the handling costs as shown.

Exhibit 17.7 shows the four items laid out under another popular method, namely by the unit size of the individual groups. It will be noted that a saving is made on the daily selection costs by changing to the second method.

Exhibit 17.8 illustrates another common technique employed. Here the location is decided by total storage requirements, the smallest need being placed in the cheapest zone and so on. Again there is a saving in the daily order selection costs.

There would seem to be suggested here that the best way of dealing with this problem would be to adopt some method of location which would combine the best points of the three systems illustrated above. Such a method has been with us for several years now and is known as the cube/order index. As the name suggests the technique relies on the relationship between total space requirement and the number of orders demanded for each particular group of products. The method is used simply by constructing a cube/order index in declining order. The cube/order is calculated by dividing the total space requirement by the number of orders; this is repeated for each item and the results arranged as described above. In the case of our four items the cube/order index would run items 2,3,1,4,20,40, 60,60.

The cube/order index is probably the most accurate technique in the location problem, but it is best suited to the situation where a large number of items are being handled. In our example here the use of this method does not improve on the total capacity method. When this occurs management has greater flexibility. It can choose to lay out inventory in either of these ways depending which method suits its individual demands best. It is because of this possibility of greater flexibility that it is always best to determine the costs involved with all four methods before the final decision is made. If, however, because of cost or time this is not possible then the best method of approach is to apply the cube/index method from the start.

ORDER PICKING METHODS

We have now decided upon the best zone location inventory, but we are still left with the problem of deciding how the orders will be assembled to our shipping area. There are basically three order picking routines: the area method, the zone technique and the multiple-order system. These methods do not necessarily need to be employed throughout the entire operation, as they can be (and are) altered to suit the individual's requirement.

In the area system, the simplest, the inventory is arranged in a logical order throughout the warehouse, each item being located in a specific area. The order picker circulates through the areas assembling the order as he proceeds. A secondary labour force continually replaces the stock consumed. Each order is completed as the picker moves through the areas, and returned to a central shipping area. The working stock is always kept up to consumption by the replacement from reserve stock.

In the zone method each picker operates within a specified zone of the warehouse which will contain inventory. As each order is received it is split into its component parts and each requirement sent off to the relevant zone, where it is assembled and transported back to a central consolidation and shipping area. A variation on this basic method is for each separate requirement to be assembled in sequence, the order being transported from zone to zone until completed. This method overcomes a disadvantage of the more simple zone method, namely that every order has to be completed before the next enters the system.

The multiple-order method is the most complex and also the most expensive. A group of orders is taken and each separate requirement despatched to the relevant zone in consolidated form. Each component is identified with the parent order by means of colour coding or labelling. When all the individual components have been assembled they are despatched to the central assembly area, where the original parent orders are assembled from each of the consolidated items. Obviously this method requires a great deal of tight control, usually on a timing basis.

It will be noticed that, for the purpose of calculating order selection costs for use in the location decision, only in the simple zone order picking method is the information easily obtainable. The ideas behind location methods still hold and it will be obvious how important they are now irrespective of the order picking discipline used. Simply because they become more complex to decide upon does not mean that they should be ignored. In fact, by using work sampling methods the relevant costs can quite easily be found by any of the methods outlined above.

Work sampling is not, however, limited to deciding order selection costs. The technique can be used for the entire warehousing operation. This is very important as one of the greatest difficulties experienced in efficient control of this function is allocation of costs. As will be seen work sampling programmes can be extended to give a full picture of the total cost situation in the warehouse.

Work sampling consists of a large number of random observations of the function being investigated. From these it is possible to build up a reliable idea of just exactly what operations take most time and money within the warehouse. If, say, on 30 per cent of the observations made on a particular programme a lift truck was standing idle, of the total time that lift truck was available for use within the warehouse, then the same proportion would be spent waiting for work. In other words if an activity takes up a certain proportion of the total observations made it is likely that this same relationship will hold over the entire working life of the system, providing that all else does not change. This proportion is based on the laws of probability and can be upheld mathematically.

The accuracy of the prediction will depend on the number of observations made. Obviously as the total number of observations made increases, so does the accuracy. Methods of deciding the number required for desired accuracy levels will be discussed below.

There must first, however, be a more detailed explanation of the technique involved. The number of observations required will depend on the degree of accuracy demanded. Whilst it is tempting to say that 100 per cent accuracy is what we want, it must be realised that this is not possible unless we are prepared to spend a great deal of time and money. This level is seldom worthwhile anyway. For example, try forecasting with 100 per cent accuracy the length of your next telephone conversation, or face-to-face meeting with other management, then assess the effect of, say, plus or minus 5 per cent in accuracy.

Unless costs are very tight 95 per cent accuracy would normally be considered more than acceptable in most situations. Therefore our discussion relating to calculating the number of observations required will be based on achievement of 95 per cent confidence levels of stated accuracy. That is, if we say that X number of observations will show that activity A takes up 50 per cent of time plus or minus 5 per cent we are 95 per cent confident that this forecast is correct. The formulae given are to be found in any standard work on statistics and are available, of course, for different confidence levels. For 95 per cent confidence levels, the number of observations required, N, is given by

$$N = 4p\,(100 - p)/L^2$$

Where L is the limits of forecast and p the estimated time of activity as a percentage of total time. Thus

$$L = 2\,[P(100 - P)/N]^{\frac{1}{2}}$$

where P is the calculated percentage time for the activity.

From the above formulae it is obvious that in the first instance we have to estimate the time that a particular activity takes up of the available time. In the second formula we use the calculated percentage.

We must therefore check fairly quickly to see if our estimate is reasonable. If not, then we recalculate the number of observations required. A convenient method is to plot the total number of observations against the estimated percentages as shown in Exhibit 17.9. At first there will be violent fluctuations but as the accuracy of the original estimate improves these will die down as shown. As this occurs the original guesstimate is confirmed and the study can proceed. If there is no settling down then obviously the original value assigned to p must be changed.

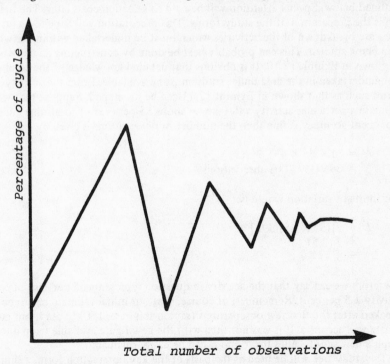

Exhibit 17.9

In practice we would continue and calculate the L value which would then give us a better basis for the alteration required to p, i.e. unless the fluctuations were severe and continued to be so.

The use of work sampling in the warehouse will enable the warehouse manager to identify those areas which are of primary concern with regard to overall utilisation of equipment within the warehouse and will help him in making the choice of specific areas where an efficiency drive will produce the greatest benefits.

For example, assume that the lift truck already mentioned was at work within a particular warehouse, and only employed 70 per cent of the possible time. Either there is overcapacity in this factor or there is a bottleneck further along the line. Which of these two situations exists does not really matter; the point is that work sampling has thrown up the question and appropriate action can be taken by the warehousing manager. Again it can frequently happen that there is a bottleneck which has been difficult to identify. The work sampling study should throw this up, since it will show how costs are, in fact, generated and not as they are assumed to be.

A work sampling scheme is a project perfectly feasible for the distribution manager to design and carry out without the help of an outside specialist. No particular skills are required except a deep knowledge of the area being investigated. The entire study consists of preparing the work sample forms which are used to record observations, the actual carrying out of the observations and the analysis and presentation of the results. Assuming that the study is aimed at the overall construction of costs, as opposed to the investigation of a specific piece of equipment, say, for example the fork lift trucks employed, the steps will be as outlined below. Special attention will be paid to selection costs later. The first job is the preparation of the study forms. This preparation will depend on an accurate breakdown of the activities which must be undertaken within the work area being studied. This can probably best be done by constructing an activity tree as shown in Exhibit 17.10. It is obvious that detailed knowledge of the total operation undertaken in the area under study must be available. From the activity tree forms such as that shown in Exhibit 17.11 can be developed. Suppose that we estimate a particular activity will take up about 55 per cent of total time and that 5 per cent accuracy is fine then the number of observations is given by

$$N = (4 \times 55 \times 45)/5^2$$
$$= 396 \text{ (say 400) observations}$$

The limits of variation would be:

$$L = 2[(55 \times 45)/396]^{1/2}$$
$$= 2 (2.5)$$
$$= 5$$

Therefore we can say that the activity in question represents 55 per cent of activity ± 5 per cent. Remember, of course, that our initial estimate has to be checked after the first few observations (say, in this case, 150) to see if our guesstimate was accurate. If it was not then with the new figure available from our graph a new set of values for N and L can be easily calculated.

The study tree will be used as the basis of the key observation form, a simple example of which is shown in Exhibit 17.12. Obviously a list is made of all the

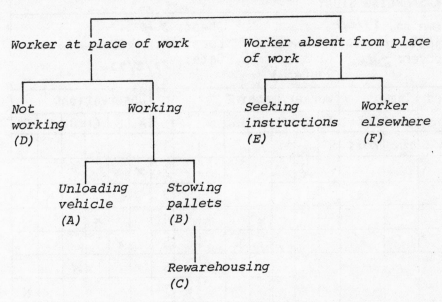

Observations

Worker at place of work   Worker absent from place
                               of work

Not   Working   Seeking   Worker
working   instructions   elsewhere
(D)   (E)   (F)

        Unloading   Stowing
        vehicle   pallets
        (A)   (B)

                       Rewarehousing
                       (C)

separate work elements that the study is intended to cover. It is essential when
this is being done to remember that the observers must be able to recognise the
work elements with ease. This means that all the activities to be observed must be
carefully defined. If it is desired to examine a particular function in depth then it
is easy to construct the requisite form, only this time breaking the element in
question down into its elementary components.

It is worth pointing out at this stage that it is of the utmost importance to inform the employees within the warehousing complex that the study is being
organised. From the very basis of the method it will be obvious that if the study
is to be successful, it is also desirable that the reasons behind the work sampling
project are explained to the workers. An air of suspicion surrounding the observers
will not help the accuracy of the scheme.

The work sample form should be as simple in layout as possible. All activities
that occur from the moment a consignment arrives at reception should be classi-
fied and located on the form, which should include written definitions of the
work components being observed and space for the appropriate recording to be
made. Again, the sample sheet included is given as a starting point.

Once the layout and composition have been decided upon, the study can be
initiated. This is done by the work sample operative making random passages
through the work place observing the activities which are going on as he passes
through. The actual activity at the time must be recorded. It is important to
stress that no interpretation is to be placed on actions at this stage. If the obser-

Exhibit 17.11 Sampling form

WORK SAMPLING STUDY

Scheme no. 53/a/1
Subject: Warehouse movements
Observer: DBK
Route: y

Sheet: 3 of ...
Location: Main warehouse
Date: 27/8/77

Round no.	Time On	Time Off	1	2	3	4	5	6	7		A	B	C	D	E	F
14	0710	0725	X							1	X					
				X						2	X					
					X					3					X	
						X				4			X			
							X			5		X				
								X		6				X		
									X	7						X
15	0818	0833	X							1	X					
				X						2						X
					X					3			X			
						X				4			X			
							X			5		X				
								X		6				X		
									X	7						X
16	0900	0915	X							1	X					
				X						2	X					
					X					3				X		
						X				4				X		
							X			5		X				
								X	X	6						

ver sees a workman in complete inactivity then this should be recorded. Later the reasons for an abnormally high number of idle observations can be looked at, but the object of the study is to find out just exactly what the work components are.

The most important condition associated with any work sampling scheme is randomness. It is of the utmost importance that the personnel involved develop a completely random series of observations. There are many reasons for this, the two major ones being related in the first instance to the work force and the second to the equipment involved in the study. If, for example, the equipment under observation has a definite operating cycle, then if the observer arrived on a regular schedule just after the machine had commenced its cycle it would always be recorded as operating. This same broad consideration would, of course, also apply to the labour force within the warehouse. In the latter case if it was obvious that the study personnel appeared at regular intervals it is likely that the labour force would be at pains to seem busy when the observer made his round.

There is another type of error that can occur through the very nature of work sampling, this being due to chance causes. These are reduced through taking as great a number of observations as is practical. A method of deciding on the number of observations to be taken will be looked at later. The essential point is that the observer must at all times preserve the random nature of his study.

It is normally worthwhile to develop a summary chart of the results of the work sampling scheme as it progresses. The chief advantage is that with a summary

Exhibit 17.12 Work sampling form: summary sheet

WORK SAMPLING PROJECT			
Scheme no. 53/a/1 Subject: Warehouse movements Observers: 2/GJM & DBK		Date: 27/8/77 Location: Main warehouse Workers: 15	
Number of observations required: 8000 Period of study: 28 days Number of trips per day: 19/day/observer			
Activity key reference	Observations: no. required	Estimated time as a percentage of total time	95% confidence as percentage of total time
A	2600	32.5	± 1.0%
B	321	4.0	± 0.5%
C	1560	19.6	± 0.8%
D	1700	21.3	± 0.8%
E	525	6.6	± 0.5%
F	1294	16.1	± 0.8%
Totals	8000	100.0	

chart the data can be handled more conveniently as it accumulates. To arrive at a percentage breakdown of the importance of the various work elements being investigated the number of times a particular function was observed is divided by the total number of observations made and multiplied by 100. Thus, if out of a total of 2000 observations, it was observed that a machine was idle on 150 occasions, then the idle time of the machine over its normal working period will be equal to 30 per cent of its total operating schedule. This summary will, of course, be used in the final presentation of the work sampling study.

When the study has been completed there are two broad activities that will result in the final presentation of the essential categories required. These in the first case will be the evaluation of the validity and reliability of the study and the translation of the data into meaningful form. This latter process consists of turning the percentage time elements of the warehouse function into money terms.

As regards the validity of the original data the most perfect way of ensuring this is to choose carefully the personnel responsible for conducting the study. The most important man here, of course, is the warehouse manager himself.

There is no point in setting up a work sampling programme if you yourself are not fully convinced of its usefulness. An attitude of reserve will only communicate itself to the other members of the observation team, resulting in a less than accurate study. If this is not to be the responsibility of the warehouse manager himself, it is important to ensure that the person chosen as director is familiar with the application of the method and can engender a degree of enthusiasm in all concerned with the project.

There are, of course, almost certain to be some errors in the study itself. As far as these go it is useful to remember that they are almost always due to some form of mistake on the part of the observers and as such could be eliminated by attention to detail. The most common example is failure to correctly identify the personnel engaged in a particular function. This can result in either the wrong appropriation of time being made or a straight misidentification of the time to be allotted to a specific work element. Another common error is not to take account of special conditions. This situation can arise if, for example, a non-recurring order happens to take place at the same time as the study is being conducted. Such conditions as these should be brought to the attention of the person responsible for the study. Again, if there is a change in the basic operations of the company during the study period, such as a change in methods of manufacture, this again should be brought to the attention of the director of the study.

The validity of the actual conclusions that can be drawn from the result of sampling study will obviously depend on the accuracy of the basic data. The governing condition here is that the accuracy of the data will increase with the number of observations that are made. This in turn will vary from component to component, depending on its proportion of the total number of observations. There are standard tables available for arriving at this number. A more convenient check is to plot the percentage occurrences of a particular work element against the total number of observations. At first there will be violent fluctuations as is shown in Exhibit 17.9, but as the accuracy of the percentage allotted to the element increases these will smooth out. As this occurs the number of observations being made is approaching that necessary for accuracy. Once these conditions are looked to, the final stage of the study can be completed. This is the translation from percentages taken up with the total cycle time to what these represent in money terms.

This is best tackled by each individual work category. The first step is to prepare the total presentation as already described with reference to the summary chart. The data arrived at represents, as we have already pointed out, the appropriation by time of the relative expenses in the overall operation of the warehouse. This is converted to money terms by applying an overhead weighting that will apportion the cost to the various work elements in proportion to the time they take up in the total scheme of operations.

The weighting factor is arrived at as follows. The cost accounts of the warehouse and the total expenses associated with the handling function are noted. This will consist of the cost of the labour force and other direct expenses and also indirect expenses. This total sum is divided by the cost of labour to give the weighting factor. Say, for example, the first category used in a particular study was unloading and this consisted of factors such as direction of lorry, opening of door and preparation of load waiting for lift truck, direction of lift truck, travelling of lift truck and so on. Assume that the respective times of these activities were as shown in Exhibit 17.13 and the total direct costs were £1800 and the weighting

Exhibit 17.13

	Percentage to total	Direct cost	Total costs
Direction of lorry	3	300	600
Opening of doors	2	200	400
Waiting	4	400	800
Direction	3	300	600
Travel	6	600	1200

factor 2. It will be noticed that the direct cost is taken as the percentage as a direct translation into the unit decided upon. This can be anything convenient for the study. For example, if the total costs of the warehouse used when the calculation of the weighting factor was being made were in £ per month then this would be the unit which the direct contribution was translated into.

It will be seen that this approach reveals the relative importance of the various components that go to make up the total costs of the warehouse. There is available a second method that will show up the proportion of time that the factors studied take up of the total operations. This is achieved from the same basic data which was collected in the first study. The individual time loadings are arrived at as follows:

$$T = 60pm/n$$

where T is the time in minutes, p the percentage of total occurrences, m the total man hours worked and n the number of material categories handled.

This approach will enable the warehouse manager to identify the particular product classes that take up more than proportionate amounts of handling time. When this information is related to the value and amount of these materials handled it is possible that discrepancies will show up. For example, suppose that a particular material represents only a small proportion of the total throughput of the warehouse both in terms of value and volume; investigation of the time spent handling it could show that it was requiring an inordinate amount of time and money to deal with it. This could be a possible area for cost reduction by eliminating this from the warehouse or if this is not in keeping with the policy of the company other steps could be taken. This would perhaps consist of an investigation of the handling properties of the product with a view to increasing their efficiency. This could be the introduction of unitisation or perhaps a change in the packaging methods used. If the company only carries the line for occasional demands, a rationalisation of the amounts held might reduce the quantities to be handled. If it is to supply outside customers a change in ordering size might help. This would involve, say, prepacking in units of convenient size (to help handling costs) and only supplying at that number. Realising that a particular product is adding to costs more than it is adding to the efficiency of the warehouse would also enable a more selective order pattern to be made up, substituting more profitable items for the cost generating ones.

As was pointed out above the work sampling technique can also be used to determine particular costs such as order picking costs. If we find that the total costs of handling in for a specific area or type of merchandise is, say, £10,000, and the total handling out costs £16,000 and we are, say, handling 12,000 items, then the order-picking costs for that particular set of conditions would be as shown in Exhibit 17.14. If on the other hand it was decided to examine each of the activities involved in turn then, of course, a study confined to that particular order picking cycle would be mounted.

Exhibit 17.14

Handling out costs	*16,000*
Handling in costs	*10,000*
Difference	*6,000*

Total number of items: 12,000
Therefore

PICKING COST/UNIT = 50p

But there is little doubt that the main application of the results of work sampling will arise from the presentation adopted in Exhibit 17.5 showing the incidence of cost centres within the warehouse. As the warehouse can bring a great deal of benefit to the firm it will sooner or later be requested to increase efficiency. As has already been pointed out, there is no sense in trying to cut costs until the work sample scheme shows up their relative importances.

In the sample form used here there are several areas which immediately show up as factors that could benefit from a study. These include elements like the great amount of time which is spent in waiting for the lift truck to arrive. What is the cause? Could a new layout help? Or type of packaging, size of lift trucks, new equipment?

Presented in this form the study will help the manager to allocate his budget to obtain the greatest results. If, for example, it is shown that packing takes up the greatest amount of time then there is a straight implication that investment in some sort of automatic machine would help. Depending on how detailed the study is, it might show that the nailing of cases is a major work element in terms of time, and by purchasing relatively inexpensive pneumatic equipment an important bottleneck will be removed and an overall increase in effectiveness achieved. The actual unloading of the materials handled might show up as an inordinately large cost centre. This can be speeded by cheap aids as opposed to the purchase of additional lift trucks, which might be the most usual reaction.

The work sample study will, then, be of advantage to the warehouse manager, chiefly because it will identify the most important areas where costs are being generated.

In practice the study will probably be in two parts, one phase being used to identify the broad factors where profits are lost, the second to probe more deeply into these activity categories. For example, in the case just mentioned where the loading/unloading operations are shown to be taking too much time a more detailed study would be initiated to establish the cause exactly. This could reveal that, for example, the trucks were held up by a lack of lift trucks, or that the lift trucks were not in use for a high percentage of the time due to the poor flow of work, that the type of load delivered was unsuitable and so on. Used on a specific work centre in this way a second-phase study can be very useful in helping to decide on whether the purchase of additional equipment or the reorganisation of work flow may be the solution to a particular problem. Very often it will be found that the need is not for more expensive equipment but for a more intensive utilisation of existing equipment.

These are some of the methods that can be employed by the warehouse manager to help him investigate the efficiency of the warehousing function, but the whole problem of warehouse profitability is much wider than this.

The overall effectiveness of the warehouse will depend on a great many outside factors that must also be looked at in any cost saving investigation. To gain an overall impression of the efficiency of any particular warehouse, not only must the economies involved with the broad categories be investigated as through-work sampling but the mechanics of each of these factors must also be investigated. This, as already mentioned, can be carried through by more studies, but there are broad general areas which can also be looked at.

The relationship between order size, destination and mode of transport can frequently produce savings through consolidations of shipments. The type of transport used will affect the inventory levels held. Slow cheap transport can only be employed at the expense of high costly inventory levels. By using a swifter, more expensive transport mode, total costs may be reduced through lower inventory. An investigation of the type of order processing involved could also throw up areas where improvement could mean lower inventory levels through a decrease in the total reorder cycle. This would not only benefit the warehouse but also the customer, since they would receive a more speedy service and could in turn reduce their inventory levels.

A careful check should be kept on new developments in the storage and handling fields. New equipment is coming on to the market constantly and one of these developments might very well be the answer to your problem. The key factor to bear in mind always is the fact that the warehouse does not add to the value of a product only to its cost. Therefore you should never undertake the warehousing function if it can be avoided, nor should you involve the company in an opera-

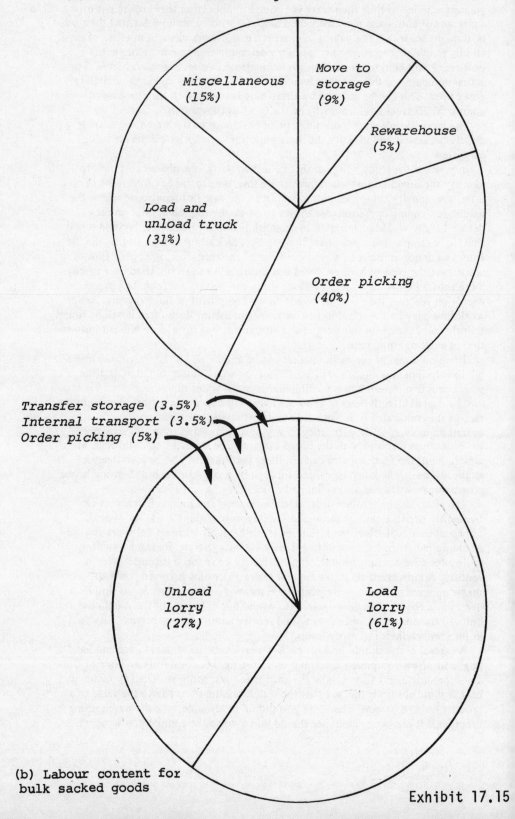

(a) Breakdown of warehousing cost

Miscellaneous (15%)

Move to storage (9%)

Rewarehouse (5%)

Load and unload truck (31%)

Order picking (40%)

Transfer storage (3.5%)
Internal transport (3.5%)
Order picking (5%)

Unload lorry (27%)

Load lorry (61%)

(b) Labour content for bulk sacked goods

Exhibit 17.15

(c) Labour content for large cartons

Unload lorry (10%)
Store goods (9%)

Order pick (28%)

Internal transport (13%)

Transfer to storage (20%)

Load lorry (20%)

Pack (2%)

Internal transport (10%)

(d) Labour content for engine units

Unload lorry (30%)

Order pick (14%)

Transfer to storage (23%)

Load lorry (21%)

Pie charts

tion that it could purchase more cheaply outside the organisation.

In conclusion, greater competition and a decreasing profit margin are forcing a great many companies to investigate their entire structure in search of cost savings. Because of a great deal of neglect in the past one of the most profitable areas for such a study is in the warehousing activities of the firm. In many cases it might be shown that the introduction of the warehouse into the distribution network is unjustified. It is more likely that the firm will find that old sales territories have increased in importance and that costs are being generated through the direct distribution of materials to the sales points as opposed to the introduction of the warehouse. Once it has been decided to establish a warehouse, the problems of location and identification of cost factors must be dealt with. Perhaps the most important facet of the drive to reduce costs in the warehouses is to keep pace with new developments in material handling equipment and distribution thought.

Part 4
ORGANISATION AND CONTROL

18 An introduction to structures

The final part of transport and distribution is the most difficult. Here we must deal with organisation and control. This is essential in order to consider putting into practice what has already been dealt with. It is the most difficult because we are now dealing with people, not abstract ideas. We can theorise to our heart's content about quantities and rules, but in the last resort they must be carried on with an organised structure. This means people, and people are the most difficult of all management problems to control. An idea may be good, it may be profitable, but its effectiveness depends in the last analysis not on inherent 'workability' but on whether the people who are responsible for its implementation give their full cooperation.

It was pointed out at the very start of this book that transport and distribution are functions so essential to the modern industrial economy that they have been a part of management ever since 'industry' started. It is because of this that they are the object of very hard and strong views. They are, in fact, one of the first policy areas within which management decisions were taken. To effect a change in their role requires a basic policy decision on the part of the firm concerned. So deep are their roots that something must briefly be said about policy decisions.

There are three types of policy decision and it is of the utmost importance for management to be sure which type they are taking. If they believe that the decision they are about to take is one type of decision and they act along those lines when in fact the problem is of a different kind then conflict is sure to ensue.

The first classification of policy decisions is those which lie completely within the control of the management of the company. This Type 1 category is much rarer than it would appear on first thought. When this type of decision is taken then the management concerned has no further worries; the decision has been taken and the next task is simply to arrive at procedures whereby the policy decision will be carried out. When these have been decided upon, the next step is to adopt methods whereby the procedures which will achieve the policy decisions will be implemented. This process involves nobody but the management concerned right up to the final implementation stage. When the firm is sure that it is involved in a Type 1 policy decision then the management will act in a certain way. These decisions are rare and usually concern very basic operations within the firm.

The most common type is Type 2, where the decision to be taken is not completely management's, but includes the interest of the other main institution within the firm, namely the unions. When the policy decision is of this type then, of course, it is very unwise not to include the unions in the discussions. This is often better done at the beginning. The question of changing the role of transport and distribution is very basic and affects the unions' interests. Therefore if they are not consulted at the start they will force management to consult them later. Why waste time and effort? Besides if they are in at the start they might make profitable contributions to the overall discussion, even if this is only to pinpoint the areas which are going to cause problems later. Therefore when the firm recognises that a Type 2 decision is being made it should ensure that all the relevant parties are consulted.

Then there is the Type 3 decision, where forces outside the immediate environment of the firm have some degree of control. In our case these will almost always be either the customer or the government or both. It is fairly obvious that for all except the very largest firms consultations with the government concerning the internal operations of the firm will be very rare. The most common way in which the government will make itself felt will be in regulations. For example, there is no use planning routes which can only be operated by drivers exceeding the permitted hours at the wheel. Customers are very important. It will be remembered that the prime object of the transport and distribution system is to supply a given service level at the minimum cost. This will, of course, depend on the customers' reactions and indeed cooperation.

The point being made is that management must not assume that it can simply decide that the time has come for a rethink of the total distribution policy of the firm and expect to put a plan into operation without meeting some difficulties. There will always be difficulties and problems associated with change. What we will try and do now is to give some broad general pointers which may help to make the initial planning a little easier.

It will probably sound ridiculous to say this, but the first step that must be taken in any plan is to decide upon the objective. If this does sound stupid then think a little about it. Think, for example, of the nationalised industries we have already mentioned. What is their objective: to make a profit, to break even or to run as a social service? They are given an objective and as soon as this is carried out and the social costs seen, they find their objective altered. Or think of the firm: is the main objective to maximise profits? There are some very large corporations in this country which if they had this as their major objective would liquidate their assets and go into premium bonds or unit trusts, which invest abroad, so low is their return. Once the objective has been decided upon then policy decisions must be made. These are the broad guidelines to be laid down. For example, we might have as our objective the introduction of a fully integrated total distribution system, but we may also lay down the policy decision that there will be as little redundancy as possible or none at all or we may set a limit to our investment and so on.

Procedures must then be laid down, i.e. there must be decisions made about organisational structure, location and so on. Finally there must be a decision as to the methods which will be used to implement the procedures decided upon within general policy rules. All of this, it will be seen, is done at the basic planning stage, care being taken, of course, about which type of decision we are taking. Consulting all interested parties in the first instance (where practicable) will save time and money at a later stage.

To give an example of this suppose we decide that to increase the efficiency of our warehousing methods we will utilise a certain size of pallet. We must ensure that this is suitable for our customers otherwise there will be trouble later. In this context one remembers the case where it was recommended that a particular size of lift truck be used to load vehicles, its capacity being much greater than that previously used. This greatly increased the efficiency of loading, but reduced over-all effectiveness because it was later found that most of the customers just did not have fork lift trucks of similar capacity so that the drivers had to break down the loads to a more manageable size. This was exceptional, but the motto is still 'as much consultation as practicable'.

Another important point to be discussed at an early stage is the status to be accorded the TDC function. The higher up the management scale this is the better. Remember we could be dealing with a function accounting for up to nearly half of the final sales cost of our particular product. The TDC manager is going to be faced with some tricky problems.

It will be remembered that air freight can often reduce warehousing and inventory cost but only at the price of high transport rates. In other words we are introducing trade off. We expect the transport manager to accept very high costs so that the firm may be better off overall. He spends a great deal so that the warehouse manager can improve his figures. Now, if the firm in question is a new one, with a completely new management, then this might not be a difficult problem. But if, as is more likely, we are dealing with old staff within a new structure then it is likely that in this situation there will be many human problems. The greater the authority behind the decisions the easier will be the task. While we are discussing this area it is as well to repeat that there must be full cooperation at all levels. This, of course, should be taken care of at the preliminary planning stage. There is absolutely no point in trying to introduce a TDC system unless there is a preponderance of opinion in favour of it at the highest levels. There will always be awkward people: it is the job of the manager to take care of this, but he must have full backing at the top. This is why it is important to agree on a clear-cut objective, then backbiting is cut to a minimum.

ORGANISATION STRUCTURES

Once all of the preliminary decisions have been taken the next stage can be started, namely basic organisational structure. This will depend on three main considerations. The first of these is investment, the second is the existing types of structure within the firm and the third the type of market and the product range.

Investment is something that the individual firm must come to a conclusion about, taking stock of its own position. A major point is, however, that the amount to be made available will depend first of all on the importance to the firm of this cost centre and secondly on the objectives set.

As with the inventory problem so with the total problem: never initiate a project the cost of whose introduction and control outweighs the benefits to be reaped. In other words a preliminary survey must be carried out to ascertain the exact commitment which the firm has in the transport and distribution functions.

The greater the costs then obviously the greater the benefits to be expected and consequently the greater will be the investment commitment. At the same time we must be careful that diminishing returns do not appear. Therefore, as always, we must remember that the more accurate and sophisticated the systems we introduce the more costly they become. We must then be careful when setting objectives not to set our sights too high. A compromise must be reached between the theoretically possible economies and the practical costs which would be involved in achieving them as the result of this decision that will affect the total investment made available.

Our next problem is more complex. This is the actual organisations involved. This is in two stages, the internal organisation of the TDC department and the position which this department holds within the total structure of the company.

Exhibit 18.1 shows the ideal structure of a TDC department, all the functions affecting each other directly coming under the overall control of one department or man. The first difficulty is, of course, one of size. We have in the exhibit five

Exhibit 18.1 Theoretically ideal structure

TRANSPORT AND DISTRIBUTION

Transport
Inventory
Warehousing
Protective pack
Order processing

different functions. In the small to medium-small firm it is quite possible that all of these functions could indeed be under the control of one individual. If this is the case then we have the situation where the greatest economies could be made, that is proportionately speaking.

We have here instant communication and the minimum of conflict. There is the problem of span of control, however, that is there is a limit to the number of functions that any individual can operate at the same time efficiently. This might be overcome by outstanding individuals but there is little doubt that we are dealing with the small firm in this situation. In the larger firms there would have to be delegation. The problem is to decide what groupings to introduce. The first obvious link to try to incorporate is transport, inventory and warehousing as one responsibility and packaging and order processing as the other. Here, however, we are still dealing with relatively small firms, so that these very complex subjects are limited in their impact.

The next step up the scale ladder would bring us to the situation where we could further specialise by allowing, say, warehousing and inventory to go to one manager and packaging and order processing to another. The transport decision would be kept under the control of the head of the department. The ultimate is when each of these functions is the responsibility of an individual with the head of the department acting as the source of control and coordination. It is as well to remember that the further we move from the one-man show then it is likely that we will also be experiencing decreases in efficiency. This is due almost en-

tirely to falling coordination which is almost inevitable as the lines of
communication are increased.

The best internal structure is to keep as few separate functions as possible, but when delegation becomes impossible to avoid to make sure greater effort goes into coordination. Probably the best for the large firm is transport as a separate responsibility, warehousing and inventory another with order processing and packaging linked if possible, but with packaging more likely to be a centralised service. At the head of the TDC department is the overall coordination function. This internal set-up will be dictated to a large extent by the particular traits within the individual firm.

The next problem is the place of this department within the overall structure of the firm. While we are forced to discuss the internal and external problem separately they do, of course, interact. Indeed the external structure will in some cases determine the number of separate functions coming under the control of the TDC department. The structures of firms fall into two broad divisions, centralised and decentralised. Centralisation can be of two types, geographical and authoritative. Neither is mutually exclusive; we can have a geographically dispersed firm which still has strong central control, or we can have a geographically concentrated firm which is fully decentralised as far as authority is concerned. The key with centralisation of authority or the lack of it is the number and quality of decisions that are allowed to be taken down the line away from the central board.

Within either of these situations we can have a concentrated or dispersed distribution function, i.e. if we have a centralised firm structure we can have either a concentrated or dispersed distribution department structure. The key influences affecting the choice will be the third mentioned at the start of this section, namely the type of market and the nature of the products.

Exhibit 18.2 shows one of these situations where we have a centralised firm structure. We have a chief executive reporting to whom are the chief of division A and the chief of division B. The services of this firm are all under central control as are the marketing and sales policies of the divisions. In other words the divisions have relatively little decision-making capability; all the major policy decisions will originate from head office and be passed out to them for action.

We could introduce much the same control for the transport and distribution functions as can be seen above in Exhibit 18.2. Here again there is central control of all the functions which come under our idea of TDC. The divisions are not allowed to make independent decisions on warehousing, inventory, transport or other distribution problems. These originate from a central division and are passed out to the divisions for action just as before. There are certain advantages to be had from this system, but they will only be gained provided that the firm's markets and products are suitable for this type of TDC structure and not all firms with a centralised control have these types of products.

The first general condition that must be met is that there must be some degree of homogeneity in the markets served. This does not mean to say that they must be close or even served by the same transport mode. But what it does mean is that there must be as few as possible local differences in the basic characteristics of the markets. That is there must be no differences that would involve a separate distribution policy for the separate markets. Suppose that one of the markets was such that there were only token inventory levels kept, whereas another was involved in high service levels with sophisticated control techniques. In this situation it might very well prove to be best to allow local control over the low inventory level

Exhibit 18.2 Individual divisions retain power only for day-to-day decisions. Distribution divisions provide all transport and distribution services to entire company

Chief Executive

DIVISION A	DIVISION B	TDC	Marketing	Services
Administration	Administration	Transport	Advertising	R&D
Planning	Planning	Warehousing	Sales	Purchasing
Manufacturing	Manufacturing	Inventory		Personnel
Fabrication	Fabrication	Packaging		Legal
Inventory		Order processing		Finance
Packaging				Corporate plans
Local transport				
Order processing				

Exhibit 18.3 Local management decides service levels for their products and operate local transport and packaging. Central division controls national transport and warehousing, i.e. national distribution

Chief Executive

DIVISION A	DIVISION B	TDC	Marketing	Services
Administration	Administration	Transport	Advertising	R&D
Planning	Planning	Warehousing	Sales	Purchasing
Manufacturing	Manufacturing	Order processing		Personnel
Fabrication	Fabrication			Legal
Inventory				Finance
Packaging				
Local transport				
Order processing				

market. By insisting that central control continued it is likely that the only result would be extra administrative costs, extended lines of communication and possibly management duplication. Again if there are very pronounced local conditions regarding selling and/or supply a greater amount of local control may be more profitable. In this situation the best plan is probably a two-step approach, the broad policies being laid down at the central office and the local branches allowed to make the necessary changes. This does, of course, have the disadvantage of increasing the lines of communication, but then all management is a compromise.

The width of product range is another important factor affecting the desirability of central control. If we have a narrow spread in market conditions and a product range having broadly the same characteristics then we have the ideal situation for centralisation of the TDC function. If on the other hand our products vary greatly in handling characteristics or the conditions required for storage, then a central distribution service may present some problems.

This is, fortunately, not a constraint that is too often met with, since even products having very wide differences in their chemical make up and ultimate purpose have, very often, broadly similar handling characteristics. These characteristics will be determined by the ease with which a product can be palletised, the weight limitations it imposes on handling equipment and any special temperature or other climatic or physical storage conditions. Where a firm has products which are not compatible in these ways and are going to very different markets, then as before there may be positive disadvantages in pursuing a policy of centralisation. Although it must be remembered that the general structure of the firm may lean towards central control, TDC is one of the functions less centralised in this situation than the others.

There will always be the firm who although its management structure is centralised in bias, its market and product conditions are such as to preclude a similar structure in distribution. In this firm the structure of transport and distribution must look more like that shown in Exhibit 18.3, where the distribution function is decentralised within a centralised firm. It will be noticed that each of the divisions is responsible for the greater part of the transport and distribution function, only transport and warehousing being kept under central control. There are many advantages in this type of structure for the multi-product and multi-market firm. It allows decisions affecting distribution to be made down the line by local management but at the same time, by keeping warehousing and transport under a central body, it provides link functions whereby the coordination of the transport and distribution policies of the firm may be achieved. In this way it is getting the best of both worlds.

If we were to allow, say, transport to be decentralised as well, then there would almost certainly be a strong possibility of duplication and waste arising. This could be of much greater importance than would seem at first glance when we remember the basic role of transport in the TDC triangle.

By following the trend indicated, local divisions make up their own estimates of service requirements, packaging and so forth; the central transport and warehousing division acts almost like the public warehouseman already mentioned, and provides a consolidated distribution service which can be much more effective than a variety of half-baked measures operated by each division. In fact, many of the larger corporations operate this system irrespective of whether the general structure is centralised or decentralised.

Exhibit 18.4 shows a decentralised firm structure with a centralised transport

Exhibit 18.4 Divisions with most decision centres under their control. Product and market fairly homogeneous, making central distribution viable and efficient

Chief Executive

DIVISION A	DIVISION B	TDC	Services
Administration	Administration	Transport	Advertising
Planning	Planning	Warehousing	R&D
Sales	Sales	Inventory	Market strategy
Personnel	Personnel	Protective	
Legal	Legal	pack	
Purchasing	Purchasing	Order	
Manufacturing	Manufacturing	processing	
Fabrication	Fabrication		
Local	Local		
transport	transport		

Exhibit 18.5 Most decisions out to the division including transport and distribution. Suitable for diversified markets and wide, dissimilar product ranges

Chief Executive

DIVISION A	DIVISION B	TDC	Services
Administration	Administration	Bulk movements	Advertising
Planning	Planning	TDC policies	R&D
Sales	Sales	TDC cost	Market strategy
Personnel	Personnel	studies	
Legal	Legal		
Purchasing	Purchasing		
Manufacturing	Manufacturing		
Fabrication	Fabrication		
Transport	Transport		
Warehousing	Warehousing		
Inventory	Inventory		
Protective	Protective		
pack	pack		
Order	Order		
processing	processing		

and distribution structure. This would be of benefit to the firm when the already
mentioned market and product conditions were in existence.

The final organisation, Exhibit 18.5, shows both a decentralised organisation structure and decentralised transport and distribution. Here, however, the problem is different because of the general decentralisation. Unlike the centralised firm with decentralised distribution, here the chief functions kept at the centre are those which are primarily planning and coordination because the general structure really brings into existence what are virtually separate firms. Therefore the functions not pushed out to the divisions are those like bulk movements, TDC planning and general distribution studies.

The main point in this discussion is that as usual the individual must have an individual solution to the problem of structure. TDC is still a relatively new area for most firms in this country even although the last fifteen years has seen a vast increase in the study of the subject. Therefore there are very few guidelines that can be laid down from experience in this field as an integrated subject. There are, however, very strong trends to be seen: the first move would seem to be the consolidation of the transport and warehousing functions. It is fair to say that the first step towards a fully integrated TDC system must be this, followed perhaps by some measure of discussion on inventory and service level decisions.

There will be conflict in any new idea being introduced into the firm. This has already been mentioned, but there is sometimes conflict from an area which we would not expect, namely marketing management.

It will be obvious by now that some of the areas which we have been discussing might be looked upon by the marketing department as their own. It is very difficult to argue against this, since the only valid view of marketing is as the entire process of getting the firm's product to the consumer. But we are in a period of change and just as marketing grew basically from sales so transport and distribution are emerging as an integrated subject.

Each TDC manager must argue his own case within the context of his own firm. There is, however, one point to be made here: all firms irrespective of their industry must make a profit to continue in existence. If such a large proportion of the sales cost for industrial firms is going on what we have chosen to call total distribution cost (average 16 per cent) and this is claimed to be within the empire of the marketeers, they have been doing a remarkably bad job of it since most firms do not have a TDC account, never mind an efficient TDC department. They must move aside. The key with distribution must be cooperation and consultation but not dumb submission.

One of the reasons why many firms in this country are saddled with ludicrously large warehousing networks has been the accent on marketing without adequate distribution information. You really do not need upwards of 60 warehouses in the UK to provide high service levels. Indeed experience of speaking to many firms in this country of various sizes gives me the impression that a great number of them think that high service levels cost little more than slightly lower ones. This may be true, but only in a small number of cases. Perhaps it is not yet within the role of transport and distribution to affect these policies, but at least we should be able to give a more accurate account of the costs involved.

19 An introduction to control

The question of control has already really been looked at throughout the book. Examining the individual compartments making up the total distribution cost triangle and keeping them operating at high efficiency is control in itself, but not the entire function. For control of the TDC function we need information systems as with the control of any other function within the firm. The only difference is the type of information required. There has been adequate discussion throughout this volume to give indications of the type of information which would be required.

There are basically three approaches to the analysis of TDC. These are the old compartmentalised approach where each department is regarded as separate, which has already been dismissed as inefficient. Then we have the extended TDC approach, where all the various factors looked at and *their interaction on each other* are considered before a decision about a particular policy or mode is deliberated. Thus before looking at the choice, say between air and sea, we would examine not only transport rates but also inventory service level costs, warehousing costs, packaging, insurance and so on. Then we would make the final choice of system.

This method of attack is much better, since it in fact allows the basic TDC approach to be used. The major difficulty likely to be met with is the simple collection of much of the information that would be required. In the test this problem was often mentioned in connection with specific techniques used in a particular area or function, but even when trying simply to investigate the overall situation of the firm the same difficulties will be met.

These really boil down to the fact that in most firms there is no separate TDC account. The costs which we have mentioned as belonging under one umbrella are usually found dispersed all over the place and in some cases not recorded at all. It will be found that at the manufacturing plant, for example, warehousing costs are sometimes included in general manufacturing accounts because they are considered to have come from the general plant allocation. Packaging costs are frequently treated in the same way. In distribution depots it is not uncommon to find these costs poorly dealt with and treated as a cost of sales, again being hidden away in an account not normally associated with transport and distribution. One of the most important difficulties is the cost of inventory. This has already been looked at in the relevant section, but many of the costs will again be dispersed throughout the general accounts.

It is often found that the methods used by accountants to allocate costs do not help the manager in our field. This is often referred to as natural allocation, i.e. the expenditure is allocated on the basis of what it buys. Therefore in looking at basic transport costs the only reference that might be found will be transport in and transport out, which for our purposes tells us less than nothing.

Therefore the only thing which can be done is to compile our own accounts for the physical distribution system with which we are concerned. These must give as much detail as we require but great care must be taken to ensure we do not smother trends by too much detail. Just exactly how detailed the accounts will be depends on the individual. Will they be for each sales area, each depot, each product and so on? The answer will, of course, depend to a great extent on the amount invested by the firm in this area, but this is a question that cannot be answered until a pilot study is carried out.

In any event we must classify the existing costs under the main headings dealt with: transport, inventory and warehousing. There should not be too much trouble encountered in assessing the total expenditure on transport for the methods already in use. The next problem, inventory, might not be so simple. First the investment in inventory must be investigated, then an estimate of the carrying costs made and finally we must conduct an analysis of operating procedures. This will be done on the basis which has already been described, first an ABC breakdown, if applicable, then the various points for reordering and safety stock will be set. This is, of course, assuming that this has not already been done. If it has and the system is working well, we will be primarily interested in possible changes in methods as discussed below. Finally we must make an investigation into the operating costs associated with the present warehousing network. This will give us something like the statement outlined in Exhibit 19.1.

There are then two courses open to the manager. He can assume that the present system as operated is satisfactory and perhaps investigate, or he can initiate a full-scale study to see where improvements can be made through the utilisation

Exhibit 19.1

	Present system	Possible 1	Possible 2
Transport			
Bulk movements			
Local costs			
Warehousing			
Fixed costs			
Inventory			
Capital invested			
Carrying costs			
Totals at given throughput			

of the techniques described in this volume and by more sophisticated methods of distribution. He might find that the present system can be improved upon, but since he will have a great deal of information about it collected why should he assume that it is the best method?

To examine alternative methods of distribution is not difficult. As always the basic problem is the collection of information but, as has been mentioned, a great deal of this will have been done already for the improvement of the existing transport and distribution network.

There are two basic methods available for the long-term comparison of different distribution methods; they do have weaknesses of course, but these will be looked at after the techniques are explained. They are the graphic and the dynamic approaches, both of which are simply extensions of the break-even analysis familiar to accountants. Both techniques require that the total costs of all systems to be compared are known. These must be broken down into their fixed and variable cost components. These terms are used reluctantly since there is really no such thing as a permanently fixed or variable cost; however compromises must be made.

There are two approaches to the problem of separating fixed and variable cost. As usual the difference resolves itself into accuracy and time considerations. The first and the most accurate method is to take every single cost incurred in the systems and separate each into fixed and variable categories. This is obviously best done by an accountant. If you imagine the entire distribution system in existence but with no product flowing through it then those costs which would still be incurred can be regarded as fixed costs at least in the short term and those which would only start to be incurred when products flowed through the system would be variable costs. This method is accurate but slow and a good breakdown can be achieved by extrapolation. The total costs for the various systems under review are estimated and note taken of their maximum and minimum values. These are then plotted on a graph and the straight line joining them drawn and extended back, as shown in Exhibit 19.2 until it meets the vertical axis of the graph (costs). The point where the line meets the axis is the fixed costs for this system and all cost values above it are regarded as variable. The line itself will, of course, show total costs, that is fixed plus variable costs. The further down the vertical axis the meeting is the lower the fixed costs, and the more steeply the total costs line rises the greater the rate at which the proportion of variable costs in the total cost rises. These two characteristics can and do have very important implications for management decisions.

Suppose we are considering the choice between air freight and direct road via the ferry services to a continental destination. Assume that Exhibit 19.3 represents the graph which we have drawn. The vertical axis represents the total costs of the systems and the horizontal axis the volume of annual shipments in a suitable unit. It will be noticed that the fixed costs for the air alternative are lower than those for the road method, but at the same time the variable costs of the air route rise much more steeply than the road and cross at X. This is called the change point.

If we assume this as the pattern between our two distribution methods, and remember these are total costs we are examining, then certain conclusions can be made. Let us look first at the total costs to the firm. Below the change point X it will be noticed that the total costs by air are lower than those by road. Therefore for volumes below those represented by the change point the distribution system

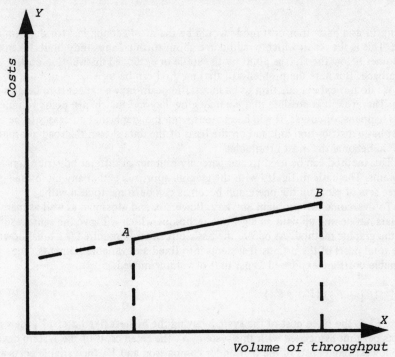

Exhibit 19.2

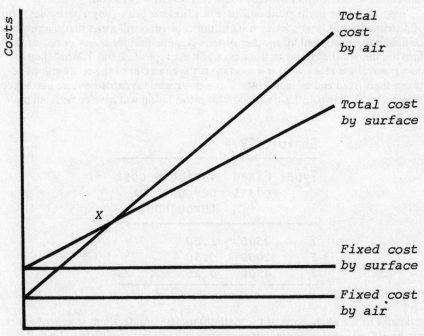

Exhibit 19.3 Utilisation of change point
in future planning

using air as a basic transport mode would be the most economical for the firm to use. This is the result which would come about through any study undertaken at volumes below the change point by the static or extended distribution costs approach. But here the problems of that method can be seen.

We do not expect our firm to be in a static position; we expect it to be growing. Therefore it is possible that we may grow beyond the change point volume. If this happens, of course, it will be obvious from the graph that air ceases to be the best basic distribution link and on the basis of the data shown the road alternative would become the most profitable.

This method can be used to compare any number of different distribution systems. The basic difficulty with the graphic approach is that any more than, say, three sets of plots on the one graph becomes cumbersome to deal with.

To overcome this problem Smykay, Bowersox and Mossman as well as many others have come up with an algebraic technique which will give the same results as the graphic method. As before the basic information required is a breakdown of the total costs of the proposed systems into fixed and variable elements. The variable costs are expressed as per unit of volume moved:

$$(F_1 - F_2)/(V_1 - V_2)$$

Here F_1 is the fixed cost of the system having the highest fixed costs, V, the variable costs per unit associated with this system, F_2 the fixed costs of the system having the lowest fixed costs of the pair under comparison and V_2 the variable costs associated with it per unit of throughput. All the various methods to be examined are ranked in increasing order of fixed costs, smallest first and so on.

Suppose we are in the position where our firm has been using a particular form of distribution but is wondering if its future expansion will mean that the present method will be replaced by another system. Assume that for policy purposes the firm has limited the choice to three possibilities: types 1, 2 and 3. What they are does not really matter; what is important is the character of the relationships between their fixed and variable costs. From investigations carried out we can expect these to be as shown in Exhibit 19.4 This information will have come from basic

Exhibit 19.4

Type	Fixed costs	Variable cost per unit of throughput
1	2500	1.00
2	3000	0.50
3	4500	0.25

estimates of the likely costs of the methods under consideration. It will, of course, not be 100 per cent accurate, but then again we are dealing with broad bands of planning decision here. Taking types 1 and 2 and substituting in the above equation:

Change point $= (3000 - 2500)/(1 - 0.5)$
$\qquad\qquad\quad = 1000$

If the same calculation is carried out between systems 2 and 3 the result is 6000. In other words, when the amount of material we are sending through our distribution network is less than 1000 units, type 1 is the best choice of system. Over this figure and below 6000 units the best choice would be type 2 and once we grow beyond the 6000 units per year level, type three is the best.

As between the two methods of tackling this question of long-term planning the most accurate and the easiest to use is the algebraic approach. The chief problem is that its accuracy must always be remembered as applying to the result with the information fed in. That is we must not start to regard the change points given by the algebraic approach as inviolable limits.

The graphic method does have one very large advantage over the algebraic and this is that any close parallel between the fixed and variable costs of the two methods will be easily seen. When this occurs there will, of course, be wide ranges of movement volumes for which the total costs between the two systems are pretty much the same. Yet if the algebraic method were employed it would still give detailed results as to when changes should be made. In practice, of course, the narrow margin between the methods would ensure that the costs of making a change outweighed any possible benefits.

USES AND LIMITATIONS OF DYNAMIC APPROACHES

The major uses to which these methods can be put are obviously all in the forward planning field. Depending on the reliability of the basic information, they can be used to plan for investment in facilities. If it is obvious that at some future date one method of transport and distribution is going to be of the greatest use, then investment in the present methods would have to be carefully looked at. In this context an important concept to be utilised in conjunction with either of the planning methods is time span.

It is all very well to look at a graph or a simple equation and say at a given volume we must use a distribution system based on air, and then when another volume is to be moved the best method will be road ferry. The key question that must be asked is over what time span we would expect the various change points to come about. The firm cannot, except in very exceptional conditions, jump in and out of investments in a variety of distribution systems unless the changes were to be very attractive indeed.

If we are faced with, say, three different change points and the time span was very short up to point 1, similar to point 2, but very long to point 3, in this situation the problem is simply solved. We could, for example, ignore the systems proposed up to change point 1. We might also ignore the system proposed between points 1 and 2 and simply concentrate on investment in the system between points 2 and 3. On the other hand, if inspection of the estimated difference in costs between 1 and 2 and 3 is attractive enough, then the firm might consider leasing the facilities required for the recommended system between 1 and 2 and concentrate on the method between 2 and 3 as a long-term plan.

The final decision will depend on the cost advantages between the alternatives. But time span is important. We might find that we expect to take so long to move between various change points that it is hardly worthwhile considering any possible alterations in our present system. We might also find that we are coming very close to an important change in point and if this is the case there is little point in trying to improve the efficiency of the existing system; much better to concentrate on the introduction of the new methods.

One of the best ways to use these methods is to project into the future the likely maximum movements to any particular market. This will give an estimate of the likely total commitment to the market; then we draw up a list of change points by either method. This will give a useful base line for any likely changes in distributive methods within the firm. We must always remember, of course, that the methods have certain disadvantages and that the change points are best looked upon as the midpoints of volume ranges within which a change of methods employed for transport and distribution may be desirable.

The only real form of control is to have the information required for the efficient operation of the distributive system and to keep a constant check to ensure that targets are met. And, if they are not, whether this is due to the target, the system or something outside the control of management.

SUMMARY

Because of the nature of the TDC concept, its many separate compartments and different techniques we have been forced in this book to deal with them as separate entities. At the same time throughout as much emphasis as possible has been laid on the interaction of the various functions. It might be worthwhile to examine the likely moves which may be expected in this field over the next few years.

There is little doubt that there will not be a sudden springing into life of TDC departments in all the firms within this country. Change does not take place like that, but at the same time there can be as little doubt that over the coming years there will be an evolution towards transport and distribution becoming a more integrated function.

In the text a variety of reasons have been given for this movement, but it is most likely that the one bearing the greatest weight will be competition. Many of our large corporations are in a poor state when a realistic view is taken of their efficiency in terms of their competitors. It is not a case of the products themselves being poor; indeed in many cases there are few to equal them in the world. The snag is that we do not produce them efficiently enough. At the same time the world markets are becoming more competitive and the consumer more sophisticated. This will in itself place a greater and growing importance on service levels and, it will be remembered, that this is the key which unlocks the door to a greater amount of attention being paid to TDC. The higher the service levels, and the more complex and expensive the product, then the more expensive is transport and distribution. As this cost goes up more attention must be paid to it.

Index